WITHDRAWN

The American History Series

SERIES EDITORS

John Hope Franklin, *Duke University*
A. S. Eisenstadt, *Brooklyn College*

Philip Weeks
KENT STATE UNIVERSITY

Farewell, My Nation

The American Indian and the United States in the Nineteenth Century

SECOND EDITION

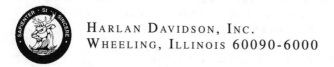

HARLAN DAVIDSON, INC.
WHEELING, ILLINOIS 60090-6000

Library of Congress Cataloging-in-Publication Data

Weeks, Philip
    Farewell, my nation : the American Indian and the United States in
the nineteenth century / Philip Weeks.—2nd ed.
        p.   cm.—(The American history series)
    Includes bibliographical references and index.
    ISBN 0-88295-956-5 (alk. paper)
    1. Indians of North America—Government relations. 2. Indians of
North America—History—19th century. 3. Indians of North
America—Relocation. I. American history series (Wheeling, Ill.)

E93.W39 2000
973'.0497—dc21   00-059635

Cover Photo: Crow (Apsaroke) warriors during a winter campaign in a
valley of the Pryor mountains in Montana. *Edward S. Curtis Collection, courtesy of the Library of Congress.*

Manufactured in the United States of America
04 03 02 01 00 1 2 3 4 5 MG

Dedicated, with love and deepest affection, to Jeanette Weeks,
Michael Weeks, John Weeks, and Rich Weeks

FOREWORD

Every generation writes its own history for the reason that it sees the past in the foreshortened perspective of its own experience. This has surely been true of the writing of American history. The practical aim of our historiography is to give us a more informed sense of where we are going by helping us understand the road we took in getting where we are. As the nature and dimensions of American life are changing, so too are the themes of our historical writing. Today's scholars are hard at work reconsidering every major aspect of the nation's past: its politics, diplomacy, economy, society, recreation, mores and values, as well as status, ethnic, race, sexual, and family relations. The lists of series titles that appear on the inside covers of this book will show at once that our historians are ever broadening the range of their studies.

The aim of this series is to offer our readers a survey of what today's historians are saying about the central themes and aspects of the American past. To do this, we have invited to write for the series only scholars who have made notable contributions to the respective fields in which they are working. Drawing on primary and secondary materials, each volume presents a factual and narrative account of its particular subject, one that affords readers a basis for perceiving its larger dimensions and importance. Conscious that readers respond to the closeness and immediacy of a subject, each of our authors seeks to restore the past as an actual present, to revive it as a living reality. The individuals and groups who figure in the pages of our books appear as real people who once were looking for survival and fulfillment. Aware that historical subjects are often matters of controversy, our authors present their own findings and conclusions. Each volume closes with an extensive critical essay on the writings of the major authorities on its particular theme.

The books in this series are primarily designed for use in both basic and advanced courses in American history, on the undergraduate and graduate levels. Such a series has a particular value these days, when the format of American history courses is being altered to accommodate a greater diversity of reading materials. The series offers a number of distinct advantages. It extends the dimensions of regular course work. It makes clear that the study of our past is, more than the student might otherwise understand, at once complex, profound, and absorbing. It presents that past as a subject of continuing interest and fresh investigation.

For these reasons the series strongly invites an interest that far exceeds the walls of academe. The work of experts in their respective fields, it puts at the disposal of all readers the rich findings of historical inquiry, an invitation to join, in major fields of research, those who are pondering anew the central themes and aspects of our past.

And, going beyond the confines of the classroom, it reminds the general reader no less than the university student that in each successive generation of the ever-changing American adventure, from its very start until our own day, men and women and children were facing their daily problems and attempting, as we are now, to live their lives and to make their way.

John Hope Franklin
A. S. Eisenstadt

CONTENTS

PREFACE

This work is not a definitive account of the United States' relationship with the Indians in the nineteenth century. Such a study would be immense. I have attempted to highlight major events and trends that explain an important cultural and political story in the American national experience, while providing an interpretive framework that I hope is helpful to individuals, especially students and teachers, seeking to understand that story and relationship better.

The decade that has passed since publication of the first edition of this book has seen a continued increase in both the scholarship and the high level of popular interest in the American Indians and the history of their relationship with the United States of America. In this edition I have considered and often incorporated the conclusions of this scholarship, and I have updated the bibliography. Primary research has been included, too. I have also selected and added photographic illustrations to the second edition, hoping that readers will be better able to envision the people and the events that take place in the narrative. While the first edition's story of the American Indian and the United States between 1820 and 1890 remains the centerpiece, the text has been sharpened and clarified. Sometimes I have rewritten the original text completely. Additionally, I have expanded the treatment both backwards and forwards chronologically. In the second edition consideration is now given to the late colonial and revolutionary eras because they provide a crucial foundation for understanding inaugural United States policies toward the American Indians. Additionally, the experiences of the tribes of the trans-Appalachian West, as they encountered and reacted to the new republic's initial thrust westward, is examined to provide a fuller understanding of the complexities of the national government's response to the Indian question in the early nineteenth century. Those events were also a crucial precondition of the United States government's adoption of the policy of Separation in the 1830s.

Finally, the Aftermath is new. I hope it helps correct a misconception that I find common among most of my undergraduate students (and which the entertainment media continues to perpetuate for the consumption of the general public), namely that the history of the American Indians (and perhaps Indians themselves) ended with the passing of the nineteenth century. Precisely because this volume is about American Indian–United States relations in that century, I believed it imperative that a profile of twentieth century trends be included in the second edition, lest any reader mistakenly conclude that the Indian experience ended with the close of Chapter Six and the nineteenth century. For those who wish greater elaboration of this subject after reading the Aftermath, they are directed to another volume of the American History Series, Peter Iverson's *"We Are Still Here": American Indians in the Twentieth Century.*

Let me close with a note on terminology. An inevitable problem in dealing with the native peoples I am writing about is what to call them. The difficulty began with Christopher Columbus, who demonstrated the enormous creative fertility of error. During his voyages to the Caribbean area, Columbus, believing that he was near the East Indies, called the local people he met *indios,* which came into English as *Indians.* So they have been almost universally called by English-speaking people. In recent decades two terms, "Native Americans" and to a lesser extent "Amerinds," have come into usage among educators, publishers, the media, and various other well-intentioned folk. The current terminology most acceptable to Indian people is "American Indians," although most refer to themselves by their tribal name: Mohawk, Cherokee, Cheyenne, Hopi, and so forth. Native American has almost become lost by Indian people since many individuals now born in the United States say that they are native Americans. A developing trend is First Nations, or indigenous Americans, or Indigenous Nations, as part of a growing movement for Indian studies programs becoming indigenous in name and looking for parallels and common themes among other indigenous peoples throughout the western hemisphere and in other parts of the world. I warmly thank Professor Donald L. Fixico, Director of the Indigenous Nations Studies Program at the University of Kansas, for his advice and for answering my questions about Indian sensibilities relating to appropriate terminology for the second edition. If anyone is dissatisfied, or worse, offended with such usages, I am sincerely apologetic.

ACKNOWLEDGMENTS

Special thanks is extended to Andrew Davidson and Lucy Herz for their commitment to editorial excellence; to John Hope Franklin and the late Arthur Link for always being encouraging mentors of my work; to James B. Gidney for taking me under his wing when I first hoped to publish and for generously (always a trait of his) allowing me to incorporate in this book some material that I wrote for a collaborative venture of ours many years ago; and to several colleagues who took time to read a draft of the manuscript and share their expertise: David Wallace Adams, Donald J. Berthrong, Blue Clark, Donald F. Fixico, the late Arrell Morgan Gibson, Park Dixon Goist, William T. Hagan, and Morrell Heald. It is with great pleasure that I acknowledge the individuals to whom this book is dedicated, for reasons that have made each special in my life:

Jeanette Weeks, my wife and my best friend, who has always supported my dreams ("Let Us Go and Rest Awhile") while making my world a bright and happy, fulfilled and loving place;

Michael Weeks, honorable, gentle and strong, who made parenting so easy, and to whom I am forever grateful for the host of treasured memories you have provided your mother and me, son;

John Weeks, a beloved companion along the miles of my life—how many joys we've shared (Oh, if the bridge had collapsed, you can rest assured that only the records would have sunk!); and,

Rich Weeks, in whose company I shared the special excitement that youth brings only once—"May the LORD make his face to shine upon you, and give you peace."

Philip Weeks

The sun rose dim on us in the morning, and at night it sunk in a dark cloud, and looked like a ball of fire. That was the last sun that shone on Black Hawk. His heart is dead, and no longer beats quick in his bosom. He is now a prisoner to the white men; they will do with him as they wish. . . . Farewell, my nation! Black Hawk tried to save you, and avenge your wrongs. . . . He can do no more. He is near his end. His sun is setting, and he will rise no more.

BLACK HAWK, SAC AND FOX

Dead Dreams

They could now get on with the task of burying the dead. For the previous three days, the last three of the old year, a ferocious winter storm had pummeled the upper plains. By the morning of New Year's Day, 1891, the blizzard had blown itself out and the sun began to break through the grey clouds. As the sky cleared, a train of wagons accompanied by individuals on horseback set out from Pine Ridge agency, situated near the southwestern corner of the Sioux's Pine Ridge reservation in South Dakota. The party's destination was the valley of Wounded Knee Creek some twenty miles to the east. There, Sioux and troops of the U.S. Seventh Cavalry had battled on December 29, 1890, leaving twenty-five soldiers dead, thirty-nine wounded, and hundreds of Sioux either killed or severely wounded.

The Sioux who fell at Wounded Knee were followers of the Paiute mystic Wovoka, whose message combining Indian mysticism and Christian millennialism had found a substantial following among western tribes in the late 1880s. All Indians, Wovoka preached, must adopt a pacific lifestyle. They must put violence behind them and purge themselves of enmity toward the whites. If they obeyed, Wovoka reported, God promised to return the earth to the Indians—the living as well as the dead—and give them back the buffalo.* In short, the nearly four-century Euro-American epoch in the New World would end as the meek inherited the earth. To hasten that day and the return of the dead, Indians must learn a special dance and perform it regularly. The more often it was danced, the sooner God would vanquish the whites and return the earth to the Indians. Whites called it the Ghost Dance because of its promise to awaken the dead.

Kindled by the despair and privation the Indians suffered in the aftermath of the Plains Wars, Wovoka's doctrine spread quickly throughout the system of western reservations in the late 1880s, where it was accepted with great rejoicing by the hungering tribes. Fervidly many Indians performed the Ghost Dance believing that God would soon destroy the whites and return the world to the Indians. What warfare had failed to accomplish, faith would, they hoped. In March 1890, eleven messengers brought word of Wovoka and his joyful, wondrous tidings to the Sioux at their five South Dakota reservations. They were impressed sufficiently to convene a council and select representatives to journey to the mystic's home to evaluate and learn his teachings. After a week's stay with Wovoka in Mason Valley, Nevada, the delegation returned, trained in the beliefs and movements of the Ghost Dance. The Sioux eagerly accepted Wovoka's revelations as divine inspiration, and many on the Sioux reservations converted to the new faith. Overnight their abject depression changed to overpowering expectation

The dance went on throughout the fall of 1890. The Sioux prepared themselves for the return of the buffalo, their dead friends and relatives, their former lands, their old way of life, and for the vanquishing of the white man. Their problems seemed small in the face of their people's imminent rebirth. As Wovoka's message spread among the Sioux, however, it dramatically altered, deviating greatly from the original doctrine. The time-honored cultural

---

*the American bison, commonly referred to as *buffalo*

values of a warrior people were superimposed upon Wovoka's vision of peace and harmony. Christlike meekness was replaced by strident activism. The Sioux transformed the Ghost Dance from an instrument of regeneration into a symbol of resistance and insurgency. Dancers soon wore special Ghost Dance shirts, which, they believed, could miraculously repel an enemy's bullet.

Alarmed by the mounting frenzy among the Sioux, federal authorities ordered the Ghost Dance halted. Most Sioux acquiesced. A few hundred refused and tried to flee to the Dakota Badlands. They were intercepted by troops of the Seventh Cavalry and taken as prisoners to the small settlement of Wounded Knee. On the morning following their capture, the soldiers moved to disarm the Sioux. A shaman, reminding them of the protection offered by their Ghost Dance shirts, harangued the men to resist. One pulled a rifle from under his blanket and fired into the massed soldiers. The Seventh Cavalry responded with a volley of rifle, pistol, and artillery fire. The Sioux and the soldiers then clashed in hand-to-hand combat. Women and children, terrified and hysterical, fled to escape the melee. Many of them became casualties. Later that day a blizzard swept over the Dakotas, freezing the bodies of the Sioux into the positions of their violent deaths. The task of burial was delayed three days until the storm passed.

Among the seventy-five Sioux departing Pine Ridge on New Year's Day, 1891, were thirty local whites. Their leader, Paddy Starr, had secured a contract from the army to bury the dead Indians at two dollars a body. The men anticipated this task would earn them a sizable sum. At least 150 Sioux, lying dead on the battlefield since December 29, would need interment. Another 100 corpses could be found scattered about the surrounding countryside. A contingent of soldiers accompanied the group to provide protection. The Sioux, led by Dr. Charles A. Eastman, a Santee Sioux and the agency's physician, journeyed toward the battlefield in a state of great emotional agitation, hoping to discover which of their relatives did not survive the confrontation.

They reached their destination shortly past noon. Robert M. Utley, in *The Last Days of the Sioux,* described the ghastly scene that riveted the attention of all in the party, as they looked in stunned silence upon the Wounded Knee battlefield: "Strips of shredded canvas and piles of splintered lodgepoles littered the campsite, together with wrecked wagons and twisted pots, kettles, and domestic utensils. Here and there the skeletons of a tepee rose starkly from the wreckage, bits of charred canvas clinging to the poles. Snowcovered mounds cluttered the ground from one end of the camp to the other; beneath them lay the shattered bodies of the victims of the battle. Other mounds dotted the floor and sides of a deep ravine along the edge of the campsite; and beyond . . . the mounds lay thick and numerous. . . . Each mound hid a human form, torn by shrapnel and carbine bullets, caked with blood, frozen hard in the contortions of violent death. They were of all ages and both sexes. The storm of shot and shell had spared none."

Yet, incredibly, a handful of people had survived the melee. Dr. Eastman searched frantically among the bodies, looking for signs of life, while all around him the pitiful wails of the Sioux he had accompanied split the cold winter air. "It took all of my nerve to keep my composure in the face of this spectacle," he remembered, "and of the excitement and grief of my Indian companions." To his horror, he found many of the dead women with their shawls pulled up over their faces, as if this last act might somehow shield them from the soldiers who stood above them with weapons raised. Amidst the piles of people frozen into hideous postures, Eastman discovered a four-month-old girl, wounded twice by soldiers' bullets, but alive. Lying next to her dead mother, still bundled tenderly in a shawl and wearing a cap embroidered in beadwork with a flag of the United States, the infant had miraculously survived her wounds, the blizzard, and three days of freezing temperatures. The searchers rescued two more children, a little girl and a little boy, as well as five adults.* The survivors were placed aboard wagons and removed to Pine Ridge agency.

---

*All three children were later adopted. The baby wrapped in the shawl found a home with Brigadier General L. W. Colby, who renamed her Marguerite Colby. Some Siouan women preferred to call her Ikicize-Wanti-Cinca, that is, "Child of the Battlefield." The other two orphans likewise found foster homes. Captain George Sword, head of the Pine Ridge Indian Police, took in the little girl; Lucy Arnold, a local schoolteacher, the little boy.

The doctor recalled the anguish of that day in his autobiography, *From Deep Woods to Civilization:* "All of this was a severe ordeal for one who had so lately put all his faith in the Christian love and lofty ideals of the white man."

The white workers likewise combed the macabre, snow-covered mounds, collecting the bodies of the dead Sioux from whom they stripped clothing and other items for souvenirs. After being gathered into a huge pile, the corpses were cast without ceremony into a mass grave dug on a hill overlooking the battlefield. Four days earlier, artillery pieces raked the Sioux from this hill. "It was a thing to melt the heart of a man, if it was of stone," remembered one observer of the burial scene, "to see those little children, with their bodies shot to pieces, thrown naked into the pit." Before dirt was shoveled atop the bodies, the workers posed around the grave for a group photograph, apparently collecting another memento of the occasion.

Wounded Knee was the last battle between the Indians and the United States Army, although no one knew it at the time. War Department annual reports throughout the 1890s indicated that the military anticipated other outbreaks of trouble. The full significance of Wounded Knee emerged in time: it was the conclusion of a struggle that had embroiled the United States since its inception over 100 years earlier, and, before that, the European imperial powers for almost 300 years. It epitomized the greatest reality of the Indian-white experience: the recalcitrance of many Indians to accept the unalterable reality of white hegemony over the continent, much less their own lives and destinies. It exemplified the long-standing incapacity of federal Indian policy to define a workable and mutually acceptable solution to what whites commonly called the "Indian question." And, it has become an historical allegory that is, at the same time, artificial and accurate. For many, Wounded Knee symbolizes the passing of "Indian America," although most tribes had experienced their own "Wounded Knee," their own culminating episode, years, decades, or centuries before. "I shall not be there. I shall rise and pass. Bury my heart at Wounded Knee," wrote Stephen Vincent Benét in his poem "American Names," providing a label for those who viewed

Wounded Knee as a microcosm of Indian history in the post-Columbian period, characterized by victimization and cultural imperialism, futile resistance and absolute defeat. This theme gained a wide popular audience with Dee Brown's 1971 best seller whose title, *Bury My Heart At Wounded Knee,* drew from Benét.

Black Elk, an Oglala Sioux holy man who witnessed that confrontation, recognized that something more than the lives of 250 Sioux ended in that remote South Dakota valley. In *Black Elk Speaks,* he offered an epitaph to the larger struggle, whose roots stretched back to earliest European colonial settlement concluding at Wounded Knee:

I did not know then how much was ended. When I look back now from this high hill of my old age, I can still see the butchered women and children lying heaped and scattered all along the crooked gulch as plain as when I saw them with eyes still young. And I can see that something else died there in the bloody mud, and was buried in the blizzard. A people's dream died there. It was a beautiful dream. . . . The nation's hoop is broken and scattered. There is no center any longer and the sacred tree is dead.

***

The expansion of the American population westward during the first century of the national experience was breathtaking in its swiftness and scope. Surging outward from the Atlantic seaboard and across the Appalachian chain, Americans moved with intense and unyielding determination to acquire and settle a vast western domain: first east, then west of the Mississippi. By 1850, the United States had realized its Manifest Destiny. The nation stretched from the Atlantic to the Pacific—"from sea to shining sea," as Americans heralded jubilantly in song. Many still dreamed of adding Canada, more of Mexico, and various Caribbean islands, such as Cuba, to the expansive republic.

Each year Americans filled in the frontier until finally, in the late nineteenth century, the superintendent of the census for the United States declared that the American frontier had ceased to exist. A Census Bureau bulletin in 1890 concluded: "Up to and including 1880 the country had a frontier of settlement, but at present the unsettled area has been so broken into by isolated bodies of settlement that there can hardly be said to be a frontier line." In a twist of irony, the announcement came in the same year as the battle at Wounded Knee, the last battle between American Indians and the United States Army.

This staggering migration of people, acquisition of territory, and settlement of the frontier was one of the greatest forces shaping the history of the United States. In 1893, three years after the superintendent of the census's pronouncement, a young historian named Frederick Jackson Turner presented a paper in Chicago before the convention of the American Historical Association entitled "The Significance of the Frontier in American History." The paper and its thesis established the reputation of Turner, who became one of the most respected scholars of his generation. A good selection of his work and ideas may be found in *Frontier and Section: Selected Essays of Jackson Turner.*

The settlement of the frontier also proved to be the foremost source of a near constant state of friction and hostility between the United States government, its citizens, and the Indians. The vast locales acquired and settled by Americans were home to various native groups, and Indians did not long forbear the newcomers who moved with such resolve to displace them, regulate them, and occupy their patrimony. In the face of this aggressive thrust westward, the pattern most representative of United States–Indian relations was set early. It was subject to the ebb and flow of events and to differing views of policy, but through it ran a strain of unremitting determination by Americans to dislodge the indigenous inhabitants of the western lands. Government might from time to time relent. Americans wanting land never did.

The Indians' resistance to westward expansion and the response of Americans combined to produce periods of desperate violence. Throughout these years, the United States followed three fundamental goals: one, promoting westward expansion and settlement; two, protecting its citizens and their business ventures; and three, guaranteeing Indians' property and treaty rights. The goals, however, were inherently in conflict. Faced with intense and unyielding pressure to support and defend Americans, their interests, and their aspirations, officials found it impossible to pursue the goals simultaneously and impartially. The Indians were marked as the eventual losers. In 1879, a Wyoming newspaper reflected upon the inevitable outcome. "The same inscrutable Arbiter that decreed the downfall of Rome, has pronounced the doom of extinction upon the red men of America. To attempt to defer this result by mawkish sentimentalism . . . is unworthy of the age."

The rapidly shrinking frontier and the interracial tensions caused by expansion meant that the United States could not temporize in addressing the "Indian question." From the birth of the republic, one central, overriding concern confronted the managers of the nation's westward expansion and the architects of federal Indian policy: what should be done with the Indians? Most whites considered them a dangerous impediment to the republic's territorial, cultural, and economic aspirations. "For a hundred years the United States has been wrestling with the 'Indian question,'" noted Commissioner of Indian Affairs John Quincy Smith in 1876 at the conclusion of the Plains Wars. Many answers to this question were advanced, both in and out of government. Some suggested creating a geographic boundary, much as the British had done in 1763 when they designated a frontier line along the Appalachians, so that Indians might maintain their accustomed way of life free from white encroachment. Others suggested that acculturating the Indians, then assimilating them into the dominant society was the wisest course; although, as Brian W. Dippie has suggested in *The Vanishing American,* "This gift of civilization—the ultimate gift, to the whites' way of thinking . . . always seemed to please the donor more than the recipient." Still others, such as Montana Territorial Governor James M. Ashley, applauded extermination. "The Indian race on this continent has never been anything but an unmitigated curse to civilization," Ashley concluded in a letter he published in a national newspaper in 1870, "while the intercourse between the Indian and the white man has been only evil [and will remain so] until the last savage is translated to that celestial hunting ground for which they all believe themselves so well fitted, and to which every settler on our frontier wishes them individually and collectively a safe and speedy transit."

Abundant suggestions, prudent and foolish, mean-spirited and generous, were offered because most Americans knew that a solution to the Indian question was needed desperately. And generations of federal officials struggled to fashion a policy to solve the Indian question, even though the permanent resolution they sought remained elusive. General William T. Sherman, in a remark to General John M. Schofield, reflected the exasperation this produced in generations of Americans, "The whole Indian question is in such a snarl, that I am utterly powerless to help you by order or advice." This question of what means could solve the Indian question, and the ensuing search for an answer, shaped, reshaped, and to this day continues to affect the relationship of the federal government with Indians.

Possibly no time period affords the student of United States–Indian relations a better vantage point for observing the complexities of this relationship, especially the government's search for the final solution to the Indian question, than the nineteenth century. Three principal solutions characterized this century. The first, the *policy of Separation,* was the answer of the 1830s to the Indian question: eastern tribes would be colonized, by force if necessary, beyond a line separating them from areas of expected white settlement. Following implementation, the Indian presence on lands east of the Mississippi River was drastically curtailed, which opened this area for exclusive use by the American population. This solution was not, however, the panacea Americans expected and predicted it to be.

The second solution, the *policy of Concentration,* emerged after massive American western migration and territorial expansion in the trans-Mississippi West during the 1840s destroyed the rationale upon which the policy of Separation was based. The United States government's new solution to the Indian question called for the drastic reduction of Indian landholdings in the West and the compulsory relocation of tribes to federal reservations where permanent residency, under strict governmental, judicial, and cultural control, would be enforced. Indian resistance to this policy, and Washington's commitment to it, resulted in the titanic struggle of the 1860s and 1870s known as the Plains Wars.

The *policy of Americanization* was the third solution advanced in the nineteenth century. With its tandem programs of land reform and formal education, it was the national government's answer to the Indian question in the aftermath of the Plains Wars and the reality of the military subjugation of the Indians. This policy, implemented during the presidency of Rutherford B. Hayes, although not translated into effective reform within the term of office of Hayes, became the policy of the federal government until the 1930s, when John Collier, Franklin D. Roosevelt's Indian Commissioner, judged this policy a failure and sought another solution to the Indian question.

The search for a solution to the Indian question forms an organic whole that transcends the history of United States–Indian relations. The republic was little more than a half-century old when the United States government settled upon the first solution, but the Indian question stretched back to colonial times.

Where today is the Pequot? Where are the Naragansetts, the Mohawks, the Pokanoket, and many other once powerful tribes of our people? They have vanished before the avarice and the oppression of the White Man, as snow before a summer sun.

TECUMSEH, SHAWNEE

CHAPTER ONE

The "Indian Question"

Arrival through the American Revolution

Scientific and linguistic analysis suggests that the first people came to America some 15,000 to 25,000 years ago. During the Ice Age, northeastern Asia and northwestern North America were joined where the Bering Strait is today. Hunter-gatherers, in small nomadic bands and over thousands of years, migrated across the Bering Strait land bridge (usually called Beringia) and began filling in the Americas. Humans reached the southernmost part of the Western Hemisphere, present southern Chile and Argentina, by 8000 B.C.

From the diffusion of people came the diffusion of languages and cultures. Following the voyages of Christopher Columbus, the first Europeans to settle in North America after A.D. 1500 found two continents where some 2,000 native languages (not dialects) existed. The Indians residing north of the Rio Grande, north of present Mexico, spoke as many as 350 separate languages. The Indian societies of what is now the United States also varied greatly in culture and way of life. Many were farmers who grew a wide variety of crops, while others engaged in fishing or hunting to obtain food. Still others combined hunting, gathering, and farming. The forms of Indian political organization varied widely, too. The Plains Indians, for example, were divided into small tribal groups, while the Indians of the southeast often organized themselves into confederacies.

The first Europeans to arrive in the Americas also found a substantial native population. About 7–12 million Indians lived north of the Rio Grande in what is today the United States and Canada. Another 25 million natives lived in Mexico and Central America. The rest, some 30–40 million people, lived on the islands in the Caribbean Sea and in South America. The Indian population declined catastrophically, perhaps 30 to 50 percent, within 100 years of the onset of colonial settlement due to the introduction of European diseases, especially smallpox.

During the colonial period, three European powers came to control the lands that would become the contiguous United States. By 1700, Spain held California and much of the trans-Mississippi West. East of the Mississippi River valley a contest raged between England and France for mastery of that substantial region. From 1689 to 1763 the French, and to a lesser extent the British, engaged many tribes to help them fight four successive wars, as each imperial rival tried to expel its adversary and to establish colonial supremacy in eastern North America.

English and French relations with the American Indians exhibited marked differences. Natives served French imperial interests well not only as soldiers, but also as partners in the lucrative fur trade business. As a result, the French developed and retained a friendship with Indians that their European rivals never earned or enjoyed. On the other hand, the Indians' strained, suspicious, and frequently violent relationship with the English and Americans stemmed primarily from a colonial population determined to acquire tribal land, hold it, and then expand it for farming and nonagricultural enterprises.

By the eighteenth century American colonists had subdued Algonquian peoples throughout the entire southern half of New England. Pequots, Nipmuks, Wampanoags, and Narragansetts, no longer able to withstand the pressure of the transplanted Europeans, finally capitulated. In the American South, warfare and the expansion of colonial settlement had expelled most tribes from their homes in the Tidewater and Piedmont regions. Indians residing in the thirteen British colonies were increasingly shattered, demoralized, and held at the mercy of the white people wherever those newcomers had collected in substantial numbers.

Only the Haudenosaunee, the New York–based League of the Iroquois (Mohawk, Oneida, Onondaga, Cayuga, and Seneca), among the eastern woodland tribes residing in the direct paths of Anglo-American expansion were able to resist expulsion from and maintain themselves in their own homelands. The so-called Five Nations,* adeptly employing the power that their political, military, and diplomatic unity provided, dominated much of the present northeastern United States until the American Revolution. They also raided westward against their political (native) enemies and fur-trading rivals, claiming hegemony over many of the western tribes and establishing a virtual monopoly of the beaver trade in lands that are now Ohio and Indiana.

After King George's War (1739–1748), the third of the four wars for imperial supremacy in eastern North America, Great Britain and France focused their attention on the Ohio Country, the land west of the Appalachian Mountains and north of the Ohio River. Both sides laid claim to this region and both envisioned future settlements there. Early in the 1750s the French crossed Lake Erie and began to build a chain of forts along the western Pennsylvania border to serve as a barrier to British and American expansion. This activity alarmed the tribes living in the Ohio Country. Although these tribes continued to welcome traders and conduct business with them, they pointedly warned the French to stay off their lands if their intent was to establish permanent settlements.

The French fortifications also alarmed the British and the Virginia and Pennsylvania colonists, who were all determined to thwart France's designs on the Ohio Country and to repel their

---

*The Iroquoian-speaking Tuscaroras fled northward from the colony of South Carolina in the 1710s and joined their kinsmen's League the next decade. Thereafter whites frequently called it the "Six Nations," although the Iroquois never changed the name.

hated adversary. In 1754, the French took control of the strategic point—now Pittsburgh—where the Allegheny and Monongahela rivers meet to form the Ohio River. At this site they built Fort Duquesne (later renamed Fort Pitt by the British). Governor Robert Dinwiddie of Virginia quickly sent a small militia force under George Washington to seize Fort Duquesne and order the French to leave. The French heatedly refused, and proceeded to push Washington's troops back into the southwestern corner of Pennsylvania, below Fort Duquesne, and defeat them. This battle triggered the fourth Anglo-French war for empire, in which most of the Indians of the Ohio Country participated on the side of the French. In light of these French-Indian alliances, Americans called the conflict the "French and Indian War."

The tribes living in the Ohio Country at the outbreak of the French and Indian War were relative newcomers there. Ohio had been virtually vacant for seventy-five years following the Iroquois raids of the mid-seventeenth century and the Five Nations' subsequent claim to the area south of Lake Erie. Other Indians for decades were apparently too intimidated to try to establish permanent villages there. This changed in the 1730s as tribes began to enter Ohio from all points on the compass, no longer able to resist the vacant spaces and abundant resources. As historian George Knepper, author of *Ohio and Its People,* observed, if nature abhors a vacuum, apparently at times societies do too.

From the east came New York Iroquois, mostly Senecas, who established villages in the Cuyahoga Valley (close to where Cleveland is today) and in the northeastern part of the future state. These people were known as "Mingoes," presumably an Algonquian word meaning "stealthy." They were drawn to Ohio because a great famine had created prolonged hardship in New York and because of the allure of goods available at white trading posts. From the Ontario Peninsula above Lake Erie, via the French settlement at Detroit, came the Wyandots. The Wyandots were Hurons whom the Iroquois Confederation, during its sweep westward in the seventeenth century, had driven from their Canadian homeland, formerly known as "Huronia." In the 1740s, with the permission of the Five Nations, the Wyandots settled in northern Ohio near

Sandusky Bay, along the shores of Lake Erie to the west of the Mingoes.

The Pickaway Plains in central Ohio became home to Shawnees from the Cumberland region of Tennessee and Kentucky and from Pennsylvania. They settled in that locale at the invitation of the Wyandots. In 1768 the future Shawnee political and war leader, Tecumseh, was born at the village of Old Piqua on the Mad River. The Odawas (or Ottawas) came down from the northern shores of Lake Huron through Michigan and settled around the fringes of the Black Swamp, a supersaturated area in northwestern Ohio. Their war chief Pontiac became a vigorous supporter of the French and an implacable foe of British expansion into the trans-Appalachian West during the 1760s. The Miamis, first seen by French explorers near Green Bay, Wisconsin, now stretched eastward out from their towns in Indiana and established settlements in the watersheds of the major rivers in southwestern Ohio. (Cincinnati would be built in this region after the American Revolution.) Led by their principal chief whom the French called "La Demoiselle" and the British called "Old Britain," the Miamis were drawn into Ohio by a desire for French and British trade goods.

Among all of the newcomers to the Ohio Country, the Delawares represented the best example of a tribe forced into numerous relocations under pressure from colonial settlement. An ancient and highly respected Algonquian people, they called themselves the *Leni Lenape,* the "Real People," when Europeans first encountered them in New Jersey in the region around the Delaware River. Driven westward into Pennsylvania, and then pushed across that colony by both colonials and Iroquois, the Delawares in the 1750s accepted the Wyandots' invitation to settle in eastern Ohio in the Tuscarawas and Muskingum valleys. While still living in Pennsylvania a number of Delawares had been converted to Christianity by Moravian missionaries, one of the most diligent of whom was David Zeisberger. His activities are recounted in two volumes by Earl P. Olmstead: *Blackcoats among the Delaware* and *David Zeisberger: A Life among the Indians.*

Born in the Kingdom of Bohemia (modern Czechoslovakia) and raised in Saxony, Germany, nineteen-year-old Zeisberger arrived in the American colonies in 1740 taking up residence in Bethlehem, Pennsylvania, the seat of the Moravian Church in America. He came eager to begin the career of a frontier missionary. Zeisberger, who had early in life exhibited a capacity for learning languages, mastered the Delaware, the Mohawk, and the Onondaga tongues and began his work in New York colony among the Iroquois.

The life of a missionary on the frontier was not only dangerous (Zeisberger was ready to ignore that), but often unproductive religiously. He found that Indians and colonists alike were suspicious of him and his Moravian beliefs, in particular his pacifism, a point of view entirely foreign to both groups. Zeisberger, laboring ceaselessly, experienced little success in New York and then only modest success in Pennsylvania. After two Moravian missions located near Bethlehem were destroyed in 1763 during Pontiac's Uprising, Moravian church leaders decided that it would be wiser not to conduct future missionary efforts near white settlements. Zeisberger, resolving to move himself and his band of converts westward, led his group to the Allegheny River and then farther west to the Beaver River. However, they were not at ease even in western Pennsylvania. Zeisberger continued to dream of a peaceful land where he, his white coworkers, and the Christian Indians could settle and prosper.

In 1771, receiving an invitation from Netawatwes, the head chief of the Delawares, to bring the "praying Indians" into the Delawares' new homeland, he left the colony of Pennsylvania and entered the Tuscarawas Valley in eastern Ohio. Zeisberger knew immediately that this was the place for his agrarian mission village. He called it *Schoenbrunn,* meaning "Beautiful Spring." A substantial Moravian migration followed which soon spread downriver into two more settlements: *Gnadenhutten* ("Cabins of Grace") and *Lichtenau* ("Pasture of Lights"). Within three years, more than 400 Indian converts were residing in these mission towns, characterized by sturdy log homes, large fenced fields, and gardens surrounded by fruit trees. Nonchristian Indians, offered hospitality and lodging at the mission towns, came and went too. Under the protection of the Delawares, especially Chief White

Eyes of the Turkey clan and Gelelemend of the Turtle clan (Netawatwes' grandson and heir to his chiefship), Indian and non-Indian Moravians alike were able to live in peace and to prosper.

To the distress of most Canadian and Great Lakes tribes, the French and Indian War ended with an absolute British victory in 1763 by terms of the Treaty of Paris: France ceded Canada and virtually all of its North American territory east of the Mississippi to Great Britain. England's rule over the tribes living west of the Appalachians and in the Great Lakes region was tenuous, often violent, and, in the end, brief. The outbreak of the American Revolution in 1775 raised the specter of a different danger for these tribes: it threatened to sweep away the British and place them and their lands under the dominion of the aggressive, land-hungry Americans.

Almost all tribes engaged in military activity during the Revolutionary War fought for the British. While regulars and German mercenaries did the campaigning against American forces in the eastern sector near the Atlantic coast, the British relied on Indian troops in the war's western sector to attack American colonists and to raid colonial farms and settlements.

Among the disasters of that long war was the split in the ranks of the Iroquois League. The American Revolution became the stage upon which a second drama, the Iroquois civil war, was acted. While the Mohawks and Cayugas remained faithful to their British alliance, the Oneidas, Tuscaroras, and some Senecas joined the American side. The Onondagas elected neutrality at the war's outset, but after American troops assaulted their towns in central New York, they backed the British. In 1778, British-led Iroquois took the war to colonials residing in the Wyoming Valley of Pennsylvania and the Cherry Valley of New York. They massacred families and burned their towns and farms. Furious upon receiving word of these attacks, General George Washington ordered General John Sullivan to take a large force into the Five Nations' homeland in New York and reciprocate. Sullivan swept from Tioga to the Genesee River in 1779, desolating Iroquois fields, orchards, and villages, and killing men, women, and children. Some Iroquois survivors fled to British Canada. Many others, left behind without adequate supplies, starved to death during the especially harsh winter of 1779–1780. The American Revolution destroyed both the solidarity of the Iroquois League and its power inside the emerging United States.

Another disaster during the American Revolution befell the inhabitants of the Moravian mission villages in the Tuscarawas Valley. The Revolutionary War was a disturbing intrusion for them and the other Ohio Indians, for their lands were directly on the Great Trail from Detroit to Fort Pitt, the former a British stronghold, the latter a center of American military activity. Most of the Ohio tribes supported the British. Brutal fighting engulfed the Ohio Valley during the Revolutionary War, as frequent British and Indian raids against colonials in Kentucky, Virginia, and Pennsylvania brought a series of American retaliatory strikes against the Indians and their villages in the Ohio Country.

As the fighting progressed, the Christian Delawares were viewed as enemies by all other natives of the region: Delawares to the south, Mingoes to the north, Shawnees to the west, and, above all, the powerful Wyandots located some 100 miles to the northwest on the Sandusky River, who were supplied and reinforced by the British at Detroit. The reason for the enmity was that the Moravians, both white and Indian, had selected the difficult and dangerous course of remaining neutral in the conflict.

By 1781 the French were providing substantial aid to the American cause, and victory in the east was becoming increasingly possible. However, the war in the west still raged, and the prospect of an American victory there was not nearly so sure. Zeisberger and the Moravians continued to hold to their position of neutrality and would not violate their pacifist beliefs, although they repeatedly invited retribution by clandestinely warning American settlers of impending British and Indian attacks. In late 1781, they were instrumental in thwarting a British and Wyandot raid on Fort Henry (now Wheeling, West Virginia). When Captain Matthew Elliot, leader of the British attack, found out from captives the role of the people from the Moravian settlements, he was enraged. He took his force to the Tuscarawas area and ordered the inhabitants of the mission towns to go with him to the Sandusky River area, where pro-British Indians could watch them.

The Moravians protested that their corn crop was standing in the field ready to be harvested; without it they would starve. Elliot refused them permission to stay, but promised them that he would personally make sure they were adequately fed, a promise he never kept. Zeisberger and other Moravian leaders spent the winter as prisoners of the British at Detroit. The commandant, Major Arendt Schuyler De Peyster, after interrogating Zeisberger and his coworkers, found them not guilty of treasonable activities. Meanwhile, the Delaware converts experienced a terrible time that winter in the camps along the Sandusky. By the following spring they were so close to starvation that the Wyandots relented and allowed 150 of them to return to their fields in eastern Ohio to harvest and bring back remnants of the last year's crops.

The Pennsylvania frontier had gone through a terrible winter, too. Although the war in the east had ended in victory for the Americans, throughout the winter months the British and their Indian allies had raided unmercifully among the settlers in the western counties of Pennsylvania. The Shawnees were a special scourge—they had not forgotten that their chief, Cornstalk, on a peace mission, had been murdered by Americans under a flag of truce in 1777 and launched retaliatory strikes because of it. It was in this atmosphere that Colonel David Williamson and his Pennsylvania militia heard of the Moravian Delawares who were by now harvesting their fields. Fairness and sound judgment had completely fled the frontier. Forgetting that the Christian Delawares had been considered good friends and had provided much useful military intelligence, 400 militiamen made their way to Gnadenhutten to punish them for the deeds of other Indians.

Arriving at night near Gnadenhutten, the militia waited quietly in the woods until morning. When the sun rose, they saw an unexpected number of Indians working in the fields. There could be no possibility of mistaken identity. The Christian Delawares had given up painting and decorating their faces and bodies; they dressed and wore their hair like whites. The militiamen carefully surrounded the village so none could escape. Six Delawares were encountered in the woods, one a woman. All were immediately put to death.

As the militiamen closed in, the Christian Delawares made no attempt to resist or run away. They readily believed the story they were told, that they were to be removed to Fort Pitt where they would be safe for the rest of the war. The Moravian Indians then went to their chapel where they calmly awaited the start of the journey to Pennsylvania. Meanwhile, outside, a kind of kangaroo court was convened and all but eighteen of the militiamen voted for the deaths of the Delawares. The eighteen argued that these Indians had been their friends during the Revolutionary War and had been peaceful toward the whites on the frontier. But their pleas were to no avail; the sentence was to be carried out as promptly as possible.

During this time the Christian Delawares still had no hint of what awaited them. After being notified of their fate, they were allowed to have the night to prepare themselves. The shocked Indians spent the time praying, singing hymns, and offering farewells. At dawn they were dragged by rope, two and three at a time, to a couple of houses in Gnadenhutten, referred to as the "slaughter houses" by the militiamen. There they were executed in cold blood by crushing blows to the head with a mallet. In all, ninety Delawares were murdered, twenty-nine men, twenty-seven women, and thirty-four children. The victims were thrown into a mass grave. Hearing of the slaughter, the people at the other mission towns fled back to the Sandusky. Some returned temporarily to eastern Ohio after the Revolution, but eventually they settled along the Thames River in southern Ontario, where their descendants live today.

Inspired by their successful sweep of the unarmed Delawares, the frontiersmen mounted an expedition to clean out the Sandusky River towns. They were led by Colonel William Crawford, George Washington's close friend and former western land agent. Although Crawford and his troops were unaware of it, Indians scouted them all the way across Ohio. Even though the Ohio tribes had never favored the Christian Indians, they nonetheless planned to take a dreadful revenge for their deaths. When Crawford's forces arrived at the Sandusky, they found no one in the towns but were met by a force of Indians and British Rangers. The Americans were nearly wiped out. For the survivors, it was every man for himself. A few, led ironically by Colonel David Williamson, made it back to Pennsylvania. Crawford was captured, taken to a nearby Delaware town, and tortured terribly before finally being burned at the stake.

Breaching the Ohio Country

As soon as the American Revolution came to an end, white settlers began to penetrate the Ohio country and other western lands in search of homes. Many were veterans of the Revolution, compensated by their debt-ridden state and national governments for their time in the military with land grants in the trans-Appalachian West. Although Great Britain granted these lands to the United States in the Treaty of Paris of 1783, the native peoples who had thought for centuries that the land beyond the Appalachian Mountains was their own were determined to resist.

The government of the United States hoped to avoid warfare with the tribes there and provide for the orderly westward expansion of the nation by the wise management of Indian affairs. Congress, with its power over the regulation of commerce and treaty making—granted initially by the Articles of Confederation and then by the Constitution—exercised sweeping control over Indian matters. It did so by two procedures. By the first it passed legislation, in particular a series of Trade and Intercourse acts enacted between 1790 and 1834. These laws, delineated in Francis Paul Prucha's *American Indian Policy in the Formative Years,* regulated white settlement on Indian land, controlled white trade in liquor with tribes, provided a detailed definition of Indian country, managed the sale of Indian land, and established a network of government-operated trading houses known as factories. The goals of this legislation were to gain the confidence and loyalty of tribes on the frontier, to control them economically, and to decrease sources of conflict so as to promote harmonious relations between them and American settlers as the nation expanded westward.

By the second procedure, Congress ratified formal treaties with Indians to nullify their titles to land. England and the other European imperial powers had recognized tribes as sovereign nations holding titles to land by right of occupancy and throughout the colonial period concluded treaties with them based on this principle. The United States government concurred, grounded its policy on this principle, and, for almost 100 years, dealt with Indian tribes as sovereign nations by means of treaties.*

As soon as the Revolutionary War ended, American commissioners conducted numerous councils with the Indian tribes on the southern and western frontiers to establish official relations between them and the United States and often to secure land cessions. In 1785 and 1786, commissioners negotiated foundational treaties with southern tribes at Hopewell, South Carolina. By the terms of the Treaties of Hopewell, the United States made peace with the Cherokees, Chickasaws, and Choctaws, defined tribal boundaries, and acquired small tracts of tribal land for the national government's use. Other treaties with other southern tribes followed. The United States government had acted in the hope of keeping peace in the South, believing its efforts would restrain the Southerners from advancing too rapidly onto Indian lands. Hardly impressed by the will of the federal government, agents from the states of Virginia, Georgia, and North and South Carolina toiled tenaciously in the late eighteenth century to acquire more and more land from Indians within their states. The actions of the national government in fact upset the states of the South. They charged that the U.S. commissioners' deals with the Indians violated their states' "sovereignty and legislative rights."

At the same time that American commissioners were establishing diplomatic relations between the United States and the

---

*This changed in 1871 when Congress passed legislation declaring that: "No Indian nation or tribe within the territory of the United States shall be acknowledged or recognized as an independent nation, tribe, or power with whom the United States may contract by treaty."

tribes of the South, other commissioners were exerting intense pressure on the western tribes for land cessions. This was because the new United States government planned to use their land, the land beyond the Ohio River, as a laboratory for developing policies and procedures on how to fashion territories from the wilderness and the conditions under which territories would enter the Union as new states. To that end, Congress organized the vast area beyond the Ohio into the Northwest Territory and passed land ordinances in 1784, 1785, and 1787 that articulated an array of policies for the orderly survey, sale, settlement, and establishment of government there.

National leaders understood that perhaps the biggest initial impediment to this ambitious program of westward settlement was the Indians living in the Ohio Country. This area would be the first developed by the United States and settled by Americans within the Northwest Territory. Commissioners were dispatched and the first attempt made to obtain the Indians' lands in three treaties from 1784 to 1786. The first treaty, with the Iroquois League at Fort Stanwix, extinguished the League's claims to territories west of Fort Pitt. At Fort McIntosh, the United States imposed the second treaty upon the Wyandots, Delawares, Chippewas, and Odawas by "right of conquest" from the Revolutionary War, a conquest that had never occurred. When Indian representatives protested and advanced their own arguments and claims, the commissioners rebuffed them, asserting, "because we claim the country by conquest, [you are here] to give not to receive." The Fort McIntosh Treaty allotted lands between the Cuyahoga River and the Maumee River, in northwestern Ohio, for the tribes present. The treaty took for the United States the remaining 30 million acres of the Indians' land. Tribal members felt no obligation to honor a treaty that had been dictated to them, especially one based, as they saw it, on the specious justification of right of conquest. Soon their leaders were conferring with British agents at Detroit, who distributed guns, ammunition, blankets, and other supplies to them, and who also parceled out hope of the British recovery of the Northwest Territory from the weak American republic—with the Indians' help, of course.

Commissioners next approached the Shawnees, who signed the Fort Finney Treaty. Told that they "should be thankful for the forgiveness and offers of kindness of the United States," the Shawnees theoretically lost all of their lands in southwestern Ohio and adjacent areas of eastern Indiana. In reality, they left the proceedings, returned to their villages, repudiated the treaty, and made war again on Kentuckians and on the settlers who now arrived to occupy their "former" lands. Repeating the pattern of the Revolutionary War years, militias of rugged frontiersmen, led by Benjamin Logan and George Rogers Clark, promptly retaliated, sacking Shawnee villages and destroying Indian property in Ohio.

By the time the United States had secured these three treaties in 1786, a loose confederacy of western Indians was developing at the Miamis' capital of Kekionga (Fort Wayne, Indiana) and along the Maumee River. These villages contained not only Miamis, but also Odawas, Chippewas, Shawnees, Potawatomis, Kickapoos, Delawares, and others. All were determined to hold the Ohio country with the support of, and with guns from, the British in Canada. Led by Little Turtle of the Miamis, Blue Jacket of the Shawnees, Buckongehelas of the Delawares, and Tarhe of the Wyandots, the allied tribes struck hard, again and again, at the ever-increasing farms and settlements in Ohio. One estimate claims that between 1783 and 1790 over 1,500 settlers perished in Indian attacks.

It didn't take long for national leaders to realize the failure of their Indian policy in the Northwest Territory. A concerned Secretary of War Henry Knox decided that the United States must respond with force, which would coerce new treaties. In the early 1790s, three American expeditions went up the Miami River to the Auglaize and the Maumee to subdue the confederated Indians. The first two expeditions, commanded respectively by General Josiah Harmar and Ohio Territorial Governor Arthur St. Clair, were unmitigated disasters. St. Clair's beating was the worst defeat ever suffered by an American army at the hands of Indians in a single battle: 600 Americans dead and nearly 300 wounded.

The news of St. Clair's defeat ignited President George Washington's well-known temper. To lead the third expedition,

Washington called on a comrade from the Revolutionary War, General "Mad Anthony" Wayne. Wayne was anything but mad; he was a solid military man who drilled his troops in forest warfare at Cincinnati before allowing them to move northward. After besting the Indians in a series of engagements as he progressed up the western side of Ohio, he routed them at the Battle of Fallen Timbers near Toledo, Ohio, in August 1794. A year later over 1,000 Indian representatives came to Greenville and signed a treaty highly unfavorable to their claims to Ohio. They were convinced that they had no option but to evacuate the lands enumerated in the Fort McIntosh and Fort Finney treaties.

Tecumseh, Gradualists, and Removalists

Among the defeated warriors was the Shawnee leader Tecumseh, who knew there could be no peace if whites continued to push farther west. He wanted white and red people to live in peace by mutually respecting a boundary line between them. Whether the boundary was in western Ohio or farther west on the Wabash in Indiana was less important than the resolve of both sides to respect it.

Tecumseh spent his youth enmeshed in the frontier wars of the trans-Appalachian West. His father, Pucksinwah, was second in command of all Shawnee warriors under Cornstalk. He died in 1774 at the Battle of Point Pleasant, perhaps the most intense engagement between colonials and Indians along the Ohio River. Thereafter mentored by his older brother Chiksika in the life of a warrior, Tecumseh along with the Shawnees raided white encampments along the Ohio River, struck frontier settlements in Kentucky, and joined Cherokees to make war on Americans in Tennessee. Tecumseh lost the man who had been both mentor and brother when Chiksika died in 1788 attacking Buchanan's Station in Tennessee. Tecumseh, a warrior with a growing reputation, and his Shawnee followers made their way northward in 1790. They wished to join with the confederated tribes that had just beaten General Harmar during his invasion of Ohio. Throwing himself into the defense of his homeland, Tecumseh participated in the next two critical engagements: St. Clair's debacle and the Battle of Fallen Timbers.

In the aftermath of the major defeat at Fall Timbers, Tecumseh began to preach a political message stressing pan-Indianism: all tribes had a collective stake in blocking the westward advance of whites, and the further sale of Indian land lacked validity unless approved by all the tribes. Tecumseh found strong backing from his younger brother Lalawethika, a drunken braggart who had experienced a religious conversion and became Tenskwatawa, known to whites as the Shawnee Prophet. He claimed divine revelations, and he preached to Indians a rejection of the white man's ways and a return to traditional native values and lifestyle. The brothers' message was crystal clear: the Indians' only source of salvation would be cultural renaissance combined with armed resistance grounded on Indian unity.

The old tribal leaders, like Black Hoof of the Shawnees, dismissed the brothers' ideas and sought reconciliation with Americans by honoring the terms of the Greenville Treaty. Even so, the brothers went forward in their determination to form a confederacy of tribes powerful enough to challenge any further acquisition of Indian land. Tecumseh journeyed tirelessly from tribe to tribe, from Wisconsin to Florida, from Indiana to Mississippi, trying to rally support to block American settlement. North of the Ohio River he gained some adherents. South of the Ohio he was listened to with respect—but gained no real support. In 1808 the brothers moved their village from Ohio to Tippecanoe Creek in western Indiana. This site became known as Prophetstown, and hundreds of people from various tribes, ranging from young warriors to whole families, traveled there to camp and to hear the encouraging message. Many whites were alarmed. Some, such as Thomas Jefferson, were sympathetic. But the president's solution to the tensions caused by American expansion, like that of other Gradualists, was anathema to Tecumseh and the Prophet. Almost from the birth of the republic, two groups—the "Gradualists" and the "Removalists"—emerged with different opinions of the proper course of federal policy to achieve peace with Indians. Ultimately the fate of the eastern tribes was shaped by the battle between these groups to dominate the national government, as each sought to influence policy toward Indians.

The Gradualists advocated peaceful coexistence between Americans and Indians until a steady assimilation of Indians into the dominant society occurred through missionary work, education, and reordering Indian land usage. Their program called for a total transformation of Indian society in the absolute confidence that the transfiguration would in all ways be superior to the "primitive" lifestyle that had preceded it. This group stressed the necessity for nonagriculturalist Indians to change their subsistence pattern from hunting, which required extensive territory and periodic migration, to farming, which would require much smaller tracts of land and encourage a sedentary lifestyle. This would free up "excess" land, which could then be acquired peacefully by whites. As Jefferson explained: "While they are learning to do better on less land, our increasing numbers will be calling for more land, and thus a coincidence of interests will be produced between those who have land to spare, and those . . . who want land." When transformation into farmers was joined with educational and missionary efforts, Indians would possess the economic, cultural, and religious wherewithal to be acceptable and productive neighbors for the settlers about them. But first, Indians must abandon their native cultures, the tribal order, and their belief in communal ownership of property. "They cannot much longer exist in the exercise of their savage rights and customs," declared William H. Crawford, James Madison's secretary of war. "They must become civilized, or they will finally . . . become extinct."

The Gradualists foresaw no unsolvable problems with those Indians unwilling to alter or abandon either nonagricultural subsistence patterns or their accustomed lifestyle. They proposed to critics that the steady movement of the American agricultural frontier toward the Mississippi would deplete the wild game that these Indians depended upon for survival. When they could not find sufficient food, they would be compelled to sell their land and move out of the settlers' way. The Gradualists confidently expected their program to achieve two critical objectives: it would civilize and assimilate a sizable number of Indians and facilitate peaceful relations between Indians and white settlers on the frontier as the westward movement proceeded.

On the other hand, Removalists argued the opposite side of how to solve the Indian Question. They, too, sought peaceful relations between Americans and Indians, but they were not persuaded that the plan advanced by the Gradualists held much likelihood of success. The Removalists contended that most Indians were little interested in being "civilized," as shown by the message of the Shawnee Prophet and Tecumseh. Perhaps the actual problem, they speculated, really was not one of disinclination, but of incapacity. Most Americans, concluded one commissioner of Indian Affairs, regarded Indians as "irreclaimable, terrible" savages. The scientific community validated this assertion. "Do what we will," emphasized Dr. Josiah C. Nott, one of the South's leading surgeons, "the Indian remains the Indian still. He is not a creature susceptible of civilization. . . . He can no more be civilized than the leopard can change his spots. . . . He is now gradually disappearing, to give place to a higher order of beings." Dr. Charles Caldwell, a University of Pennsylvania medical professor, an influential lecturer and author, a leading phrenologist,* and the founder of a medical school in Kentucky, concluded the same. After examining a variety of Indian skulls, he determined that "when the wolf, the buffalo and the panther shall have been completely domesticated, like the dog, the cow, and the household cat, then, and not before, may we expect to see the full-blooded Indian civilized, like the white man."

To accept this line of reasoning required one to reject the Gradualists' program. Indians, incapable of being civilized, were doomed to extinction and therefore any effort to civilize them must prove futile. This judgment was not meant to be malicious, it was thought to be only common sense. It led to another matter of contention: did uncivilized and uncivilizable people enjoy any inherent right to the land they occupied? Most Americans thought not. The noted author Hugh Henry Brackenridge, for example, ar-

---

*Phrenology was the study of the conformation of the skull, which was believed to indicate character and mental ability.

guing in his article "The Animals, Vulgarly called Indians" that tribes had no right to the soil, asserted that it was as ridiculous to "admit a right in the buffalo to grant lands" as it would be to bestow the same right on "the Big Cat, the Big Dog, or any of the ragged wretches that are called chiefs and sachems." Brackenridge concluded his argument with a question: "What would you think if going to a big lick or place where the beasts collect to lick saline nitrous earth and water, and addressing yourself to a great buffalo to grant you land?" The answer, he expected confidently, was obvious to all discerning people.

The Removalists also argued that the unrelenting westward thrust of white settlement would occur too rapidly to permit peaceful coexistence on the frontier. It was common knowledge that taking too much tribal land at one time led to warfare. To avoid further bloodshed and depravations on the frontier and, equally as important, to throw open more Indian land for white settlement and enterprise, the Removalists offered their own solution: Indians must exchange their lands east of the Mississippi for territory west of that river. If some tribes proved recalcitrant, as might be anticipated, the Removalists urged forced evacuation as an appropriate option. This solution, again, was not seen as malice, but as common sense. Removalists judged removal as a benevolent course—one predicated on the assumption that Indians would remain "savages," perpetuating their accustomed way of life. Removal, therefore, was thought to be the best way of assuring peaceful relations between Americans and Indians. Some Americans took a hard line against any Indians who might resist removal. Congressman David Levy of Florida contended that Indians were "demons, not men. They have the human form, but nothing of the human heart. Horror and detestation should follow the thought of them. If they cannot be emigrated, they should be exterminated."

Because Thomas Jefferson supported the Gradualists' program, in his annual messages to Congress he offered vigorous praise and support for those measures that would advance "the arts of civilization" among Indians. He reiterated this view in messages to the Indians. The president stated to the Miamis, Weas, and

Potawatomis: "We shall with great pleasure see your people become disposed to cultivate the earth, to raise herds of useful animals and to spin and weave, for their food and clothing. These resources are certain, they will never disappoint you, while those of hunting may fail, and expose your women and children to the miseries of hunger and cold." Yet if in time Indians refused the opportunities provided by white society to civilize themselves, Jefferson would demand that they be evicted from their land. "This then is the season for driving them off," he wrote.

In Indiana Territory, William Henry Harrison had been appointed territorial governor in 1801. Harrison had fought under General Wayne at Fallen Timbers and had been present for the signing of the Greenville Treaty. Able and determined, Harrison understood the nation's plan for expansion and the president's strategy for the Indians. Also a compassionate man, Harrison on one occasion adopted the son of a dying Delaware chief and raised the boy with his own family. The governor sought to develop a peaceful relationship with the tribes living in the Indiana Territory. He also kept a close eye on the activities at Prophetstown and the comings and goings of Tecumseh. "For four years he has been in constant motion," Harrison noticed. "You see him today on the Wabash and in a short time you hear of him on the Shores of Lake Erie, or Michigan, or the banks of the Mississippi. And where ever he goes, he makes an impression favorable to his purpose." The strident messages coming from Prophetstown and the nearly 1,000 warriors residing there alarmed him. Trouble could not be far away, Harrison reasoned. He inevitably came to the conclusion that, in Jefferson's lexicon, the season was nearing for driving off Tecumseh, the Prophet, and their followers.

In 1811, Tecumseh traveled south again in an attempt to bring the Chickasaws, Cherokees, Choctaws, and Creeks to his cause. All Indians were on the brink of catastrophe, he warned. "The mere presence of the white man is a source of evil to the red man. . . . The only hope for the red man is a war of extermination against the paleface. Will not the warriors of the southern tribes unite with the warriors of the Lakes?" Only the Red Sticks, a faction of the Creeks, embraced Tecumseh's proposal. Many people of the southern tribes rejected his call because they were turning to the program of the Gradualists. In one of the most significant episodes in Indian–United States relations, these Indinans not only tried such acculturation during the early nineteenth century, but some, like the Cherokees, did it with phenomenal success. Even then, Americans still insisted that the Cherokees abandon their homes in the southern highlands to settle beyond the Mississippi. Tecumseh's strategy met with no greater success.

Harrison used the opportunity of Tecumseh's absence to move against Prophetstown. Commanding regular troops, frontier militia, and volunteers, Harrison led a force of nearly 1,000 men across Indiana Territory. Tecumseh had admonished his brother to avoid a conflict with Harrison during his absence. The Prophet disobeyed. After convincing the warriors at Prophetstown that they would be immune to the bullets of the approaching troops, at dawn on November 7, 1811, he ordered an attack on Harrison's encampment. The Indians fought furiously and out in the open, a stark departure from their custom, and one no doubt prompted by the conviction that they were invincible. Ultimately Harrison's men repelled them, marched on Prophetstown, and burned it. Numerically, many more soldiers than Indians died that day. But emotionally, the Battle of Tippecanoe disillusioned Tecumseh's followers and shattered his movement. Soon thereafter, most of the tribes' support for it faded away.

Tecumseh now turned to the British. With his remaining followers, he crossed the Detroit River into Canada and put himself under British command. His last resource was a war between the United States and Great Britain which, in the event of a British victory, might create an independent state for the American Indians in the Northwest Territory. Six months later the War of 1812 broke out. In it Tecumseh distinguished himself for valor, but he lost his life on October 5, 1813, at the Battle of the Thames in Canada against a United States army commanded by William Henry Harrison. This victory, plus the Battle of Tippecanoe, would make Harrison president of the United States twenty-eight years later.

While the British might properly have claimed victory on the east coast—they burned the White House and the U.S. Capitol— they and their Indian allies lost absolutely in the northwest. When

Great Britain raised the question of an Indian state during peace talks at Ghent, Belgium, U.S. representative John Quincy Adams angrily prepared to leave. His partner Henry Clay counseled him not to, that the British were merely bluffing in the hope of securing various concessions from the Americans. They were. Harrison's victory at the Thames, coupled with Andrew Jackson's triumph less than a year later over the Red Stick Creeks at the Battle of Horseshoe Bend in eastern Alabama, brought to an end the dream of the pan-Indian confederacy.

Toward a Policy of Separation

Forces stimulating American expansion were never long dormant, and during the early nineteenth century the frontier pushed relentlessly beyond the Appalachian chain into Indian country. It pressed deeper into the Northwest Territory with the collapse of significant Indian resistance under Tecumseh and the Shawnee Prophet. It spread across the Old Southwest, especially with the rapid expansion of the Cotton Belt after Eli Whitney's invention of the cotton gin. By 1820 settlers had pushed as far west as the valley of the Mississippi River. The census of that year indicated that almost one-fourth of the American people lived in the trans-Appalachian West, and there was no hint that the flow of settlers into the area would diminish.

This activity fanned interracial conflict, and for a growing number of Americans solidified the conviction that gradualism could not solve the Indian question. For the first two decades of the nineteenth century, the Gradualists had dominated the national government and the formation of Indian policy. But proponents of removal pronounced the program of the Gradualists a failure. It had failed to prevent warfare on the frontier or to bring natives in any appreciable numbers into the American mainstream. Unacculturated Indians remained on the much-coveted land of the frontier, impeding white settlement. For most Americans this situation evidenced gradualism's greatest failing. It seemed clear that the two races could never live in close proximity to one another. "The deep rooted prejudices, and malignity of heart, and conduct, reciprocally entertained and practiced on all occasions by the Whites and Savages will ever prevent their being good neighbors," surmised one official. "Either one or the other party must remove to a greater distance." Removalists stepped up calls for Washington legislators to initiate a comprehensive plan to colonize eastern Indians on lands west of the Mississippi River.

In those same years Gradualists also concluded, slowly and painfully, that colonization might be appropriate. This development did not signal an abandonment of their beliefs and goals. It did, however, reflect their doubts about the possibility of success of their program amidst the swirl of settlement on the frontier. They could not refute charges that so far, most Indians would not, or could not, be civilized. Even when certain Indians had altered their lifestyles, few were accepted into white society. More often than not, their attempts only heightened tensions with white neighbors. The Gradualists also knew that these assimilated Indians were the exception. Most Indians experienced increasing distress, privation, and societal disintegration. "Two centuries have gone round," observed Thomas L. McKenney, President Monroe's Indian commissioner, after traveling among the tribes in the Old Northwest, "and the remnants of these people, that remain, are more wretched than when they were a great and numerous people." His report described the depth of their debasement: "They catch fish—and plant patches of corn; dance, paint, hunt, fight, get drunk when they can get liquor and often starve. . . . There is no sketching that can convey a clear perception of the misery and degradation in which [they are] involved."

In light of this dismaying reality, removal took on new significance and purpose for Gradualists. Because their long-term objective remained the incorporation of detribalized, acculturated Indians into white society, removal seemed the only means of achieving that end. It became the panacea to the Gradualists, but its success and the mitigation of the trauma to tribes, which removal would certainly cause, depended on future contingencies, as scholar Bernard Sheehan points out in *Seeds of Extinction.* "The Indian must be allowed a period free from the pressure of the frontier, and the civilizing program must move west with the tribes.

Should these expectations be fulfilled, the inconvenience of removal . . . would have been only incidental to the long-run accomplishment." Increasingly, Gradualists believed that not only did the ultimate success of their program seem to rest on supporting removal but the very survival of the eastern Indians depended on it as well. Therefore, the Gradualists and the Removalists, for different reasons, found themselves occupying common ground. Henry Schoolcraft, for years an Indian agent at Sault Sainte Marie, Michigan Territory, echoed mounting public opinion. "It is now evident to all, that the salvation of these interesting relics of Oriental races lies in colonization west," he wrote. "Public sentiment has settled on the ground; sound policy dictates it; and the most enlarged philanthropy for the Indian race perceives its best hope in the measure [forced removal]."

President James Monroe, like his mentor Thomas Jefferson, supported the Gradualist program as the best course for saving the Indians and promoting peaceful relations between them and whites. Monroe stressed that to civilize the Indians it was "indispensable that their independence as communities should cease," their accustomed lifestyle and cultural values be abandoned, and the government provide "some benevolent provisions." Congress responded to his calls with the Indian Civilization Act of 1819. It appropriated $10,000 annually to employ "capable persons of good moral character" to educate the Indians in reading, writing, arithmetic, and agricultural techniques. The question was: were these measures too late to save the Indians in the East? The president, increasingly troubled by reports from Commissioner McKenney and others about the deterioration among tribes, finally acknowledged that settlement "on every side by the white population" would not allow sufficient time for acculturation programs to improve the situation. Like other Gradualists, he concluded that removal, to be followed by government-assisted civilization programs in the West, offered the best solution.

In 1824, Monroe proposed a plan for the relocation of tribes westward. "The hunter or savage state requires a greater extent of territory to sustain it, than is compatible with the progress and just claims of civilized life, and must yield to it," Monroe explained, offering Congress his rationale for advocating relocation. "It was right that the hunter should yield to the farmer, for the earth was given to mankind to support the greatest number of which it is capable, and no tribe or people have a right to withhold from the wants of others more than is necessary for their own support and comfort." He stressed, however, that relocation must be voluntary on the part of eastern tribes and that their new western land must equal the extent and quality of that forfeited in the East. The government's plan for the Indians did not rule out persuasion, but at this juncture it did not contemplate force. Forced removal, Monroe declared emphatically, would be "revolting to humanity, and utterly unjustifiable." The direction charted by the president mollified the Removalists, but it displeased them that it left the choice of relocation up to the Indians. The next chief executive's attitude did not satisfy them at all.

The crusty, honest New Englander John Quincy Adams succeeded Monroe as president. Like his predecessor Adams acknowledged voluntary relocation as an appropriate solution to the Indian question, although he showed far less enthusiasm for the plan. Also like Monroe, he refused to force tribes westward against their will, but he opposed the idea with greater vehemence than Monroe had. Adams was not sentimental regarding Indians, and he held no illusions about the present state of Indian-white affairs. The president, an ardent legalist, categorically rejected forced removal simply because it would amount to a violation of earlier treaties with the tribes, a breach of the nation's solemn pledges Adams considered unconscionable.

Although not coerced into doing so by the Adams administration, tribes of the Old Northwest during the 1820s began forfeiting their remaining lands, agreed to removal treaties, and started relocating beyond the Mississippi to lands that later became Kansas. Many factors compelled them to this course of action. Harried by settlers, many corrupted by alcohol and other aspects of white culture, and void of strong leadership like that of Tecumseh, the Indians acknowledged that continued resistance was futile. Most had already abandoned hope of saving themselves and remaining in their lands by accepting the Gradualists' civilization measures.

They had decided that the inevitable could be forestalled only so long. One Wyandot chief chided federal officials, saying he saw little point in supporting acculturation or urging his people to make progress toward that goal when it was clear that whites intended to evict them whether they were civilized or not. Some individuals resisted removal by hiding, marrying whites, and even by committing suicide. Most abandoned the Old Northwest between 1829 and 1843, withdrawing to the trans-Mississippi West.

In sharp contrast, while some southern Indians emigrated to the West by the late 1820s, a significant majority of the region's tribes refused voluntary removal and elected to stay on their lands, most especially the five major tribes of the region: the Cherokees, Chickasaws, Choctaws, Creeks, and Seminoles. That decision made them a target for southern Removalists. Americans residing in the Southern states still regarded these Indians as barriers to further (white) settlement and economic gain. They demanded the elimination of the Indians in order to open more lands for agriculture, particularly cotton.

In the face of mounting demands for their eviction, the tribes devised various strategies to buttress the right to remain in their homelands. For example, they changed their traditional forms of government. The Cherokees, Chickasaws, and Choctaws, between 1808 and 1829, fashioned systems of national laws based on a written constitution. National judicial systems and national police forces also were inaugurated in the same period. Another strategy was supporting the interests of the United States. During the War of 1812, for example, parties of the Cherokees, Creeks, Chickasaws, and Choctaws came to the aid of General Andrew Jackson, assisting his militia to guard the southern frontier against British invasion and to combat factions of anti-American Indians, such as the Red Stick Creeks.

Perhaps the most salient strategy was that of altering their lifestyle in the hope of making it more acceptable to white neighbors. In this the Cherokees provide the most distinct illustration. Occupying 15 million acres in northern Georgia, southwestern North Carolina, northwestern Alabama, and eastern Tennessee, many Cherokees adopted housing and clothing typical of white society. Some sent their children to white schools, a few of whom were sent as far away as the foreign mission school at Cornwall, Connecticut, which the American Board of Foreign Missions opened in 1817. After 1821, the Cherokees had a written language of their own, utilizing the eighty-five symbol syllabary developed by Sequoia, and they published their own newspapers. The most widely read and well known of their publications was the *Cherokee Phoenix,* which first appeared in 1828 and was edited by the mixed-blooded Elias Boudinot. Boudinot printed the paper's columns in both the Cherokee and English languages. Historian Arrell Morgan Gibson reported that the Cherokees achieved near total literacy in their own language in less than half a decade. In 1827 the Cherokees drafted and adopted a written constitution, modeled after the United States Constitution, that reaffirmed their nation's sovereignty. Increasingly, they conducted political affairs in much the same manner as Americans. Like their white neighbors and some members of other major southern tribes, some Cherokees owned African slaves. The Cherokee nation also developed a thriving economy, monopolized by the mixed-bloods, based on stock raising, grain and lumber mills, and a plantation agricultural system. A northern visitor during the 1820s observed that they lived "in comfort and abundance, in good houses of brick, stone, and wood," admitting that the Cherokees "seemed to have more money than the whites in our own settlement."

Americans who opposed forced removal applauded these advancements, often exaggerating the extent of such gains among tribal members in order to bolster support for gradualism and assert their contention that Indians could indeed acculturate. Those favoring forced removal often discounted reports of the level of civilization achieved by the Cherokees and other southern tribes. One Southerner declared, for example, that it was "a mistake to imagine a nation civilized because it has black cattle, or plants a few potatoes in the weeds, or spins a gross of broaches of very indifferent cotton." Misleading reports about Indian advances, Removalists argued, did not mitigate the need to acquire more Indian land or the right to require their eviction.

Secretary of War John C. Calhoun noted the irony of the situation in the South to President Monroe. "It cannot be doubted," he wrote, "that much of the difficulty of acquiring additional cessions from the Cherokee nation, and other southern tribes, results from their growing civilization and knowledge, by which they have learned to place a higher value upon their lands than more rude and savage tribes." Calhoun was correct in his assessment. As southern Indians became more acculturated, they became more conscious of a unitary tribal identity, eventually combining it with the white man's concept of national sovereignty. Certainly the Cherokee nation was more determined than ever not to yield to the Removalists. "The Cherokees have long since come to the conclusion never again to cede *another foot* of land," declared Principal Chief John Ross. To protect Cherokee landholdings, in 1819 the Cherokee nation made the unauthorized sale of lands by Cherokees to whites a capital offense. Georgians, on the other hand, declared the actions of the Cherokee nation to be a threat to state sovereignty. An earlier compact between Georgia and the United States further complicated the knotty situation in that state. In 1802 Georgia waived its claims to western lands, thus reducing its territory to that of the present-day state. For this cession, the state coaxed the federal government into promising that title to all Indian lands within its newly fixed borders would be conveyed to Georgia. No other state managed to extract such a concession. But Georgia's triumph proved more frustrating than satisfying. For twenty years the federal authority made broad grants of Indian land to Ohio, Indiana, Illinois, Kentucky, North Carolina, Tennessee, Alabama, and Mississippi. Georgians watched anxiously, and with increasing anger, while almost one-third of their state remained in the hands of Indians.

Removing the Southern Tribes

Southern state officials could do little in the 1820s except harass the Indians to remove themselves because one president after another simply refused to force them west against their will. James Monroe had ignored mounting demands from fellow Southerners and steadfastly refused to budge from his position of strong disapproval of forced removal. And John Quincy Adams, deeply troubled by developments in Georgia, showed little sympathy for Southerners' avarice for Indian land, guaranteed to Indians, as he pointed out, by solemn federal treaties. Then the fate of the southern tribes reversed as a result of the 1828 election. Adams lost his bid for a second term to Andrew Jackson of Tennessee, an advocate of forced colonization of the southern tribes. The Cherokees were well aware of what the ascendancy of Jackson forbode. "A crisis seems to be fast approaching when the final destiny of our nation must be sealed," predicted Chief John Ross. He addressed the situation in his annual message of 1829 to the Cherokee nation:

The preservation and happiness of the Cherokee people are at stake, and the United States must soon determine the issue—we can only look with confidence to the good faith and magnanimity of the General Government, whose precepts and profession inculcate principles of liberty and republicanism, and whose obligations are solemnly pledged to give us justice and protection. . . .

President Jackson gave personal attention to passage of federal legislation authorizing forced removal, stressing in his annual messages the need for Congress to endorse a policy of Separation to solve the Indian question. It might have troubled him to betray tribes that had come to his aid during the War of 1812, when the survival of the republic was at stake. Chief Junaluska, who had saved Jackson's life when a hostile Red Stick Creek sneaked into the general's tent and tried to stab him, now reacted with bitterness: "If I had known that Jackson was going to drive us from our homes, I would have killed him that day at the Horseshoe." Chief John Ross likewise was appalled. "I have known Genl. Jackson from my boyhood—my earliest and warmest friends in Tennessee are generally his advocates—during the late war [the War of 1812] I held a rank [lieutenant] in the Cherokee regiment and fought by his side," he wrote the legendary frontiersman Davy Crockett. "How the President of the U[nited] States can reconcile it to his feelings to withdraw from us the protection pledged by treaty, and to allow the state of Georgia to usurp from us the rights and liberties of freemen . . . I cannot understand."

Andrew Jackson was a hybrid, not a pure Removalist. In his proposed agenda for the Indians he coalesced the Removalist and the Gradualist positions, producing the policy of Separation. Like

Monroe, Adams, and earlier nineteenth-century presidents, Jackson believed firmly that Indians were capable of acculturating and could be assimilated into white society. He did not think them irreclaimable savages. But, considering the desperation with which whites coveted their lands and the virulence directed against Indians by many Americans, Indian assimilation was impossible as long as the Indians remained east of the Mississippi. Unlike his recent predecessors in the White House, Jackson would not leave the choice up to the Indians. Relocation was no longer an option. Indians would be forcibly relocated to the western wilderness by the federal authority. Once physically separated from Americans, Indians would no longer impede white settlement and enterprise. At that point Gradualists would have sufficient time to implement their civilization measures successfully. By the time, far in the future, white settlement again reached the Indians, thought Jackson, they would be culturally, religiously, politically, and economically ready to take their place in the dominant society. For these reasons, the president stressed, a policy of Separation as the only solution to the Indian question, one which Congress must affirm.

Andrew Jackson's current reputation, shaped by textbooks, teachers, and the media, is that of a scourge to the Indians of the South because of his strong advocacy of their removal to western lands. However, Jackson viewed himself as a true friend and protector of the Indians, a benevolent advocate acting with paternalistic wisdom in their best interest. Michael Paul Rogin develops this theme in *Fathers and Children.* Although the policy of Separation appeared to be "an act of *seeming* violence," Alfred Balch, a Jackson supporter, wrote the president, "it will prove in the end an act of enlarged philanthropy." While many whites and most Indians would have disputed Balch's predication, Andrew Jackson concurred emphatically:

May we not hope . . . that all good citizens, and none more zealously than those who think the Indians oppressed by subjection to the laws of the States, will unite in attempting to open the eyes of those children of the forest to their true condition, and by a speedy removal to relieve them from all the evils, real or imaginary, present or prospective, with which they may be supposed to be threatened.

Indian Removal 1832-1842

Removal of the Tribes of
the South and Old Northwest

Location of Indians in the
Indian Territory, after Removal

The debates in Congress over proposed legislation to ratify the policy of Separation sparked rancorous debate and strong sectional antagonism, as much of the North lined up in opposition. Northerners identified Southerners as bullies and bigots; Southerners were convinced that Northerners, having already eliminated Indians from their states, were pious hypocrites. Lewis Cass, Jackson's secretary of war, echoed Southern opinion when asserting in the *North American Review* that "it is difficult to conceive that any branch of the human family can be less provident in arrangement, less frugal in enjoyment, less industrious in acquiring, more implacable in their resentments, more ungovernable in their passions, with fewer principles to guide them, with few obligations to restrain them, and with less knowledge to improve and instruct themselves [than the Indians]." He concluded his argument, stating that one could not find "upon the face of the globe, a more wretched race than the Cherokees. . . . Many of them exhibit spectacles as disgusting as they are degrading." Elias Boudinot, writing in the *Cherokee Phoenix,* attacked these ideas in his criticism of Georgia's manifesto, which demanded the immediate eviction of the Cherokees for reasons similar to those advanced by Cass.

What a pernicious effort must such a document . . . have on the interests and improvements of the Indians? Who will expect from the Cherokees a rapid progress in education, religion, agriculture, and the various arts of civilized life when resolutions are passed in a civilized and Christian legislature (whose daily sessions, we are told, commence with a prayer to Almighty God) to wrest their country from them, and strange to tell, with the point of the bayonet, if nothing else will do? Is it in the nature of things, that the Cherokees will build good and comfortable houses and make them great farms, when they know not but their possessions will fall into the hands of strangers & invaders? How is it possible that they will establish for themselves good laws, when an attempt is made to crush their first feeble effort toward it?

More attention was aroused by the speech of Theodore Frelinghuysen on the floor of the Senate. "We have crowded the tribes upon a few miserable acres on our southern frontier; it is all that is left to them of their once boundless forests; and still, like the horseleech, our insatiated cupidity cries give!" The senator

from New Jersey continued, "Our fathers successfully and triumphantly contended for the very rights and privileges that our Indian neighbors now implore us to protect and preserve to them."
None of this, however, could move Southern legislators and those
Northern colleagues who supported their efforts. To them, perhaps
above all other justifications for forced removal, the interests, indeed the rights, of the individual states were paramount, regardless
of federal treaties. Thus, in the end, the Removalists carried the
day; the Indian Removal Bill, having passed in the House, was
ratified in the Senate by a margin of eight votes. President Jackson
signed it into law on May 28, 1830, effecting the policy of Separation. The government of the United States was now legally
empowered to appropriate tribal lands by negotiating a new set
of treaties and to exile the Indians of the South to the trans-
Mississippi West.

The South's triumph in the removal fights—over justice for
the Indians and over formidable opposition from the North—
forbode an alarming future, however. The North, increasingly resentful of two generations of southern control of Congress and the
presidency, was frustrated by its defeat to the South on the removal question. As one of the fruits of its victory, the South carried a heavier burden of anxiety about the possibility of more
Northern political "assaults" upon the region's economic and territorial aspirations and its institutions, for someday would not the
question of blacks' rights be raised as Indian rights had? Its fears
soon materialized, as determined Northern antislavery agitation
mounted in the aftermath of heightened sectionalism caused by Indian removal. A year after passage of the Removal Act, William
Lloyd Garrison of Boston established his controversial abolitionist
newspaper, *The Liberator.* Then, in 1833, abolitionists formed the
American Antislavery Society with its goal the immediate, un-
compensated ending of slavery in the United States.

Within two years of the passage of the Indian Removal Act, three
of the five major southern tribes had forfeited their lands. The
Choctaws in 1830 and then the Chickasaws and the Creeks in
1832 concluded treaties with the federal government mandating

their resettlement, an eventuality that would kill thousands and prove horrific for all three tribes. Choctaw George Harkin lamented his people's circumstance: "We hope, in the name of justice, that another outrage may never be committed against us; and that we may for the future not be driven about as if beasts, who benefit from a change of pasture. We go forth sorrowful, knowing that wrong has been done."

Only the Cherokees and the Seminoles remained. While each selected different tactics, both tenaciously resisted removal. The Seminoles rejected their removal treaty and withdrew into the depths of the Florida swamps where, from 1835 to 1842, they fought courageously but unsuccessfully against the United States Army. When military operations finally halted, the government had removed most of the tribe to the Indian Territory (present-day Oklahoma), although several hundred Seminoles were never apprehended and remained in Florida.

The Cherokees were equally determined to resist removal. "The Cherokees are not foreigners but original inhabitants of America," a delegation of tribal members declared to the secretary of war. "They now inhabit and stand on the soil of their own territory . . . and the states by which they are now surrounded have been created out of land which was once theirs." The Cherokees no longer relied solely on appeals to conscience, which had failed them in the states, in Congress, and at the highest executive office. They now decided to seek redress in the federal courts. "Nothing can and nothing will sattisfy [sic] this nation upon the subject of the controversy which has been forced upon them by Georgia, than a fair and honest decision upon the principles of the Constitution, laws & Treaties of the U.S. by the Supreme Court," John Ross replied to William H. Underwood, who had inquired of the chief what response the Cherokees would offer to the threat of forced removal.

The Cherokee appeal was no routine matter. American courts can at any time be "seized" of questions for which there are neither clear laws nor established precedents. State courts had jurisdiction in state matters, federal courts in federal matters. But what was the status of an Indian nation? Certainly it had treaty rights.

These were sometimes disregarded, but they were not rejected. Moreover, the Constitution was clear that an international treaty supersedes an act of Congress. But a number of Southerners, Jefferson, Madison, and Calhoun among them, believed that the states must be judges of the constitutionality of federal acts. The vexed question of the Cherokees' status would be settled by the United States Supreme Court. In *Cherokee Nation* v. *the State of Georgia* (1831), the court under Chief Justice John Marshall ruled in the Cherokees' favor, stating that Indians were not subject to state law and so affirmed the right of the Cherokees to hold their land in the state of Georgia. Although he made no secret of his sympathy for the Cherokees, the chief justice delivered a blow to their claims to sovereignty, ruling that they were not independent but a "domestic dependent nation in a state of pupilage"—in other words, wards of the United States government. Still, the Cherokees received the decision with rejoicing, for had not the highest tribunal in the land ruled to quell those who aspired to crush them? John Ross announced to his nation: "Our adversaries are generally down in the mouth—there are great rejoicings through the nation on the decision of the supreme court upon the Cherokee case." A year later, the Supreme Court in *Samuel A. Worcester* v. *the State of Georgia* (1832) again ruled against Georgia. The Cherokees dared to hope that protections guaranteed them by treaty were safeguarded. What could block access to their rights?

Unfortunately Andrew Jackson could. The president may have said, as so often quoted, "John Marshall has made his decision; *now let him enforce it!*" The rejoinder is probably apocryphal, but it accurately depicts his attitude and his behavior—he simply refused to enforce the court's decision. When it became clear to Georgia that President Jackson would not fulfill his constitutional duty, but instead would ignore a federal court, the state quickly turned the Cherokees' domain over to white land speculators. A malleable tribal faction, led by Major Ridge, one of the wealthiest Cherokees and speaker of the Cherokee National Council, and encouraged by state and federal officials, signed a removal treaty at New Echota, Georgia, the Cherokee capital, on December 29, 1835. On behalf of the Cherokee nation they ceded to the United

States all the lands owned, claimed, or possessed by them east of the Mississippi River, and agreed to remove west of that river. Their action exacerbated Cherokee factionalism, as the overwhelming majority of the tribe, led by Principal Chief John Ross, refused to vacate their homeland. Three years later it fell to President Martin Van Buren, Jackson's hand-picked successor, to implement his mentor's design for these people. On April 10, 1838, Van Buren ordered the reluctant Major General Winfield Scott to the Cherokee homeland to remove the inhabitants beyond the Mississippi River. For Scott it was a sad task, but one from which he could not shrink. Although he made it clear to his troops that they must show compassion to the Cherokees as they rounded them up and held them in detainment camps until the journey westward commenced, too often the troops' behavior belied this order. Ethnologist James Mooney gathered firsthand accounts from survivors of the ensuing ordeal. In his words:

Families at dinner were startled by the sudden gleam of bayonets in the doorway and rose up to be driven with blows and oaths along the weary miles of trail that led to the stockade. Men were seized in their fields or going along the road, women were taken from their wheels and children from their play. In many cases, on turning for one last look as they crossed the ridge, they saw their homes in flames, fired by the lawless rabble that followed on the heels of the soldiers to loot and pillage.

Soldiers surrounded houses to make sure that no one escaped. In one typical example, a woman, seeing herself trapped, called her chickens for their last feeding. Then taking one child on her back and leading two others by the hand she joined her husband and followed the soldiers. Cattle, hogs, horses, household effects were all lost. The Cherokees were to start with nothing but the clothes on their backs. A Georgia volunteer, Private John G. Burnett, later a colonel in the army of the Confederate States of America, remembered: "I fought through the civil war and have seen men shot to pieces and slaughtered by thousands, but the Cherokee removal was the cruelest work I ever knew." Some Cherokees did evade the dragnet and fled into the mountains of North Carolina. Scott did not pursue them vigorously. Their descendants now reside on a reservation located in the northwestern portion of that state just south of the Great Smokies National Park.

General Scott, hoping that the removal would be carried out with the least possible pain to the emigrants, agreed to allow John Ross and leaders of his faction to supervise the operation. A number of Cherokee parties, numbering at most a few hundred individuals in each case, had already made the trip to the West; hence Scott, Ross, and others found little reason not to believe that this removal could be made without too much difficulty. But those who had already emigrated were relatively few in number and had chosen the time for departure and, to some extent, the route. The movement of a body of people numbering well into the thousands would be much more difficult.

Following a delay of almost half a year, the Cherokee migration began in October 1838. Despite Scott's hope for an endurable journey, the rigors of the operation could hardly be mitigated. The trek westward, a trying one even under the best of conditions, was hindered even before it began by a lack of sufficient provisions. In addition, a terrible drought blasted the Southeast through the early fall of 1838, a condition that would have hampered even a much smaller migration. To herd a party of 18,000 people through hundreds of miles of scorched vegetation and dried-up streams with only the minimum of provisions and comforts was to invite disaster. Because of the excruciating horror of death and suffering through which they trudged, the Cherokee trek is recalled as "The Trail of Tears." The missionary Elizur Butler, witness to a portion of the odyssey, confessed, "I have felt I have been in the midst of death itself." A reporter for the *New York Observer,* under the heading "A Native of Maine, traveling in the Western Country," recorded his impressions: "When I past [sic] the last detachment of those suffering exiles and thought that my native countrymen had thus expelled them from their native soil and their much loved homes, . . . I turned from the sight with feelings which language cannot express." Four thousand of those who left their Georgia homes died on the dreadful trail—about one-quarter of those who set out. Thomas H. Crawford, Van Buren's commissioner of Indian Affairs, reflected a different reality in his official report:

"Good feeling has been preserved, and we have quietly and gently transported 18,000 friends to the west bank of the Mississippi."

In 1840 the lands east of the Mississippi had been lost by those people who had lived in them for centuries. By then, federal officials and the American public overwhelmingly were convinced that the policy of Separation solved the Indian question. A few individuals did not share their optimism. Jared Sparks, editor of the *North American Review,* mused that "after all, this project only defers the fate of the Indians. In half a century their condition beyond the Mississippi will be just what it [was] on this side. Their extinction is inevitable." Jeremiah Evarts, corresponding secretary of the American Board of Commissioners for Foreign Missions, predicted that another solution would "soon be necessary." Evarts offered his rationale:

If the emigrants become poor, and are transformed into vagabonds, it will be evidence enough, that no benevolent treatment can save them, and it will be said they may as well be driven beyond the Rocky Mountains at once. If they live comfortably, it will prove, that five times as many white people might live comfortably in their places.

Most Americans preferred to trust Andrew Jackson's judgment, not that of these doomsayers. He exuded confidence that the policy of Separation had successfully dealt with the Indian question: It provided safety for Americans and the United States, and prevented the annihilation of the Indians. "The States which had so long been retarded in their improvement by the Indian tribes residing in the midst of them are at length relieved from the evil," Jackson assured a grateful nation, "and this unhappy race—the original dwellers in our land—are now placed in a situation where we may well hope that they will share in the blessings of civilization and be saved from degradation and destruction."

We do not think of the great open plains, the beautiful rolling hills, and winding streams with tangled growth, as "wild." Only to the white man was nature a "wilderness" and only to him was the land "infested" with "wild" animals and "savage" people. To us it was tame. Earth was bountiful and we were surrounded with the blessings of the Great Mystery. Not until the hairy man from the east came and with brutal frenzy heaped injustices upon us and the families we loved was it "wild" for us. When the very animals of the forest began fleeing from his approach, then it was for us the "Wild West" began.

LUTHER STANDING BEAR, OGLALA SIOUX

CHAPTER TWO

The Changing West

And so tribes from the East arrived in the western wilderness, a foreign land that they were now to call home. "Your father has provided a country large enough for all of you," President Andrew Jackson promised. "There your white brother will not trouble you; they will have no claim to the land, and you can live upon it, you and all of your children, as long as the grass grows or the water runs, in peace and plenty. It will be yours forever." To provide a solution to the nation's Indian question, the United States in the 1830s settled on a policy of Separation, uprooting and removing, often by force, more than 50,000 Indians beyond the Mississippi River. The Indian removal yielded approximately 100 million acres in the eastern United States, for which Indians received some 32 million western acres.

The question of whether or not to implement a policy of Separation had stirred heated debate. But once the policy became an accomplished fact, the American public overwhelmingly judged it a workable and humane solution to long-standing and vexing problems between Indians and whites. Americans backed the policy in the faith that separation of the races was the best solution that could be had, and certainly that it was the best possibility for the Indians. The Euro-American experience of several centuries had demonstrated conclusively, so they believed, that neither race could live peacefully in proximity with the other. With the bulk of eastern woodland tribes located beyond the Mississippi, warfare with them and conflict over land use in the East became a problem of the past. Other, less palatable reasons also helped sanction the policy of Separation: racial and cultural biases, political expediency, and perhaps above all, the enormous profits to be reaped from the confiscated Indian lands. By 1840, with the removal of these tribes accomplished, Americans, although compelled by different reasons in their support of the policy, believed that the government had solved the nation's Indian question.

Fashioning the Indian Territory

The decision to implement Separation and remove the Indians of the South and the Old Northwest required that federal officials allocate land for their colonization. This colonization zone would be for exclusive use by Indians, and it would be protected from white intrusion. The idea for an Indian country or state was not new. For decades it had been bantered about in a variety of forms, most notably by Thomas Jefferson, who considered the newly purchased Louisiana Territory—stretching from the Mississippi River to the Rocky Mountains—as the best locale for an Indian country. During the concluding years of James Monroe's presidency (1817–1825), the federal government developed a plan to establish a permanent Indian domain from lands not included within the boundaries of any state or organized federal territory. John C. Calhoun of South Carolina, Monroe's secretary of war, resurrected Jefferson's idea and reminded the government and the public that west of the Mississippi lay millions of acres stretching over endless prairies and plains to the Rockies. Americans, secure in the belief of "national completeness," considered the land east of the Mississippi River fully adequate for the needs of the republic, especially its agricultural needs, and so were satisfied that the

United States encompassed its suitable inhabitable limits. There seemed little, if any, reason in the foreseeable future for settlement to press much beyond the Mississippi. Because Americans perceived the western prairies and plains of the Louisiana Territory worthless and uninhabitable for an agricultural society, this area offered an obvious solution to the question of where to establish an Indian colonization zone. By removing the tribes of the South and the Old Northwest and settling them on a portion of this great expanse, American society could expand without interference from natives on the habitable lands east of the Mississippi. Indian society, concentrated on the "wild" land of the prairies and plains west of American settlement, could flourish in its own way, with an economy and a way of life alien to white society. The rationalization appeared flawless to Americans of that era.

To state that Americans could never exist west of the ninety-fifth meridian and east of the Rockies seems incredible today, but such was the belief of the time. During the first half of the nineteenth century, virtually all Americans believed that the Great Plains were dry, barren, and forbidding. In 1820, Major Stephen H. Long led an expedition that explored the central and southern portions of this area, journeying up the Platte River and returning through present-day Oklahoma on the Canadian River. He described the region as "almost wholly unfit for cultivation and of course uninhabitable by a people depending upon agriculture for their subsistence. . . . The scarcity of wood and water . . . will prove an insuperable obstacle in the way of settling the country." Long judged the area so worthless that he dubbed it "The Great American Desert." Although erroneous, the name stuck—along with the misconception.

In spite of his discouraging assessment, Major Long did see some attributes to this locale. "Viewed as frontier," he reasoned, this region "may prove of infinite importance to the United States, inasmuch as it is calculated to serve as a barrier to prevent too great an extension of our population westward." Secretary of War Calhoun, partly because of Long's report, urged Congress to set aside an area west of the Mississippi as a huge compound for Indians. Congress subsequently endorsed Calhoun's idea and withdrew millions of acres from potential American settlement, fashioning out of them the "Indian Territory." By 1840 the boundary of this sanctuary, after some adjustments, had been determined. The U.S. government reserved for Indians an enormous parcel of land west of the states of Louisiana, Arkansas, and Missouri. On the north, the Platte River bounded the Indian Territory and on the south the Red River defined it. The western border of the United States as of 1840 also served as the western boundary of the Indian Territory—the one hundredth meridian running northward from the Red River to the Arkansas River, then westward along the Arkansas to the Rockies. Here both the colonized eastern tribes and the indigenous western tribes living within the jurisdiction of the United States would reside.

The federal government also took steps to protect all Indians residing within the Indian Territory against white encroachment and against aggression from other tribes. Congress passed legislation that limited white settlement in much of this area, thus buttressing the right of Indians to its exclusive possession. Responsibility rested with the United States Army for safeguarding the Indian Territory, and especially for protecting the colonized Indian communities against attack by more numerous western tribes that resented the intrusion of these refugees on their hunting ranges. Soldiers were garrisoned in a chain of installations established along the eastern frontier of the Indian Territory. The forts extended southward from Fort Snelling on the Mississippi in what became in 1849 the territory of Minnesota, to Forts Atkinson and Leavenworth along the Missouri on the central plains, to three posts in present-day Oklahoma—Forts Gibson and Smith on the Arkansas River and Fort Towson on the Red River, ending at Fort Jesup near the western border of the state of Louisiana. This line of forts with their available military personnel would, in the judgment of the government in Washington, "both insure the safety of the western frontier, and enable the government to fulfill all its treaty stipulations, and preserve its faith with the Indians."

A variety of native peoples lived in the new Indian Territory. In that portion north of thirty-seven degrees latitude (the present border separating the states of Kansas and Oklahoma), the Indians from the Old Northwest were colonized, including Wyandots, Delawares, Potawatomis, Kickapoos, Sac and Fox, and Shawnees. Weakened and traumatized by their removal, and now located precariously close to the hunting ranges of the Plains Indians, the newcomers experienced frequent assaults from the powerful Cheyennes, Arapahoes, and Sioux. Missionaries, trying to improve their condition, toiled among the relocated peoples. The missionaries believed that the best means for betterment was education, especially manual labor schools where, in addition to instruction in reading, writing, basic arithmetic, and Christian precepts, the Indians would be taught how to "build and live in houses, to sleep on beds; to eat at regular intervals, to plough, and sow, and reap; to rear and use domestic animals; to understand and practice the mechanic arts; and to enjoy, to their gratification and improvement, all the means of profit and rational pleasure that are so profusely spread around civilized life." A number of local tribes, such as the Osage and Kansa, resided near the Indians who came from the Old Northwest. The government had recently resettled these local tribes on reduced territory to make room for the immigrant tribes.

In the northernmost portion of the Indian Territory, west of the Missouri and straddling the Platte River, lived other local tribes like the Pawnees, Otos, Missouris, Omahas, and Iowas—who for centuries were agriculturalists, but who in more recent times had adopted many of the characteristics of the Plains Indians' buffalo and horse culture. Life for them had become increasingly precarious by the early 1840s, as Plains tribes constantly harried them. "They were completely invested by enemies so much so that they are in danger of losing their scalps as soon as they put their heads outside their mud hovels," agent Thomas Fitzpatrick observed. "It seems to me that their feasting on buffalo, are nearly at an end. The Platte River, the headwaters of the Kansas, and even south west to the Arkansas were formerly the great hunting grounds of the Pawnies [sic]; but now those of the Sioux, Cheyennes, and Arapahoes are all gradually nearing the Pawnies, with a full determination of wiping them out," Fitzpatrick concluded pessimistically.

The government set aside the southern part of the Indian Territory, below thirty-seven degrees latitude, for the Cherokees, Chickasaws, Choctaws, Creeks, and Seminoles. After arrival in their new western lands, the surviving members of these tribes, with quiet heroism, began to reconstruct their lives from the ashes of their past. Diligently and energetically they set themselves to the awesome task of rebuilding their society, economic base, and governments; and they accomplished an astonishing, phoenix-like recovery. Within a few short years of their arrival, they transformed the wilderness of the southern Indian Territory into a flourishing and prosperous homeland. Towns, farms, plantations, and ranches provided the base for a thriving economy. They established an educational system for their children. Soon after arrival these tribes reestablished their constitutional governments, fashioning five independent Indian republics, each with a national capital: Tahlequah for the Cherokees, Tishomingo for the Chickasaws, Doaksville for the Choctaws, North Fork Town for the Creeks, and Seminole Agency for the Seminoles.

William Armstrong, federal superintendent of the Western Territory, greatly impressed by the remarkable progress of the five tribes, noted with approval in 1840: "Where but a few years past the forest was untouched, in many places good farms are to be seen; the whole face of the country evidently indicating a thrifty and prosperous people, possessing within themselves the means of raising fine stocks of horses, cattle, and hogs, and country producing all the substantials of life." Their extraordinary efforts and achievements, and the manner of society, government, and economies fashioned in the southern portion of the Indian Territory by these five republics led to their designation by Americans as "The Five Civilized Tribes." If Americans needed an example to prove the wisdom of the policy of Separation, they pointed readily to these republics as evidence of the potential for Indians to adapt to the ways of the dominant society, especially when the unyielding pressure from white settlement was eliminated. "There was nothing to distinguish appearances from those of many of our border people," Ethan Allen Hitchcock noted in 1841 during an investigative trip for the government, "except the complexion and superior neatness."

To the west of the tribes residing in the eastern end of the Indian Territory lay the domain of the Great Plains tribes. Some of these tribes had just recently made room, often with belligerent protests, for the relocated Indians from east of the Mississippi, whom they viewed as intruders and competitors for the already limited food resources of the region. Although the Great Plains tribes were nominally under the jurisdiction of the United States since the Louisiana Purchase of 1803, federal officials so far had few dealings with them—a state of affairs that would change soon, as much of the government's attention in Indian affairs for the next half-century would focus on these people. Most Americans were only vaguely aware of the Great Plains tribes, if they knew of them at all: "picturesque but unimportant savages" might be the most accurate characterization of public perception. Those who did have direct contact offered impressive descriptions. For example, the artist George Catlin in 1834 recorded his observations of the Cheyennes. His portrayal would have applied as accurately to the other bison-hunting tribes of the region.

There is no finer race of men than these in North America, and more superior in stature, excepting the Osages; scarcely a man of the tribe, full grown, who is less than six feet in height. The Shiennes [Cheyennes] are undoubtedly the richest in horses of any tribe on the Continent, living in a country as they do, where the greatest numbers of wild horses are grazing on the prairies. . . . These people are the most desperate set of horsemen, and warriors also, having carried on almost unceasing war with the Pawnees and Blackfeet, time out of mind.

Sedentary farming peoples, like the Mandan, Hidatsa, and Arikara, occupied the timbered Missouri River valley and some of its major tributaries on the eastern plains. Nomadic bison-hunting societies, collectively referred to as the Plains Indians, dominated the remainder of the region. The Dakota, or Sioux, controlled the northeastern portion of the plains. Numbering 25,000 people, which by far made it the largest group on the Great Plains, the Sioux had three principal tribal divisions. The Sisseton, or Santee, lived in present-day Minnesota, a Dakota word meaning "waters many." To their west, spanning the Missouri River on the prairies of what is now South Dakota, were the Yankton and Yanktonai.

The most populous division resided to the north and west. These were the Teton, comprising seven divisions or subtribes: Blackfeet, Brule, Hunkpapa, Miniconjou, Oglala, Sans Arc, and Two Kettles. The Teton Sioux's strength of numbers made them a formidable obstacle to any white expansion on the northern plains. On the lands along the western Missouri River and ranging on both sides of the United States–Canadian border were other tribes: the Blackfeet, Assiniboines, and Atsinas. The Crow inhabited the Bighorn Mountain country of what became Wyoming and Montana, although the Teton Sioux challenged them for control of it. To their south, on the western edge of the buffalo plains, resided the Shoshonis.

The Cheyennes and the Arapahoes, long comrades and allies and residing on the same lands, controlled present-day eastern Colorado, western Kansas, and southeastern Wyoming, but ranged widely over the central plains. The Cheyennes had two branches. The Northern Cheyennes preferred to reside near the Teton Sioux and trade with other Indians. The Southern Cheyennes remained on the central plains, trading directly for American goods at Bent's Fort, a trading post established by William Bent in 1834 on the Arkansas River in what is now southeastern Colorado. Across the Arkansas River to the south lived the traditional enemies of the Cheyennes and the Arapahoes: the Kiowa and the Comanche tribes. The Kiowas lived in northwestern Oklahoma. The Comanches, the dominant tribe on the southern plains as well as the most populous with 7,000 members, resided south of the Red River in Texas. Together Kiowas and Comanches raided into Mexico and Texas for horses, mules, and human captives long before coming into contact with settlers from the United States. Over the southwestern plains ranged the Apaches. Unsurpassed at guerrilla warfare, they were a match for any enemy, Indian or white. They hunted and gathered from the Pecos River in New Mexico over the northern Rio Grande area and eastward into Texas.

The nomadic bison-hunting tribes of the Great Plains produced a remarkable synthesis of political, social, and religious characteristics, especially when one considers the size of the region and the diverse geographical origins and cultural backgrounds of these tribes. The Plains Indians had only recently entered into the buffalo and horse culture, ironic perhaps since that way of life became so completely identified with these tribes (and often generalized to all North American Indians) in the minds of Americans and Europeans.

The highly specialized way of life they developed, reaching its climactic form in the nineteenth century, centered on two animals: buffaloes (bison), which were native to the North American plains, and domesticated horses, which were not. Just when American Indians first obtained horses is not certain, but by 1700 most tribes had acquired them. All the Indians that the French and the English encountered west of the Missouri River in the eighteenth century rode horses. Centuries earlier, the Plains Indians first obtained horses from the Spanish. Both Coronado and DeSoto used horses on their treks to the Great Plains in the 1540s, as did Spanish soldiers and then settlers in Mexico. Through theft, barter or sale, or escape, horses ultimately made their way northward onto the Great Plains and into the possession of the Plains Indians, who from that point on rapidly made the horse an integral part of their lives. Before the buffalo-and-horse-culture period, few tribes actually lived on the Great Plains. Those who did kept close to the fertile valleys of the major rivers—the Missouri, Platte, Red, and Canadian—rarely leaving those locales other than to venture out onto the plains in search of buffalo and other wild game. Then around 1700, coinciding with the spread of the horse, more than two dozen tribes moved out onto the plains, abandoning most, and in many cases all, of their previous cultural traits, to forge the buffalo and horse culture.

The horse transformed two main elements of the life of Indians on the Great Plains: transportation and food gathering. Before the introduction of the horse, Indians lived a meager life always near the brink of want, whether as farmers or hunters. They traveled and hunted on foot. While on the march they transported their belongings on their backs, on the backs of their dogs, or on a *travois,* an A-shaped frame that could be strapped to and dragged behind a person or a dog. Obviously, travel was slow, tedious, and difficult. The horse changed these conditions forever. It freed the natives from bondage to the periphery of the plains and allowed them to move at will over its immense reaches. It also transformed the Plains Indians into formidable fighters: American military personnel characterized them, often with awe, as the "finest light cavalry in the world." Use of the horse also increased competition among tribes for territory and game, and intensified intertribal warfare as raiding parties could now move with much greater speed and tactical dexterity against enemies. Horses were so valuable that the plains tribes ultimately measured wealth by the number of horses owned.

The coming of the horse altered the food gathering process as well. Archaeological and historical evidence indicates that buffalo was always part of the diet of the plains people, as were antelope, elk, and smaller game. But these animals were hard to catch in sufficient quantities by hunters on foot. Wild seeds, grains, dried berries, and edible roots composed the rest of the diet. All provided an unreliable, minimal fare. But on horseback, a hunter could kill in a single day of buffalo hunting what had previously required a week or longer. Thus, use of the horse discouraged tendencies toward a more sedentary life and strengthened roving and migratory habits. The Plains Indians "have no fixed habitations. Hunting and fighting they wander incessantly, through the summer and winter," noted Francis Parkman. "Some follow the herds of buffalo over the waste of the prairie; others traverse the Black Hills, through the dark gulfs and sombre gorges, and emerging at last upon the 'Parks,' those beautiful but most perilous hunting grounds." The buffalo, found in enormous herds throughout the region, became the dietary staple of the mounted Plains Indians. The buffalo also satisfied most of their material needs. From hides came clothing, robes, moccasins, saddles, walls of teepees, bedding, vessels to hold water, and boats to cross streams. Buffalo hooves were made into glue, horns were carved into cups and spoons, and muscle tendon was made into bowstrings, cordage, and trailropes for the Indians' horses. Dried manure—"buffalo chips"—provided fuel. Stomachs were fashioned into water bottles. "The buffalo supplies them with the necessities of life," Parkman also observed. "When the buffalo are extinct, they too must dwindle away." So vital were the buffalo and the horse to the Plains Indians' way of life, that during the Plains Wars of the 1860s and 1870s the United States Army made it a military objective to eradicate the buffalo herds and kill the Indians' horses.

Dashed Hopes

Both the American public and the United States government anticipated that the policy of Separation would assure a state of long-term peaceful relations with Indians. They believed it because most tribes under United States jurisdiction resided in or to the west of the Indian Territory, and because Americans saw no value in these lands for future settlement. Their anticipation proved frustratingly brief. Within a decade of the implementation of the policy of Separation in the 1830s, events in the trans-Mississippi West undermined the premises upon which it rested. Two factors contributed most to its rapid collapse. The first is called Migratory Fever. The second came to be labeled Manifest Destiny. Their effects ignited a new Indian question for the nation, which in turn compelled another search for a solution.

The 1840s witnessed a dramatic increase in westward movement by the American people. Phrases such as "Oregon Fever" and "California Fever" aptly portrayed the impassioned spirit of exploration that compelled thousands of citizens to migrate from their homes in the East and cross the Indian Territory and the domain of the plains tribes to settle the Far West. This uncontrolled stream of population destroyed forever the undergirding of the policy of Separation: a sanctuary where Indians could be left to themselves in lands of their own. Reports had spread eastward of the abundance of fertile, almost empty lands beyond the Rocky Mountains and the Sierra Nevada. Americans wasted no time in resolving to fashion new and, they hoped, better lives for themselves and their families in these lands, or in recognizing the commercial opportunities available there.

The first noteworthy trail to carve its way across the Great Plains in the early 1840s led to the Oregon country in the Pacific Northwest (which Great Britain and the United States jointly controlled) and took its name from its destination—the Oregon Trail. Although trappers and fur traders had been exploiting the rich natural bounty of the region for some time, the first real American interest in Oregon came as a result of the activities of Protestant missionaries who labored there to convert local Indians to Christianity. The missionaries sent reports of their efforts back east, including in them enticing descriptions of the beauty and economic potential of Oregon. Religious journals and secular newspapers printed and reprinted these observations, stimulating increasing interest in migration. The Oregon Territory, well watered and forested, appealed in particular to New Englanders and midwestern farmers, especially those who had been badly hurt by the recent depression—the Panic of 1837. To these people who longed for a new start in life, Oregon seemed an answer heaven-sent. As reports spread of this bountiful locale, Americans began to catch Oregon Fever. It started as a trickle, but by 1843 the first substantial migration had begun. With each passing year thousands of covered wagons wound their way along the trail, crossing the Indian Territory and the lands of the Plains tribes in order to reach the Oregon country.

Other westward trails soon developed. In the same decade, a persecuted religious group resolved to migrate to the West, beyond the jurisdiction of the United States. Members of the Church of Jesus Christ of Latter-Day Saints, more commonly known as the Mormons, had endured nearly twenty years of persecution by other Americans for their beliefs. To escape such hostility the Mormons had already moved their community several times: from New York State to Ohio, to Missouri, and then to Illinois. Finally, in 1846, their new leader Brigham Young organized and led an emigration party on a 1,500-mile trek from Illinois to Mexican territory in Utah. In successfully completing the journey Young's group had blazed a second major trail across Indian country, the Mormon Trail. Earlier in the decade the explorer John C. Frémont said the Utah region possessed "good soil and good grass, adapted to civilized settlements." To their chagrin the Mormons instead found a barren, sun-baked plain, "the paradise of the lizard, the cricket and the rattlesnake." It seemed to them that Stephen Long, not John Frémont, had been the more accurate observer. Dismayed, many urged their leaders to forsake this "dry, worthless locality" and press on for greener lands along the Pacific coast. Meanwhile, other Americans crossed the vast prairies and plains with the Mexican province of California as their destination. Some followed the Mormon Trail to the Great Salt Lake. From there they pushed across the Nevada desert and over the Sierra Nevada to the Pacific, thus forging the California Trail. Other overland immigrants followed the Oregon Trail to the Pacific Northwest, then headed southward into California.

The stream of Americans journeying through Indian country became a deluge after James Marshall discovered gold at Sutter's mill in northern California in January of 1848. Few words had the capacity to stir greater commotion or to evoke greater rapacity than "GOLD!" "Never, I think," commented a local resident, "has there been such excitement in any country of the world." One San Francisco editor, noting with displeasure how thousands had abandoned their daily work to become gold hunters, wrote, "The whole country, from San Francisco to Los Angeles, and from sea shore to the base of the Sierra Nevada, resounds with the sordid cry of *gold!* Gold! GOLD!' while the field is left half planted, the house half built, and everything neglected but the manufacture of shovels and pickaxes." Within six months of Marshall's discovery, Californians had rushed to the area of the American River to "strike it rich," and by the end of 1848 news of a gold strike in California had reached the East. The next year the "forty-niners" swept across the overland trails in unprecedented numbers. Fourteen-thousand non-Indians lived in California before the gold strike of 1848; nearly half a million occupied it two years later, when California became the thirty-first state. Subsequent discoveries of gold and silver in western territories prompted even greater numbers to migrate across Indian country in the hopes of making their fortunes in the mountains and rivers of the Far West.

No sooner had Americans reached Oregon, California, and other western locales, than the seeds of international crisis began to sprout. Americans residing in these areas no longer wished to live under British or Mexican rule. In this determination they were supported by an increasingly large following back in the United States. Calls for the United States to annex these regions, with military force if necessary, rose toward a crescendo along a vast arc from the Oregon country, down through Mexican California, and over to the independent Republic of Texas.

In this same decade, Americans came to believe that it was the destiny of the United States to rule the continent from ocean to ocean. It did not matter if these lands belonged to other nations; the United States—asserting that expansion was under divine sanction and providential direction, and proclaiming the superiority of American culture and institutions—intended to control them. This set of popular ideas became known as Manifest Destiny. John L. O'Sullivan, the influential editor of the *New York Morning News* and *The Democratic Review,* initially coined the phrase in an 1845 political editorial. According to O'Sullivan, American expansionism

... is by the right of our manifest destiny to overspread and to possess the whole of the continent which Providence has given us for the development of the great experiment of liberty and federative self-government entrusted to us. It is a right such as that of the tree to the space of air and earth suitable for the full expansion of this principle and destiny of growth.

International events and the rationalizations that clustered under the rubric of Manifest Destiny soon transformed the Far West and radically undercut the policy of Separation and the reasons for establishing and maintaining the Indian Territory.

Territorial expansion became the major issue in the presidential election of 1844. The Whig party nominated Henry Clay of Kentucky. Clay wanted the nation to expand westward, but he believed it should do so slowly. It was thought that rapid expansion might lead to war with Great Britain or Mexico. James K. Polk of Tennessee, the Democratic party's candidate, ran as an outspoken expansionist and a vigorous proponent of American Manifest Destiny. His victory over Clay made rapid territorial expansion inevitable. While President Polk was clearly willing to provoke a war with Mexico to obtain California and the Southwest (as he would soon demonstrate), he just as clearly wished to avoid an armed conflict with Great Britain if possible. The United States demanded the Oregon country from Britain and threatened war. The British, not eager to fight a war over a remote wilderness so far from home, offered a compromise. In 1846, Great Britain and the United States agreed to divide the Oregon country at the forty-ninth parallel of latitude. The British retained that portion north of the compromise line; Americans acquired sole right to the territory south of it down to the border of California.

Texas was admitted to the United States in March 1845. In the spring of 1846 escalating American-Mexican tension over the southwestern border of Texas erupted in war. American troops put the capstone on more than a year of successful and brilliant campaigning when Mexico City fell to them in the autumn of 1847. The Treaty of Guadalupe Hidalgo in 1848 ended the conflict and required the Mexican government to sell the entire area from New Mexico to California to the United States for $15 million. The Treaty added 1.2 million square miles of land to the area of the United States. Polk apprised Congress in his annual message of 1848 that the Mexican War secured "a country more than half as large as all that which was held by the United States before their acquisition." America's east-west boundaries now extended from the Atlantic to the Pacific Ocean, in the Far West now encompassing a great crescent of territory from the Pacific Northwest to Texas. The acquisition of these lands dramatically altered the American perception of the Indian sanctuary on the prairies and plains. In the 1830s Americans viewed an Indian country as advantageous to the United States because it provided part of the solution to the nation's Indian question. A decade later, the Indian country had become an impediment to unifying a transcontinental nation, an open space that someday had to be filled.

The fruits of Migratory Fever and Manifest Destiny proved exceedingly bittersweet. Certainly their foremost consequence was to overheat sectional animosity by raising enormously divisive questions, such as: will the recently acquired land be free or slave? should Congress open these lands to slavery or ban the institution from them? Southern and Northern efforts to resolve this concern to their section's satisfaction created a chain of events that in little more than a decade led to Southern secession, then civil war. Probably a lesser concern to most Americans than the extension of slavery was the effects of overland migration and territorial expansion on relations with Indians. Even so, the events of the 1840s severely jeopardized the policy of Separation and the nation's first solution to the Indian question. They also placed considerable stress on the tribes in the Indian Territory and on the plains, disrupting their lives and environment, heightening intertribal hostilities, and reawakening tensions between Indians and Americans.

Amid the array of forces transforming the West in the 1840s, one thing remained constant, at least for the moment: Americans did not desire Indian lands on the prairies and plains. Americans looking to make new homes for themselves in the Far West pushed quickly beyond the plains to more familiar terrains, such as Oregon. They hastened westward along the overland trails partly in excited anticipation of a better life, but also out of a primal terror of Indians. It affected all people on the overland trails. "We had been told," Heinrich Lienhard confessed in his diary, "that somewhere along the Little Blue there was a large camp of [Indians] whose hostility toward the whites was generally feared. . . . Everybody kept his rifle loaded and ready." To the vast majority of Americans of this era, living in what they still called the Great American Desert held absolutely no appeal. "What this God-forsaken country was made for," concluded one exasperated voyager, "I am at a loss to discover." Why challenge Indians for it? This locale was to be crossed and crossed as fast as possible. The throngs of westward immigrants had no desire to disturb the equilibrium established over the previous decade between Indians and whites. And yet the mere act of crossing Indian country disrupted the Indians and the policy of Separation on which this equilibrium rested.

One important part of the Indian lifestyle the travelers distrubed was the buffalo. The immense size of the herds astonished Americans on the overland trails. The large, lumbering beasts seemed to be everywhere. "Every acre was covered, until in the dim distance the prairie became one black mass from which there was no opening, and extending to the horizon," noted one traveler on the Santa Fe Trail in 1846. The never-ending tide of immigrants moving over what became well-trod, developed trails panicked the herds roaming the central plains. The animals soon avoided these trails, restricting their grazing to areas either to the north or south of them. White hunters also began their assault on the herds at this time. In 1846 Thomas A. Harvey, western superintendent of Indian affairs, noticed the disappearance of buffalo from some areas of the plains. "All experience proves that game rapidly disappears before the firearms of the white," Harvey concluded. "He kills for the sake of killing." So intimately were the culture and physical existence of the Plains Indians tied to the buffalo that the disruption of the herds, and in many instances the complete elimination of buffalo from tribal hunting ranges, produced a massive disruption in the Indians' lives. It forced tribes to secure new hunting areas by driving away those Indians who presently relied on them. Three years later Subagent John E. Barrow reported to superiors: "Our old friends, the Pawnees, have had a hard time of it during the past winter. When they returned from their hunting grounds, their trail could be followed by the dead bodies of those who starved to death. Children, young men, and women have shared this fate." It is little wonder that tribes increasingly identified the overland travelers as the source of their mounting misfortune. Harvey, in 1848, addressed the nature of the rapidly worsening situation for tribes:

The immense traveling of emigrant companies over the prairies, and the consequent increased destruction of buffalo, has excited the anxiety of several of the western tribes for some years past. . . . The country occupied by the buffalo is gradually and rapidly being circumscribed, which shows their great diminution. The time cannot be distant when they will be insufficient to subsist the numerous tribes that now depend upon them for food.

Harvey also urged the government to begin considering new solutions for the Indians, because a crisis was fast approaching as

Migratory Fever eroded the premises grounding the old solution of Separation.

Diseases introduced by the white migration and American expansion created more misery and disruption. Separated from the Old World for thousands of years, Indians had no natural immunities to diseases such as measles, whooping cough, and scarlet fever. These diseases were seldom fatal to whites, but they drove the Indian population into sharp decline. Epidemics of smallpox and cholera, which also plagued white settlements, added to the Indians' tribulations. The epidemics swept through the various tribes, devastating them with deadly speed and deadly results. A series of epidemics ravaged tribes along the Pacific coast from Oregon to California, eventually spreading across the Southwest. Historian William T. Hagan points out the frightful Indian casualties from an epidemic that struck the Upper Missouri. "Of 1,600 Mandans, only about 100 survived a smallpox epidemic which also struck down perhaps half of the Blackfeet," he records. "More than half of the Kiowas and Comanches were the victims of Asiatic cholera, and other plains tribes suffered proportionally." Agent Henry Schoolcraft set the number of Mandan survivors at thirteen, noting also that Crows, Minnetarees, Assiniboines, and Arikaras likewise were struck hard. White-introduced disease devastated the Pawnees and other tribes along the Platte. Schoolcraft, calling smallpox "the scourge to the aborigines," described uninhabited villages where wolves roamed "fattening [themselves] on the human carcasses that [lay] strewed about." Other afflictions, such as venereal disease, became common too among a people previously uninitiated to its horrors, rapidly proving itself a plague of a different variety.

Disease, not warfare with whites, was the great devastator of the Indian population. Don Russell, in "How Many Indians Were Killed" (*American West,* July 1973), estimated that Indians suffered roughly 4,000 deaths in warfare with American soldiers between 1789 and 1898, less than 1 percent of the Indian population during that time span. Death from disease produced catastrophically higher figures, perhaps as high as 30 to 40 percent of the Indian population, and even more among some tribes. "The vast preparations for the protection of the western frontier are superfluous," one American wrote from New Orleans in 1838 following the Indian smallpox epidemic of that year. "Another arm has undertaken the defense of the white inhabitants of the frontier; and the funeral torch, that lights the red man to his dreary grave, has become the auspicious star of the advancing settler." Disease proved the most accurate and deadly harbinger of advancing white settlement to tribes.

Perhaps worse even than epidemics was the introduction of alcohol on a scale that proved corrupting, demoralizing, and destructive to bodies and cultures not accustomed to it and its effects. "In epidemic form," stated historian Bernard Sheehan, "it ravaged tribe after tribe until the drunken, reprobate Indian became a fixture of American folklore." Modern studies have advanced possible explanations for Indian drinking patterns, ranging from physiological causes (Jerry McLeod and Stanley Clark, "It's in the Blood," *Canadian Welfare,* September–October 1974) to a method of protesting white domination (Nancy Oestrich Lurie, "The World's Oldest On-Going Protest Demonstration: North American Indian Drinking Patterns," *Pacific Historical Review,* August 1971). The Oklahoma Center for Alcohol-Related Research postulated that genetic factors lay at the root of the drinking habits of many Indians ("A Metabolic Clue to Indian Endurance and Intolerance for Alcohol," *Psychology Today,* July 1972). Whatever the actual cause, many Indians were ardently attracted to alcohol. Commentators as diverse as Jesuit missionaries in Canada during the seventeenth century and the influential nineteenth-century American politician Lewis Cass made similar reports that "Indians in immediate contact with our settlements, old and young, male and female, the chief and the warrior, all give themselves up to the most brutal intoxication, whenever this mad water can be procured." Cass recounts an especially telling episode of a Potawatomi chief's pitiful pleas during treaty negotiations at Chicago in 1821: "Father, we care not for the money, nor the land, nor the goods. We want the whiskey."

Reformers, missionaries, and government officials all agreed that whiskey was socially and physically injurious to the Indians. Perhaps more important to them, alcohol severely undermined their attempts to improve the condition of the Indians. "I cannot too strongly impress upon you," Indian Commissioner William Medill wrote one of his agents in 1846, "the importance of the duty imposed upon you. The prevention of the use of strong drink has almost been the one thing needful to ensure the prosperity of the Indian race and its advancement in civilization. The use of it has tended more to the demoralization of the Indians than all other causes combined." The Indian Affairs Office forbade the introduction of liquor into the Indian country and the sale of it to Indians. White traders generally disregarded the injunction for two simple reasons: they reaped enormous profits from liquor sales to Indians and, if they were caught, the government imposed a minimal penalty. "The profits of the trade are so great," said Commissioner Medill, summing up the problem, "that the risk of detection and loss of the article is, and will be incurred without hesitation."

Migratory Fever, by introducing catastrophic diseases and liquor, coupled with the mounting disruptions it caused to the tribes' ecological base, irrevocably altered Indian-white relations in the trans-Mississippi West. Although early overland travelers had wanted to avoid contact with Indians as they crossed the Great American Desert, they nevertheless left a devastating imprint. It distressed few Americans. Medill saw the Indians' mounting problems and misfortunes as nothing more than the natural consequence of approaching civilization. "The injury complained of," he concluded, "is but one of those inconveniences to which every people are subjected by the changing & constantly progressive spirit of the age."

A New Solution

The developments of the 1840s—Migratory Fever and the overland trails, Manifest Destiny and territorial acquisitions—opened a door to a succession of consequences in Indian-white relations that could never be closed. The rationale for the policy of Separation and the reasons for establishing and maintaining an Indian sanctuary on the western prairies, which sounded so convincing and so immutable in 1840, were crumbling fast as the decade wore on.

The Plains Indians and Western Trails

Those Indians who observed the first stream of covered wagons passing through their lands could little have imagined the cumulative effect this migration would have on their people and on the continuance of their way of life. At first, the tribes showed little concern, reacting placidly to the overland travelers. But by the mid-1840s, as trails through the central plains became fixed and more attractive to migrants, and as these migrants increasingly disrupted the Indians' economy, ecology, and lives, leaving in their wake untold masses of sick, dying, or dead people, Indian reaction changed. Unease and bitterness steadily mounted among increasing numbers of Plains Indians. While en route to California, John C. Frémont noted unrest among the powerful Teton Sioux, and especially their growing anger toward the overland travelers whom they blamed for driving away the buffalo. In 1846, Sioux along the Oregon Trail approached agents of the federal government, asking that restrictions be placed on the haphazard killing of game on the plains by whites, and requesting either payment from the travelers or compensation from the government for use of trails through their lands. Some Brules and Oglalas complained directly to President Polk:

For several years past the Emigrants going over the Mountains from the United States, have been the cause that Buffalo have in great measure left our hunting grounds, thereby causing us to go into the Country of Our Enemies to hunt, exposing our lives daily for the necessary subsistence of our wives and Children and getting killed on several occasions. We have all along treated the Emigrants in the most friendly manner, giving them free passage through our hunting grounds. . . . We are poor and beg you to take our Situation into Consideration, it has been Customary when our white friends make a road through the Red man's country to remunerate them for the injury caused thereby.

The government did nothing to appease the Sioux, who therefore took it upon themselves to demand and collect "tolls" from travelers. Prudently, the emigrants usually paid the fee required of them, but rarely with grace or with any feeling that the payment was just.

Americans who stayed home were no more sympathetic to the Indians' claims. To them, the idea that these unimportant "savages" had legitimate grievances was ludicrous and presumptuous. Complaints and petitions flooded the offices of congressmen and filled the pages of frontier newspapers, demanding that the government guarantee the right of free and unmolested passage on all trails through Indian country. "The advance company of emigrants, which were for Oregon, . . . comprising forty wagons, *were stopped in the road,* on arrival at Laramie by the Sioux, and not *permitted to pass until tribute had been paid,*" went one complaint. Another American grumbled: "The Sioux say they must have tobacco, &c., for the privilege of traveling through their country. . . . This may cause trouble, and Government should attend to it at once." Western editors snapped to the task of offering advice to Washington. "We think it is high time the attention of the Government was called to the matter," the *St. Louis Reveille* editorialized, "and that they should take some other measures with the Indians than making them presents and smoking with them the peace pipe."

The Indian question again faced the nation, and once more Americans expected a solution. Haltingly, the government in Washington responded. Compelled by growing demands for action, officials dispatched negotiators such as Major Philip Kearny to reason with tribes on the central plains, but the government's principal response was to establish forts along the overland trails and then charge the army with guarding travelers and punishing those Indians who annoyed or threatened them. "Such a course I am convinced would have a very salutary effect," applauded Thomas Fitzpatrick, agent for the Upper Platte and Arkansas, "and be the cause of accomplishing more good to the Indians . . . than all the treaties and councils that could be invented." Officials anticipated that Indians would be intimidated by this show of force and thus stay away from the overland trails.

This new procedure went into effect in 1847 with the establishment of forts along the trail to Oregon, manned by mounted rifle units called "dragoons." Campaigns against those Indians living near the trail commenced according to plan, but the soldiers' efforts met with little success. The Indians proved too elusive on the wide expanse of the plains, and as mounted warriors they were superior to the soldiers sent to suppress them. The military's increased presence on the central plains simply failed to intimidate the tribes. The dragoons' work had one chief effect: it sharply increased native hostility toward the United States government and the migrants on the overland trails. Retaliatory attacks on soldiers and travelers escalated alarmingly.

By the late 1840s the plains bustled with change and movement, no longer just from emigrants and various travelers, but also by speculators planning to build railroads across the Great Plains. With increasing attacks on overland travelers, the intrusion of large-scale commerce, and the specter of full-scale war with Indians, the region became a new burden for the government. Federal officials took a hard look at the situation, realizing they must do something quickly. They had conspicuously few alternatives: the premises of the policy of Separation must now either be rejected or affirmed. Either Americans must be permitted to traverse the region unhindered, or the right of Indians to hold this land indisputably and to live upon it undisturbed by whites must be enforced by the federal authority.

The proposal offered by Indian Commissioner Medill in 1848 began the reversal of the government's earlier decree of a protected Indian territory and initiated a sequence of federal decisions that three years later culminated in the government's new solution to the Indian question: the policy of Concentration. Medill speculated that the answer to the dilemma lay in establishing two large Indian reserves, one on the northern and the other on the southern plains. Seven years earlier, in 1841, Thomas H. Crawford, Indian Commissioner for Presidents Van Buren, Harrison, and Tyler, suggested the same idea. But in the face of mounting turmoil beyond the Mississippi, Medill settled on a more expeditious plan: treaties with potentially hostile tribes to secure a right-of-way through their lands. But he never had the time to implement the idea. Zachary Taylor's victory in the 1848 election placed federal patronage under the control of the Whig party. Redistribution of political spoils soon swept Medill and other Democrats from government service.

Secretary of Interior Thomas Ewing, one of the new president's most trusted advisors, personally directed Indian affairs for the Taylor administration. In dealing with the turbulent trans-Mississippi state of affairs, the secretary decided to go beyond Medill's plan for right-of-way treaties. Instead, Ewing wanted accords with the plains tribes that established areas with well-defined boundaries as their residence and hunting grounds. This plan, he felt, would limit Indian-white contact, reduce intertribal warfare, and provide government the means to limit negative white influence on tribes. A bill encompassing Ewing's recommendation was submitted to the Senate on March 18, 1850. It passed quickly in that chamber, which gave its approval in late

April 1850. The House, however, embroiled in fierce debates over the extension of slavery into the lands acquired as a result of the Mexican War, tarried on the proposed legislation. By the time that body took up the Ewing proposal, new leadership directed the country and federal Indian affairs.

President Taylor died unexpectedly on July 9, 1850, less than a year and a half into his term of office. He was succeeded by his vice president, Millard Fillmore, who brought Alexander H. H. Stuart into his cabinet as secretary of interior, replacing Ewing. Luke Lea, whom Taylor had appointed just before his death, remained as commissioner of Indian Affairs. Secretary Stuart considered the policy of Separation no longer tenable. The Indians were "encompassed by an unbroken chain of civilization; and the question forces itself upon the mind of the statesman and the Philanthropist, what is to become of the aboriginal race?" wrote Stuart. "This question must now be fairly met. . . . The policy of removal [Separation], except under peculiar circumstances, must necessarily be abandoned."

Commissioner Lea set to the task of defining a new solution to the Indian question. Proceeding from Medill's and Ewing's earlier ideas, he formulated a comprehensive plan. Lea, in his annual report of 1850, explained the policy of Concentration and the new course to be followed in Indian affairs by the federal government:

There should be assigned to each tribe, for a permanent home, a country adapted to agriculture, of limited extent and well-defined boundaries; within which all [Indians], with occasional exceptions, should be compelled constantly to remain until such time as their general improvement and good conduct may supersede the necessity of such restrictions. In the mean time the government should cause them to be supplied with stock, agricultural implements, and useful material for clothing; encourage and assist them in the erection of comfortable dwellings, and secure to them the means of facilities of education, intellectual, moral, and religious.

Lea worked closely with Robert W. Johnson, chairman of the House Committee on Indian Affairs, to assure congressional approval. In 1851 Congress passed the Indian Appropriation Act, sanctioning the new policy and appropriating $100,000 to negotiate Concentration treaties.

The United States sought to safeguard overland traffic and to open up new areas in the trans-Mississippi West to American settlement and enterprise. Consequently, the Indian Bureau moved with deliberation to implement the policy of Concentration by concluding comprehensive treaties with the western tribes. By 1856, over fifty treaties had been negotiated that extinguished Indian title to 174 million acres of land. The first major council to implement Concentration provides a good example of what happened to tribes when negotiators appeared in their land with a treaty to sign.

In September 1851, the largest gathering of natives seen on the Great Plains until that time participated in a council held near Fort Laramie in southeastern Wyoming. Its purpose was to organize the northern plains and secure the important Oregon Trail for American travelers. Almost 10,000 Indians—Cheyennes, Arapahoes, Teton Sioux, Assiniboines, Shoshonis, Crows, and Arikaras—came in for this council. The Kiowas and the Comanches did not attend, refusing to meet with their tribal enemies. The government's negotiator, David D. Mitchell, asked the Indians to allow free, unmolested travel over the Oregon Trail; to stop all intertribal warfare; and to agree to the establishment of exact territorial boundaries for each tribe. "In times past you had plenty of buffalo and game to subsist upon, and your Great Father well knows that has always been your favorite amusement and pursuit," Mitchell explained to the gathered tribes. "Your condition has changed, and your Great Father desires you will consider and prepare for the changes that await you." The government, perhaps aware of what it asked, did attempt to use such natural boundaries as existed on the northern plains, such as the Arkansas, Powder, North Platte, and Yellowstone rivers, in making its determination. In return for signing this crucial treaty, the tribes were guaranteed an annuity payment of $50,000 a year in food and goods for the next fifty years, permanent right to their defined lands, and peace with the United States. When the Fort Laramie Treaty came before the United States Senate for ratification, the senators considered its terms too generous; hence the length of time for the annuity was reduced from fifty to fifteen years.

Democrat Franklin Pierce's victory in the presidential election of 1852 assured the departure of Commissioner Lea and other Whigs from the federal bureaucracy. Just before leaving office, Lea evaluated the government's new solution to the Indian question and addressed the ethical considerations raised by the policy of Concentration. "When civilization and barbarism are brought in such relation that they cannot coexist together, it is right that the superiority of the former should be asserted and the latter compelled to give way," he wrote in his final annual report. "It is, therefore, no matter of regret or reproach that so large a portion of our territory has been wrested from its aboriginal inhabitants and made the happy abode of an enlightened and Christian people."

Concentration in the Indian Territory and Texas

George W. Manypenny, recommended to Franklin Pierce by members of the Ohio Democratic delegation to Congress, assumed his duties as commissioner of Indian Affairs within a month of the presidential inauguration in March 1853. Commissioners tended to have little contact with Indian matters after leaving the post, but not Manypenny. He developed a life-long concern with Indian affairs, the Indians' welfare, and the government's relationship with and treatment of tribes. He summarized his ideas and activities in *Our Indian Wards,* published in 1880.

Commissioner Manypenny continued the work of concentrating western tribes. Emissaries from the Indian Bureau negotiated fifty-two treaties with them during his four-year tenure. Manypenny also addressed the emerging threat to the Indian Territory on the eastern side of the Great Plains, which so far had remained untouched by the Concentration policy. The public's perception of the center of the country had changed considerably by midcentury. What had been viewed as the Great American Desert was now judged as the nation's fertile heartland. Settlers discovered that this area, long thought of as unproductive, could support certain types of farming. Americans, lusting after tribal holdings in the Indian Territory, complained bitterly that there was more land there than the Indians could ever use productively. Increasingly they demanded that Washington move to concentrate these tribes as well, then organize the land taken from them into a federal territory in preparation for the creation of new states on the Great Plains.

The American business community had plans for the region too, and its aspirations probably carried the greater influence among politicians in the nation's capital. Railroad companies, backed by midwestern senators David R. Atchison of Missouri and Stephen A. Douglas of Illinois, chairman of the influential Senate Committee on Territories, were making long-range plans to build a transcontinental railroad across the Great Plains. They anticipated that the line would originate at a midwestern city, perhaps Chicago, St. Louis, Memphis, or New Orleans, and from there run westward to California. Railroad executives exerted enormous pressure upon the federal government to open the Indian Territory for their use. Outgoing President Millard Fillmore, bowing to their lobbying, asked permission of Congress to concentrate all tribes residing in the northern portion of the Indian Territory on reservations. Congress gave its authorization on March 3, 1853.

Secretary of Interior Robert McClelland charged Commissioner Manypenny with the responsibility of implementing the Concentration plan. Manypenny dutifully carried out his orders, but the assignment gave him pause for reflection and, so it seems, for remorse as well. "By alternate persuasion and force," he lamented, "some of these tribes have been removed, step by step, from mountain to valley, and from river to plain, until they have been pushed halfway across the continent. They can go no further; on the ground they now occupy the crisis must be met, and their future determined." The commissioner did as duty demanded, however, spending the final months of 1853 implementing "the new order of things," as he called it, with the Delawares, Iowas, Kaskaskias, Kickapoos, Miamis, Missouris, Omahas, Otos, Sacs and Foxes, Shawnees, Peorias, Piankashaws, and Weas. His work accomplished, he reported that tribal leaders, "without enthusiasm," had signed treaties ceding their lands, thus opening that portion of the Indian Territory north of thirty-seven degrees latitude to whites and their enterprises.

As a result of the treaties, these tribes forfeited over 15 million acres to the United States. Their new reservations provided them with less than 1.5 million acres. One year later, in 1854, the United States Congress passed the Kansas-Nebraska Act, which established two large federal territories from what previously was the northern portion of the Indian Territory. Americans eagerly rushed in to claim this bonanza, which until 1854 had been withheld from them. By the end of the decade, 136,000 people had settled in those territories, mostly in Kansas. All was not well there, however. Soon people began calling it "Bleeding Kansas," as violence and bloodshed swept across that territory in the wake of disputes over the extension of slavery. George Manypenny noted sarcastically that Indian deportment contrasted "favorably with the disorderly and lawless conduct of many of their white brethren, who, while they have quarreled about the African, have united upon the soil of Kansas in wrong doing toward the Indians!"

The once immense Indian Territory had now been reduced to the domains of the republics established south of Kansas by the Five Civilized Tribes. In light of past events, they, too, had cause to wonder just how much longer Washington would maintain the sanctity of their new homelands. Troubling signals already abounded. "Necessity will soon *compel* the incorporation of their [the five Indian republics'] country into the Union," one federal official concluded. The Cherokee newspaper scathingly predicted that soon "a Commissioner will be sent down to negotiate, with a pocket full of money and his mouth full of lies. Some chiefs he will bribe, some he will flatter and some he will make drunk; and the result will be . . . something that will be called a treaty." Many in positions of leadership within the five republics' governments realized the need to secure an ally capable of helping defend their nations against encroachment by the United States. The eventual answer to their desperate situation appeared in 1861 with the onset of the Civil War in the form of the Southern Confederacy.

If the policy of Concentration was to solve the Indian question, as officials in Washington confidently expected, its success would rest on one of two exigencies: either unilateral enforcement by the United States government, probably through its military arm, or bilateral resolve and forbearance by Indians and Americans. Indians would have to cooperate by living and hunting in their specified territory, and Americans would have to utilize the land accorded to them and restrain from trespassing on tribal lands. Unfortunately, too seldom did either side cooperate with the government's expectations. To the distress of Americans, many western tribes still moved about freely, as they had always done, without heed to boundaries or borders, over lands now reserved for white settlement and enterprise by recent treaties. In turn, Indian resentment increased as the number of whites who attempted to displace them from areas within their specified territories grew. The behavior of both parties exasperated Manypenny, but especially that of his fellow citizens, theoretically the more civilized of the two groups. "Trespasses and depredations have been committed on the Indians," the commissioner stated with displeasure in 1856. "They have been personally maltreated, their property stolen, their timber destroyed, their possession encroached upon, and divers other wrongs and injuries done them." A later Interior Secretary, Carl Schurz, explained why so little cooperation came from Americans. "The average frontiersman looks upon the Indian simply as a nuisance that is in his way," he surmised. "It would be difficult to convince [many] that it is a crime to kill an Indian, or that to rob an Indian of his lands is not a meritorious act."

Nowhere were the difficulties of making the policy of Concentration a workable and permanent solution to the Indian question more apparent than in Texas. Here, during the previous decade, the United States had inherited a vicious, ongoing struggle between Texans and Indians—the fruits of Migratory Fever and Manifest Destiny. The Texas situation cried for resolution. Washington, understandably, applied its new solution of Concentration, but the policy failed to solve the Indian question in Texas. Nonetheless, this failure did little to shake federal officials' confidence in the efficacy of the policy. Perhaps it should have, for what happened in Texas foreshadowed United States–Indian affairs in the 1860s and 1870s, two of the most turbulent and violent decades in the history of Indian-white relations.

In the early 1820s a group of American colonists under the empressario Stephen F. Austin settled along the Colorado River in

Coahuila-Texas, a northern province of Mexico. Over the next decade the Mexican government prohibited further American colonization to the province, outlawed slavery there, and attempted to strengthen Mexican central authority over the American settlers already in Texas, prompting them to armed revolution to secede from Mexico in 1835. Almost as soon as Texans achieved independence the following year, they requested annexation by the United States. Northern politicians blocked the attempt, fearing that the vast Texas Republic would be divided into numerous slave states. Therefore, for the time being, the Lone Star Republic remained an independent nation. Sam Houston, the hero of the recent revolution, became the first president of the Republic of Texas. He moved quickly to establish peaceful and harmonious relations with the Indians of Texas, who included Kiowas, Comanches, Lipan Apaches, Wacos, Caddos, and Wichitas. Of these, the Comanches, who inhabited the northern and western portion of the republic, were the most dominant and populous tribe. Their livelihoods consisted almost exclusively of hunting and raiding. In earlier times they had raided Spanish, then Mexican, settlements. Recently they had turned to the newer Texas settlements with enthusiasm. In 1837 Houston successfully concluded a treaty with the Indians guaranteeing them their lands in western Texas. Texans, who had routinely disregarded Mexican law, now disregarded their new government's treaty and unceremoniously shoved their president's wishes and promises aside as they pressed into the forbidden land. Warfare soon swept across the West Texas plains as tribes brutally retaliated against the land-hungry settlers.

In 1838 Sam Houston lost his bid for reelection and the new president of Texas, Mirabeau Lamar, carried out his campaign promise to conduct a war of extermination against the Indians. Terrible fighting engulfed western Texas for the next four years, until war weariness prompted the people to turn again to the leadership of the peace-minded Sam Houston. Once back as chief executive he sought an enduring peace by creating a boundary line within the republic to separate the two warring races. He charged the highly autonomous Texas Rangers, notorious for their treatment of Indians and Mexicans, with the responsibility of guarding the border and keeping whites out of Indian lands. Had President Houston been able to effect this measure, peace might have been secured, since Indians would live west of the boundary line while Texans would remain east of it. Most Texans, however, refused to recognize the Indians' right to any land in Texas, and many claimed homesteads in Indian territory, threatening to "shoot the first Indian that came on the land." The Texas Rangers compounded the difficulty by enforcing Houston's plan only haphazardly. As a result, whites continued to overrun the lands reserved for the Texas tribes. The Indians, convinced that Houston and the Texas government had betrayed them, increased their efforts to repulse the settlers.

The United States assumed the "Texas troubles" when it annexed the republic in 1845 and made it the twenty-eighth state. From their first day as Americans, Texans, intense supporters of states' rights, were not eager to submit to federal authority on the Indian question. Washington was handicapped because it lacked ownership and jurisdiction over public lands in the state. As one of the conditions of annexation, Texas had retained "all the vacant and unappropriated lands lying within its limits, to be applied to the payment of the debts and liabilities of said Republic of Texas, and the residue of said lands, after discharging said debts and liabilities, to be disposed of as said State may direct." Therefore, Texans' attitude toward the Indians conflicted with that of the United States government, which recognized the Indians' claims to land in Texas by right of occupancy. Texans were highly critical of such an assertion by the federal authority. The state legislature angrily countered by declaring that it did not and would not recognize any Indian right to land within Texas.

The situation in Texas between 1846 and 1854 split into a series of interrelated conflicts between the United States government, the Texans and their state government, and the Indians of Texas. The United States attempted to bring lasting peace to the new state by negotiating a series of peace initiatives with the Indians, even while trying to placate Texans. The first talks took place in 1846. Two United States commissioners, Pierce M. Butler and M. G. Lewis, convened a council of the Texas tribes on the Brazos

River at a spot known as Council Springs. The treaty they negotiated offered "perpetual amity and friendship" with the Indians by promising to remove them from the jurisdiction of the state of Texas. It also pledged that the United States would protect both Texans and Indians. Texas took a vigorous states' rights position, bitterly denouncing federal interference in an internal matter and federal usurpation of a state's prerogative to administer Indian affairs within its borders. The state government declared it did not recognize the validity of the federal treaty. Hostilities resumed. The Indians quickly recognized that Texans intended not only to take all of their land, but to conduct a war to exterminate them. They responded by vicious attacks against white settlements. The Comanches, angered by the ineffectualness of the United States government in fulfilling its treaty promises, bitterly addressed their concerns to special federal agent Robert Simpson Neighbors:

For a long time a great many people have been passing though [our] country; they kill all the game, and burn the country, and trouble me very much. The commissioners of our great father promised to keep these people [Texans] out of our country. I believe our white brothers do not wish to run a line between us, because they wish to settle this country. I object to any more settlements.

The federal government was obliged to acknowledge its failure to protect the Indians of Texas. Just as clearly it also realized that Texas would not protect the Indians, especially when, in the summer of 1847, the state granted white speculators vast tracts of public land, even though Indians resided there. This recognition, coupled with ongoing hostilities, prompted American authorities to apply the new policy of Concentration within Texas. Only in this way, they concluded, could Indians be protected from further white aggression. After long delay and arduous negotiations, the United States in early 1854 finally assumed a tenuous jurisdiction over the Texas tribes, only after the state legislature agreed to the establishment of two large federal Indian reserves within the state. The Indian Bureau under Manypenny created one reserve on the Clear Fork of the Brazos River for the Comanches and a second on the main fork of the Brazos for the smaller tribes. But no sooner was this accomplished than Texans decided they wanted to settle this portion of the state themselves. Whites soon entered the federal reserves in an attempt to eliminate the Indian presence completely.

In a desperate attempt to protect the Indians from the Texans, frustrated federal officials sanctioned the complete removal of all Indians from that state in 1859. The United States had made a bitter enemy of the Comanches. Even so, the tribe had been treated with such ruthlessness by Texas that even after the long confrontation ended, Comanches never failed to distinguish between Americans and their most despised enemy, Texans.

As the decade of the 1850s closed, the western tribes were adjusting to the changes forced on them. Minor altercations occurred between troops and Indians, but there was no serious outbreak of violence. Federal officials confidently maintained that the policy of Concentration was <u>the solution</u> to the Indian question. While conceding that the policy had failed in Texas, they judged that episode an anomaly, not an augur. If anything, officials believed Texas taught an important lesson about the policy of Concentration: Washington could not count on the resolve and forbearance of either Indians or Americans. To solve the Indian question, the United States would have to enforce the policy unilaterally. But that question seemed unimportant as other, more serious problems confronted the nation. With the United States moving rapidly toward a civil war, governmental attention to Indian affairs all but disappeared. The Indian question, however, did not. If anything, the Civil War years only exacerbated the matter, reinforced the lesson of Texas, and, unexpectedly for the federal authority, further advanced the policy of Concentration.

Yes; they fight among themselves—away off. Do you hear the thunder of their big guns? No; it would take you two moons to run down to where they are fighting, and all the way your path would be among white soldiers as thick as tamaracks in the swamps of the Ojibways. Yes; they fight among themselves, but if you strike at them they will all turn on you and devour you and your women and little children just as the locusts in their time fall on the trees and devour all the leaves in one day.

LITTLE CROW, SANTEE SIOUX

CHAPTER THREE

The Civil War Years

Ominously, one event had built upon another during the 1850s, straining sectional antagonism to the breaking point. Then came the election of 1860 and the crisis that lengthened into the American Civil War. Abraham Lincoln's victory and the ascendancy to power of the Republicans, a purely Northern party dedicated to preventing the extension of slavery into the West, posed a threat too great to many Southerners. Before Lincoln took office as sixteenth president of the United States in March 1861, seven Cotton Belt states dissolved their ties with the federal union and, at Montgomery, Alabama, quickly proceeded to establish the Confederate States of America.

Lincoln was no sooner inaugurated than the emergency focused on Fort Sumter, a three-story pentagon-shaped masonry stronghold towering fifty feet above low water, constructed upon a shoal in the harbor of Charleston, South Carolina. Confederates demanded the immediate evacuation of the garrison's federal troops. Lincoln not only rejected the demand but dispatched a convoy of merchant ships to reprovision his troops. "The gage is thrown down," responded the *Charleston Mercury,* "and we accept the challenge." In the early morning hours of April 12, 1861, shore batteries around the harbor commenced a massive bombardment of Sumter. After thirty-four hours of shelling, Federals lowered the flag of the United States and surrendered the fortress. Lincoln declared the Deep South to be in a state of rebellion and immediately issued a call for 75,000 army volunteers. Four states of the Upper South, seeing Lincoln's call as an act of war, also seceded from the United States and joined the seven Cotton Belt states in the Confederacy.

A wave of war fever swept across the North and the South when people heard the news of Fort Sumter. People cheered. Bands played. Flags waved. "The military excitement here is intense," Senator John Sherman of Ohio wrote from Washington. "Civil War is actually upon us, and strange to say, it brings a feeling of relief: the suspense is over." Northerners and Southerners alike expected the war would be but a few glorious battles; people repeatedly fixed estimates of its duration at sixty days. In a short time, however, as Americans grimly battled Americans, the terrible reality of this destructive struggle settled over the land.

The combination of military, political, racial, social, cultural, economic, demographic, and constitutional consequences wrought by the Civil War made it a pivotal event in the national experience. It also proved crucial in Indian affairs. Here too the events of the Civil War years produced several important outcomes. After the five Indian republics allied with the Confederacy, the United States gained license to "solve" the Indian question in the Indian Territory, as it judged appropriate. The land taken from the five republics after the Civil War provided the government with the means in the postwar years to designate a zone for further implementation of the Concentration policy. In the absence of the federal presence during the war, white westerners tried to adjust Indian matters themselves, increasing hostility between the two groups. The heightened Indian hostility toward whites convinced the United States government that it must vigorously pursue and enforce the Concentration policy, which helped to precipitate the Plains Wars of the 1860s and 1870s.

Civil War in the Indian Territory

While the Civil War in the West paled in military significance to that of the eastern theater, both the United States and the Confederate States judged the West as being strategically important. The government in Washington, determined to hold its western domain, was especially concerned with protecting the supply of gold and silver from western mines, which it vitally needed to help finance the war against the Southern states. The government in Richmond, driven by its own vision of Manifest Destiny, intended by force of arms to acquire territory in the West for the expansion of its institutions, especially slavery; territory that, to the South's bitter aggravation, was denied it before the war by the federal government. Additionally, the Confederacy aimed to secure a land corridor to the Pacific, stretching westward from the Confederate state of Texas across New Mexico and Arizona to California. Finally, the Confederacy was determined to seize the Union's western silver and gold mines to shore up the South's pitiful lack of capital to prosecute its war for independence.

Since early in 1861 Southern officials had courted the leaders of the five Indian republics in the Indian Territory. "Your people, in their institutions, productions, latitude, and natural sympathies, are allied to the common brotherhood of the slaveholding States," argued Arkansas Governor Henry M. Rector in a letter he sent to Principal Chief John Ross of the Cherokees, hoping to coax this crucial leader over to a pro-Confederate position. "Our people and yours are natural allies in war." Similar messages went out to the other tribes. The Lincoln administration tried to counter the Confederates' arguments, especially on the slavery question. William P. Dole, Lincoln's Indian commissioner, hoping to hold the tribes' allegiance, wrote them that "the government would under no circumstances permit the smallest interference with their tribal or domestic institutions." He cautioned them that Confederate agents were spreading an "erroneous impression" about the Republicans' position on slavery. Dole's reassurances never reached the tribes, however; Southern agents intercepted them en route.

Great Plains, ca. 1860-1875

    To help realize his nation's objectives in the trans-Mississippi
theater, Confederate Indian Commissioner Albert Pike traveled to
the Indian Territory in 1861. There he hoped to draw the Five Civilized Tribes into the conflict against the United States. Pike had
fertile ground on which to work. Many tribal members still har-
bored deep animosity toward the United States for the removal
trauma of the 1830s, as well as for the federal authority's general
nonobservance of treaty obligations in the years following removal. Economically the five republics had much stronger ties to

the South than to the North. A number of the Indian republics' citizens were slaveholders, providing yet another ingredient. These Indians felt a natural affinity for the Confederate cause and a like dread of the alleged threat posed by Lincoln and the Republicans to the maintenance of slavery in the United States.

The case against the United States did not end there. Confederates exploited several other provocative issues in an attempt to compel the Indian republics to sign treaties of alliance with them. One was the threat posed by the United States to the tribes' sovereignty and sanctity. Pike and his agents apprised the tribes of the recent campaign promises of William H. Seward, a leading New York Republican who now served as Lincoln's secretary of state. During the 1860 election Seward, in a speech at Chicago, had advocated appropriating the land of the Five Civilized Tribes and opening it to white homesteaders. "The Indian Territory . . . south of Kansas, must be vacated by the Indians," rang his declaration. Confederates also reminded tribes of how the United States government had forsaken them in the sectional crisis. In the spring of 1861 the federal Indian Bureau withdrew all Indian service agents from the Indian Territory and Secretary of War Simon Cameron ordered the abandonment of Forts Washita, Arbuckle, and Cobb in the Indian Territory, transferring their garrisons to Fort Leavenworth in Union-held Kansas. Confederate forces now occupied those installations. This action not only freed the five republics of their treaty obligations to the United States, Confederate agents argued, it also left the tribes vulnerable and fully exposed to assault from the Confederacy, which surrounded them on three sides and maintained troops within their homeland. "Indeed," reflected Union Commissioner Dole, acknowledging the convincing nature of the Confederate arguments, "the only matter of surprise to me is, that they [the five republics] have not more readily and heartily espoused the cause of the rebels."

There seemed few alternatives for the Five Civilized Tribes. In fact there appeared to be a number of advantages in allying with the Confederates, in part because they promised more liberal treaties than the United States ever had extended to the five tribes, but also because the Confederacy pledged to preserve and defend the

independence of the Indian republics. The Chickasaw government, reflecting a strong desire among the great majority of its
citizens to ally with the Confederacy, made its decision on May
25, 1861. "The Lincoln Government, pretending to represent said
Union, has shown by its course toward us, in withdrawing from
our country the protection of the Federal troops, . . . a total disre-
gard of treaty obligations," the Chickasaw legislature concluded.
"Therefore, Be it resolved," it continued, declaring independence
from the United States, "that the dissolution of the Federal Union .
. . has absolved the Chickasaws from allegiance [while] the current of the events of the last few months has left the Chickasaw
Nation independent [and] the people thereof free . . . to take such
steps to secure their own safety, happiness, and future welfare as
may to them seem best."

Like the Chickasaws, citizens of the Choctaw nation also
overwhelmingly supported the proposed alliance. It took formal
action against the United States on June 14, 1861. On July 12 delegates of both nations signed a joint treaty with Albert Pike committing their governments to the Confederate cause. The turn of
events in the Indian Territory did not surprise Pike's Federal coun-
terpart, William Dole. In his annual report for 1861 the commissioner of Indian Affairs concluded:

Cut off from all intercourse with loyal citizens; surrounded by emissaries
from the rebels, who represented that the government of the United
States was destroyed, and who promised that the rebel government would
assume the obligation of the United States and pay their annuities; assailed by threats of violence, and seeing around them no evidence of the
power of the United States to protect them, it is not surprising that their
loyalty was unable to resist such influence.

Not all tribes in the Indian Territory possessed the same confidence as the Chickasaws and Choctaws. Whatever fragile unity
had existed since removal within the Creek, Seminole, and Cherokee tribes was shattered by the Southern overtures. Deeply divided
over the question of allying with the Confederacy, each tribe split
along factional lines, with one side supporting an alliance and the
other demanding neutrality. Albert Pike, in July 1861, at last won
over influential mixed-blood chiefs, among them Daniel McIn-

tosh, who allied the Creek nation with the South. But many Creeks, led by the respected full-blooded chief Opothleyahola, resisted interfering in this "white man's war," and so declared themselves neutral. During the partisan struggle within their tribe that spring and summer, the neutrals sought support from Washington. None came. Now, with their people split over the question of allying with the South, the neutrals bitterly condemned the Union's actions as a betrayal. Opothleyahola, in a long letter to Abraham Lincoln, demanded to know why they did not hear from him. The chief reminded the president that previous chief executives promised that "in our new homes, we should be defended from all interference from any people, and that no white people in the whole world should ever molest us unless they came from the sky." Perhaps Southern agents were correct after all, he stated briskly. Perhaps the "Government represented by our Great Father at Washington has turned against us."

The stand of Opothleyahola and his followers put them in a precarious, even perilous, position. Hoping to avoid a confrontation, the neutrals decided it wise to distance themselves from those Indians who backed the Confederacy. They journeyed into the northern portion of the Creek nation and established a camp along the North Fork of the Canadian River near the present town of Eufalaula, Oklahoma. The number in camp soon swelled to between 800 and 1,200 people with the arrival of neutral Seminoles under chiefs John Chupco and Billy Bowlegs, who had separated from their pro-Confederate kinsmen.

No less severe was the split among the Cherokees, which fused disagreement over a potential Cherokee-Confederate alliance with a bitter intratribal fight that stretched back three decades to the Removal crisis. One faction in this long-standing battle was the so-called Ross party, the other the so-called Ridge or Treaty party. Back in Georgia during the 1830s, the New England-educated Cherokee John Ridge had painfully come to see the hopelessness of the Cherokees' position in retaining their homeland, especially after President Jackson's refusal to enforce the Supreme Court's *Worchester* v. *Georgia* decision (see Chapter One). Believing that the Cherokee nation's only salvation lay in surrendering its land and relocating quietly in the West, Ridge moved cautiously but purposefully to line up influential support within the tribe for a removal treaty. He persuaded his father, Major Ridge, one of the wealthiest Cherokees and speaker of the Cherokee National Council, the nation's ruling body, as well as Stand Watie and his brother, Elias Boudinot, editor of the tribal paper, the *Cherokee Phoenix*. The Ross party, led by Principal Chief John Ross, opposed them. This group categorically rejected removal, strenuously denounced the Ridge party and federal advances to endorse a removal treaty, and emphatically warned the Ridge party that signing the treaty would be tantamount to signing their death warrants. Understandably, officials in Washington sided with the Ridge party to consummate their design. Disregarding the wishes of the majority of Cherokees, the Ridge party signed the Treaty of New Echota in 1835, which sold the tribe's homeland for $5 million and authorized removal of the Cherokee people to the Indian Territory.

The Cherokees carried the feud from Georgia to the Indian Territory, and now, in 1861, the Ross and Ridge parties again engaged in an intense struggle to chart the national course for the Cherokees. Stand Watie, following the 1839 assassinations of the Ridges and Boudinot in retaliation for their signatures at New Echota, inherited leadership of the Ridge party. He supported the Confederacy and pressed for an alliance. John Ross, as in the old days in Georgia, opposed him absolutely. The Civil War terrified Ross. He worried that the sea of violence that now drowned Americans might also engulf his own people in fratricidal conflict. The principal chief saw no alternative but to declare the Cherokee nation's neutrality. "I am—the Cherokees are—your friends," he reassured Confederates, "but we do not wish to be brought into the feuds between yourselves and your Northern Brethren. Our wish is for peace. Peace at home and Peace among you." At the same time he enjoined his people to the "faithful observance" of treaties with the United States and requested that they abstain from "partisan demonstrations."

The Creek and Seminole neutrals applauded John Ross's decision. Not unexpectedly, reaction from within the Cherokee nation was severely divided. Watie, sensing a growing public shift to his pro-Southern position, especially after the Union military catastrophe at Bull Run in April 1861, moved quickly to shape events. Watie offered military assistance to the Confederacy on behalf of the Cherokees and, in return, on July 12 received a commission in the Confederate Army at the rank of colonel. General Ben Mc-Culloch, Confederate military commander in the Indian Territory, then authorized him to raise a regiment of Cherokees.

The Chickasaws and Choctaws, less than a month after allying themselves with the Confederacy, also organized a regiment of "mounted rifles." On August 1, 1861, Commissioner Pike notified Confederate President Jefferson Davis that the Indian regiments stood ready for battle. Later that month they went into action for the first time at the Battle of Wilson's Creek, fought near Spring-field, Missouri. There a Confederate army, with the aid of the Indian regiments (although Watie himself was not present) mauled Union forces under General Nathaniel Lyon. The news of victory and the performance of its sons thrilled the Cherokee nation. Just as war fever swept across the North and the South that spring following Fort Sumter, martial ardor mounted throughout the Indian Territory in the late summer.

Watie's actions and Cherokee participation in the victory at Wilson's Creek effectively reversed John Ross's declaration of neutrality. Desperately hoping to block the ascendancy of Watie, Ross dramatically altered his stance. On August 21, 1861, two weeks after Wilson's Creek, he addressed his nation, telling the Cherokee people that he would seek an alliance with the Confederacy. General McCulloch reported jubilantly on August 31: "The Cherokees have joined the South." The Cherokee nation formally dissolved its ties with the United States on October 7 by signing a reciprocal treaty of alliance with the Confederate States. Both parties pledged "perpetual peace and friendship, and an alliance, offensive and defensive." After the signing ceremony Ross and Watie shook hands as a demonstration of tribal solidarity.

Those Cherokees who still maintained that the only satisfactory course for their nation was neutrality went into exile. Bearing the news of John Ross's defection, the neutrals sought haven with Opothleyahola. All too soon the worst fears of Ross came to pass. The specter of civil war among his people loomed unmistakably as Confederate Indians organized an expedition to assault the neutrals' encampment, hoping to put the "traitors" to flight. Ross, in a letter that fall to Opothleyahola, pleaded with the neutrals' leader: "Brother—My advice and desire, under the present extraordinary crisis, is for all the red Brethren to be united among themselves in the support of our common rights and interests by forming an alliance of peace and friendship." But time had run out.

The internal strife in the Indian Territory exploded on November 19, 1861, when Confederate Indians supported by Texans under Colonel Douglas H. Cooper engaged the neutrals at the Battle of Round Mountain. Less than a month later the two sides clashed again at Chusto Talasah. The decisive engagement came on December 26. Now reinforced by 1,600 Southern cavalrymen, the Confederate Indians routed Opothleyahola's neutrals—destroying their camp, belongings, supplies, and livestock—and drove them from the Indian Territory. The neutrals fled up the Verdigris River, ultimately settling in refugee camps in Kansas, where they faced destitution throughout the next three years. William Coffin, Southern superintendent for the United States, visited the Kansas camps. What he saw there profoundly moved him: "The destitution, misery, and suffering amongst them is beyond the power of any pen to portray; it must be seen to be realized." Army surgeon A. B. Campbell witnessed the plight of the refugees, too. After visiting the Verdigris River camp during the refugees' first winter in Kansas, he tried to convey the agony of the experience: "It is impossible for me to depict the wretchedness of their condition. Their only protection from the snow upon which they lie is prairie grass, and from the wind scraps and rags stretched upon switches; some of them had some personal clothing, most had but shreds and rags, which did not conceal their nakedness; and I saw seven, ranging in age from three to fifteen years, without one thread upon their bodies." After arrival in Kansas their leaders cast off neutrality and offered to assist the United States.

The year 1862 proved fateful for the Confederate Indians and Southern fortunes. The hopes that the alliances with the South offered and the excitement of the early victories began to fade. In early spring, while Ulysses S. Grant battered Confederate defenses along the Tennessee and Cumberland rivers in an attempt to

secure Kentucky and Tennessee, Federal forces to his south prepared to invade Missouri and northern Arkansas. The showdown
came on March 6, 1862, as blue and grey armies collided at
Elkhorn Tavern, Arkansas. Samuel R. Curtis's 10,000 Federals
withstood an assault on the first day of the Battle of Pea Ridge by
Earl Van Dorn's 16,000 Confederates, whose troops included
3,500 Indians. Although outnumbered, General Curtis counterattacked on the second day, inflicting heavy casualties on the Southerners and forcing them into full retreat. The performance of Colonel Watie's Cherokee Mounted Rifles proved to be one of the few
bright spots during the Confederate debacle at Pea Ridge. Watie's
men captured a strategic Federal artillery position that raked
Southern lines and later skillfully covered the Confederate withdrawal. General Curtis noted in his report on Pea Ridge how impressed Federal officers were with "the hordes of Indians, cavalry,
and infantry that were arrayed against us."

Confederate fortunes in the western theater continued to
plummet that spring as Federal forces captured most of the Upper
Mississippi and Admiral David Farragut's fleet blasted its way up
the Lower Mississippi and seized New Orleans. These victories
doomed the Southern cause in the West. Thereafter Confederates
abandoned conventional tactics in the border states of Kansas,
Missouri, and Arkansas and waged their fight through guerrilla
warfare. General McCulloch relied heavily upon Colonel Watie
and his Cherokees, whom he ordered to "destroy everything that
might be of service to the enemy." Many of the forays came from
guerrilla bases within the Indian Territory, as raiders under commanders like Stand Watie and Charles Quantrill attacked Union
border settlements and disrupted federal supply lines and bases.
Unlike the atrocities committed by Quantrill's band, Watie rejected such tactics. As a result of his notable war record, in 1864
his superiors promoted him to brigadier general.

Meanwhile, the Confederate defeat at the Battle of Pea Ridge
opened the Indian Territory to invasion from Kansas. The United
States saw two principal advantages in this tactic. One, as Lincoln
told Congress, was to lead the Confederate Indians back into the
Union. "It is believed that upon the repossession of the country by

the federal forces," the president explained, "the Indians will readily cease all hostile demonstrations, and resume their former relations to the government." The second advantage, one pressed for fervently by the two United States senators from Kansas, James Lane and Samuel Pomeroy, was to hasten the removal of the refugee Indians from that state.

Opothleyahola and other pro-Union chiefs met with General David Hunter and agreed to assist with the invasion. A month later the commander of the Department of the Mississippi received his orders: "It is the desire of the President . . . that you should detail two regiments to act in the Indian country, with a view to open the way for friendly Indians who are now refugees in Southern Kansas to return to their homes and to protect them there. Five thousand friendly Indians will also be armed to aid in their own protection and you will please furnish them with necessary subsistence." By spring, cavalry and infantry regiments from Ohio and Wisconsin arrived, swelling the ranks of the invasion force. Superiors attached them to troops from Kansas and the pro-Union Indians to form the "Indian Expedition."

Pushing southward during the summer of 1862, the Federals and their Indian allies advanced into northeastern Indian Territory as far as Tahlequah, capital of the Cherokee nation, where they arrested John Ross without incident. Thousands of Cherokees, realizing the futility of supporting the Southern cause, defected to the Union. The government sent Ross to Fort Leavenworth, Kansas, then to Philadelphia. There, with great personal relief, he repudiated his nation's alliance with the South. For the remainder of the war he directed a pro-Union Cherokee government in exile, ultimately serving as emissary to the United States. Not to be undermined by his rival, Stand Watie disavowed Ross's actions, declaring himself rightful chief of the Cherokees. A meeting of Cherokees at Tahlequah on August 21, 1862, elected Watie principal chief and reaffirmed the treaty of alliance with the South.

John Ross, upon his arrival in the East, immediately sought to develop a cordial relationship with Abraham Lincoln and to secure aid for his people. Interior Secretary Caleb Smith wrote to Lincoln, asking permission for Ross to visit the White House. The president responded coolly. "I will see Mr. Ross at 9 a.m. to-morrow, if he calls." Lincoln's chilly demeanor continued in the meeting. The two met on September 12, 1862, and Ross reaffirmed the Cherokees' loyalty to the United States. He explained to Lincoln that the Cherokees signed the treaty with the South under duress, only after the United States failed to protect his people under obligations set forth in earlier treaties. Ross's arguments failed to sway Lincoln. The president disclaimed any failure of the national government, nor was he satisfied with Ross's reasons for the alliance. Lincoln closed the meeting assuring Ross that he would investigate the matter thoroughly.

Later that year Ross again approached Lincoln to seek a pardon for the Cherokee people. After a special meeting with his cabinet, Lincoln assured Ross that he would do everything in his power to protect pro-Union Cherokees; however, any determination of the fate of those who had aided the rebel cause must wait until the war's conclusion. It would be placed on the government's Reconstruction agenda. The United States eventually granted a parole to John Ross, but, to Ross's distress, after the war the victorious Union punished the Cherokee nation and the other Indian republics more harshly than it did the states of the defeated Confederacy.

Federal troops and pro-Union Indians followed their successful invasion of 1862 by launching another operation against the Indian Territory in the summer of 1863. At the Battle of Honey Springs, fought on July 17, the Indian Expedition defeated the rebel army and its Indian allies. Then it advanced steadily southward, at last reaching the Canadian River, which separated the Cherokee and Creek nations from those of the Choctaws and Chickasaws. The Confederate Indians, fleeing in disarray in the wake of the invading force, eventually reassembled in refugee camps farther south and west, not unlike those in which their kinsmen languished in Kansas. The Indian Expedition might have pressed deeper into the Confederate Indians' territory and claimed absolute victory if military developments in the East had not intervened. Earlier that month in Pennsylvania, Federal and Confederate soldiers assaulted each other at the Battle of Gettysburg.

Confederate commander Robert E. Lee withdrew his battered forces back into Virginia and prepared for the inevitable Union counteroffensive. In March 1864, Lincoln ordered General Ulysses S. Grant in from the western theater, assigning him responsibility for directing what the president hoped would be the conclusive operation against the Confederacy. Consequently, Northern and Southern commanders chose to abandon operations in the Indian Territory and the border states and reassign men to the more critical eastern theater.

The Canadian River now stood as the rough boundary line separating Indian combatants in America's civil war. The Indian Territory descended into its own bloody and destructive fratricidal struggle, as pro-Union and pro-Confederate Indians assailed one another. Each side swept back and forth across the river for the next two years, turning the once bountiful Indian Territory into a no-man's-land of terror, disruption, and desolation. At last the Civil War concluded as Union forces triumphed. General Lee surrendered his army on April 9, 1865. Over the next six weeks other Confederate commanders capitulated to the Union. Stand Watie was the last Confederate general to succumb, signing articles of surrender on June 23, 1865, near Doaksville, the capital of the Choctaw nation.

Like the South, the Indian Territory was prostrate after the terrible fighting of the Civil War years. Great portions of it lay devastated: homes destroyed, fields overrun or untended, stock dead or running loose. The war left countless families bereft, while thousands from the five republics suffered as refugees. One can sense from John Ross the feelings of anguish and dislocation so widespread among members of the Five Civilized Tribes as he traveled back to the Indian Territory. "I know that I am fast approaching my country & my people," he wrote from Arkansas in late August 1865, "but, where is that delightful Home . . . the family Homestead ruthlessly reduced to ashes by the hand of rebel incendiaries. And whilst the surviving members of our family circle are scattered abroad as refugees—I am here journeying as it were, alone to find myself, a stranger & Homeless, in my own country."

Reconstruction under Abraham Lincoln might have been less calamitous for the Five Civilized Tribes and for the South, but by war's end he was dead from an assassin's bullet. Instead of a spirit of conciliation, one of vindictiveness toward the vanquished too often prevailed in Washington, and certainly it characterized post-war dealings with the Five Civilized Tribes. The federal government, virtually charging the tribes with treason, asserted that they "had compromised their rights under existing treaties." James Harlan, President Andrew Johnson's secretary of war, made clear to Indian Commissioner Dennis N. Cooley the government's agenda in reconstructing the Five Civilized Tribes: "The President is willing to grant them peace, but wants land for other Indians, and a civil government for the whole Territory." Thus the Civil War provided a resolution, unplanned but not unwelcomed by white Americans, to certain Indian problems that lingered from the 1850s. Through the process of Reconstruction the United States would further advance the policy of Concentration.

To reestablish their relationship with the United States, Washington required each of the five tribes to sign a Reconstruction treaty. Following preliminary discussions with a federal peace commission headed by Indian Commissioner Cooley at Fort Smith, Arkansas, in the fall of 1865, representatives of each tribe came to Washington in 1866 to sign the documents. In most respects all treaties were similar. Their terms allowed the United States to solve, in its judgment, the long-standing Indian question in the Indian Territory with the Five Civilized Tribes and provide for new contingencies. The treaties contained five major provisions. They established peace with the United States and among the five Indian republics; they abolished slavery, granted tribal citizenship to blacks formerly held in bondage by Indians, and ordered their integration into the five tribes on an equal footing; they acknowledged preliminary steps for a unified government in preparation for territorial status and possibly an Indian state; and they mandated tribal acquiescence to rights-of-way for future railroad construction across the Indian Territory.

The fifth provision dealt with land occupancy. The Indian Reconstruction treaties contained substantial land cessions by all five tribes. Their collective forfeiture amounted virtually to the western half of present-day Oklahoma. The United States planned to advance the policy of Concentration in this area. After reducing by half the five Indian republics' domains, Washington set aside roughly the western third of the Indian Territory for future use as federal reservations. A central corridor in the Indian Territory was also organized as a zone to settle tribes such as the Kickapoo, Pawnee, Potawatomi, Sac and Fox, and Shawnee, among others. A quarter-century earlier the United States had removed these tribes under the policy of Separation from the East to the northern part of the Indian Territory. In the 1850s Commissioner George Many-penny dissolved that portion of the Indian Territory and concentrated them on lands that became Kansas. Now, at the end of the Civil War, Congress evicted them from Kansas in answer to the successful lobbying of senators Lane and Pomeroy of that state and provided them with another "permanent" home, this time in lands once granted in perpetuity to the Five Civilized Tribes.

The burden of peace, like that of the war years, proved heavy for the people of the Indian Territory. John Ross concluded that the "victory perched upon the banners of the United States . . . has been achieved at the sacrafice [sic] of hundreds of precious lives, the loss of wealth and resources of the [Cherokee] Nation and amid pain, suffering and destitution hitherto unknown to our people." Elias C. Boudinot succinctly summarized the net effect of the Civil War—the "white man's war" that Ross, Opoth-leyahola, and others so desperately tried to avoid—on the Five Civilized Tribes in a letter to Stand Watie in 1866: "We have been beaten."

The Santee Sioux Uprising

The Five Civilized Tribes were the only Indians actually drawn into the Civil War itself. The Civil War was not, however, the only arena of Indian-white conflict between 1861 and 1865. Other severe altercations erupted as well, although none related directly to the war. The United States government, locked in a struggle with a determined Southern Confederacy, of necessity was forced to give Indian affairs a low priority. In the absence of a federal authority to enforce regulations, Indian affairs suffered. Meanwhile, settlement of the trans-Mississippi West, although slackening slightly, continued throughout the war years. Under the buffeting of those Americans who looked for land to farm or gold to dig, Washington found it increasingly difficult to maintain the integrity of treaty obligations and the reservations defined in the 1850s under the policy of Concentration. Indians, who long had complained of un-corrected injustices, took advantage of the recall of army regulars from frontier posts to adjust matters themselves. This situation re-sulted in two eruptions of interracial violence. One involved the Sioux, the other the Southern Cheyennes. Both incidents posed a significant threat to the Concentration policy and convinced the federal government that it would have to enforce the policy unilat-erally in the postwar years.

While the Union and Confederate armies battled through the opening years of the war, the first of the serious clashes between white settlers and Indians occurred in Minnesota. During the 1850s, when the federal government began the policy of Concen-tration, the Santee Sioux had agreed to two sets of treaties with the United States, both of which contributed to the deadly events of the late summer of 1862. In the first set of treaties, concluded at Traverse des Sioux in 1851, the tribe had ceded 24 million acres to the United States and, in turn, were allotted two reservations along both sides of the Upper Minnesota River, measuring twenty miles wide by 150 miles long. In 1858, the Santee Sioux saw this reser-vation reduced by half as they forfeited the territory north of the river in the second set of treaties. Both sets contained assimilation measures that directed the government to build blacksmith shops and saw mills, establish manual labor schools on the reservations, and introduce the concept of private property among the Santees by allotting eighty-acre farm plots to individual families. "The theory, in substance," explained Thomas J. Galbraith, the Santee Sioux's agent, "was to break up the community system among the Sioux; weaken and destroy their tribal relations; individualize them by giving each [head of household] a separate home and hav-ing them subsist by industry—the sweat of their brows; till the soil; make labor honorable and idleness dishonorable; or, as it was expressed in short, *'make white men of them,'* and have them adopt the habits and customs of white men."

It did not take long for problems to arise on the reservation. The assimilation measures of the recent treaties provided one source of intratribal tension, producing antagonism between the "farmer" and "blanket" factions of the Santees, who disagreed over whether to shed or keep the old tribal ways. Food shortages among the Santee Sioux produced the second problem. A constantly increasing white population in the rich Minnesota Valley during the 1850s and early 1860s steadily diminished the amount of game on or around the reservation. This development, coupled with the Santees' mounting inability to grow sufficient food to feed themselves on their compressed reservation, made it inevitable that government annuity payments came to mean the difference between survival and starvation. Tribal members typically used annuity monies to purchase food supplies.

The Civil War destroyed many things, among them the federal government's plan for feeding the Santee Sioux. Ever since that conflict broke out, the United States, preoccupied with prosecuting the war and in dire need of every available dollar, had become increasingly tardy in providing annuity payments. Combined with bad harvests, this situation produced severe food shortages among the Santee in the early 1860s. Hunger on the reservation increased, as did the Santee Sioux's hostility toward white settlers who, it seemed, had forged lives of plenty on former Sioux lands even as the Indians' condition slipped from deprivation to destitution. By the summer of 1862, the severe hunger precipitated a catastrophe in Minnesota.

In early August of 1862, Santees from the Upper Agency, the northern portion of their reserve, broke into the government's warehouse and, with the reluctant approval of their agent Thomas Galbraith, took enough pork and flour to save their people from starvation. Less than two weeks later Santees from the Lower Agency requested emergency food allotments. Galbraith rejected their appeal, and a local contingent of armed traders backed him up. Andrew Myrick, one of the more vocal of the group, closed the discussion by suggesting contemptuously, "So far as I am concerned, if they are hungry, let them eat grass or their own dung."

Soon many young warriors talked openly of trying to drive white settlers out of the Minnesota River valley and back across the Mississippi. The Lincoln administration's recall of federal units from the region to fight the Confederates made the success of such an undertaking more plausible. A local missionary reported that stories about the white man's war "operate very powerfully upon the . . . Indians." But this talk was checked by Little Crow, or Taoyateduta, chief of the Mdwekanton, a tribal division of the Santee Sioux. Little Crow solemnly warned the angry young men that any engagement would be nothing short of suicide. "We are only little herds of buffalo left scattered, the white men are like the locusts when they fly so thick that the whole sky is a snowstorm," he explained. "You may kill one—two—ten; yes, as many as the leaves in the forest yonder, and their brothers will not miss them. . . . Count your fingers all day long and white men with guns in their hands will come faster than you can count." For the moment the young warriors heeded Little Crow's warning.

An uncertain peace lasted for two weeks. Then the inevitable explosion occurred on August 17—"like a spark of fire, upon a mass of discontent, long accumulated and ready for it," characterized Minnesota Lieutenant-Governor Ignatius Donnelly—near the town of Acton, Minnesota, forty-five miles north of the Santee's reserve. A small hunting party of Sioux stole eggs from settlers, quarreled with them, and in a mindless act of revenge murdered five whites. That evening the hunters returned home and went immediately to Little Crow to recount the deed. He called a meeting of chiefs of the Lower Agency for later that night to decide what action should be taken. After heated debate between a war and a peace faction, the majority decided upon a preemptive strike before whites could retaliate for the murders. Little Crow himself agreed to lead the fight against the settlers of Minnesota, even though he still maintained it was a lost cause.

The attacks began during the early morning hours of August 18. The Santees initially struck at settlers residing at nearby farms. One of the first to die was the trader Andrew Myrick who, when found later, had prairie grass crammed into his mouth. The warriors sent overtures to followers of the peace faction chiefs to join in the rampage, but they firmly rejected the offer. As the day advanced, the range of the massacre, with its accompanying raping and plundering, widened. The Santees' attack caught settlers by surprise. "We were beginning to regard the poetry of the palisades as a thing of the past," one settler recalled to John Nicolay, Lincoln's personal secretary, "when, suddenly, our ears were startled by the echo of the warwhoop, and the crack of the rifle, and our hearts appalled by the gleam of the tomahawk and the scalping knife, as they descended in indiscriminate and remorseless slaughter, on defenseless women and children on our border."

Fighting frantically, the Santee Sioux swept down the Minnesota Valley in an attempt to wipe out all the settlers. Minnesota governor Alexander Ramsey wired Secretary of War Edwin Stanton, apprising him of the raids with alarm: "The Sioux Indians on our western border have risen, and are murdering men, women, and children." Many in Washington feared, incorrectly, that the uprising was a Confederate conspiracy to disrupt the Union war effort. Interior Secretary Caleb Smith was one such official: "I am satisfied the chief cause is to be found in the insurrection of the southern states." While the United States and Minnesota prepared to respond, Little Crow, in a wise tactical move, suggested directing a concentrated attack against the strategic Fort Ridgely. Here, at the compound erected to protect the populous valley, terrified settlers had sought shelter. The younger warriors overruled him, preferring to loot and plunder, a serious and ultimately fatal error that afforded time for reinforcements to swell the number of defenders at the fort. Not until August 20, the third day of the uprising, did the Santees assault Fort Ridgely. The garrison repelled the attack after three days of intense fighting. With their path to advance through the valley blocked, the Sioux changed direction and raided to the northwest. Between 400 and 800 citizens of Minnesota perished in what Commissioner Dole called "the most atrocious and horrible outbreak to be found in the annals of Indian history."

Responsibility for carrying the war to the Santee Sioux fell to Governor Ramsey and to General John Pope, commander for the newly created military Department of the Northwest. "Attend to the Indians," Lincoln advised upon hearing of the uprising, "necessity knows no law." The general concurred. "It is my purpose utterly to exterminate the Sioux if I have the power to do so," Pope declared. His orders to Colonel Henry Hopkins Sibley, commander of the Third Minnesota Volunteer Regiment, were blunt and explicit: "Destroy everything belonging to them and force them out to the plains, unless, as I suggest, you can capture them." Although there was little need to elaborate on such orders, Pope apparently felt a need to add to the savagery. "They are to be treated as maniacs or wild beasts," he exhorted. The Minnesota militia defeated the outmatched Santee Sioux in a pitched battle at Wood Lake, Minnesota, on September 23, 1862. Large numbers of Sioux surrendered. Little Crow and many of the hostiles escaped into the Dakotas to join their plains cousins, the Teton Sioux.

The rest of the tribe chose not to flee. For many, staying was the natural course of action, since they had not been belligerents and supposed they would be treated as neutrals. They understood clearly that those who had rampaged could hardly expect much mercy from the whites. In October John Pope informed Henry W. Halleck, general-in-chief in Washington, that he had taken about 1,500 Santee prisoners. Pope adamantly recommended "executing the Indians who have been concerned in these outrages." Minnesotans agreed, demanding vengeance against the perpetrators. "Exterminate the wild beasts," urged Jane Swisshelm, editor of the *St. Cloud Democrat,* "and make peace with the devil and all his hosts sooner than with these red-jawed tigers whose fangs are dripping with the blood of the innocents." Pope faced a tricky problem in meting out justice. "I don't know how you can discriminate now between Indians who say they are and have been friendly, and those who have not. I distrust them all." Undeterred, he convened a military court of justice that, in ten days, tried 392 Indian prisoners accused of committing crimes during the uprising. When it finished its work the commission had sentenced sixteen Indians to imprisonment and condemned 303 to death by hanging.

Abraham Lincoln was not convinced that justice had been served in Minnesota and ordered that no executions be made without his sanction. On November 10, he sent a request by telegram to General Pope: "Please forward, as soon as possible, the full and complete record of these convictions." Pope obeyed and dispatched the transcripts to Washington so the president and his attorneys could review them. The general also warned Lincoln: "The people of this State . . . are exasperated to the last degree, and if the guilty are not all executed I think it nearly impossible to prevent the indiscriminate massacre of all the Indians—old men, women, and children." Episcopal Bishop Henry B. Whipple, taking an extremely unpopular stand in the eyes of fellow Minnesotans, vigorously interceded with Lincoln on behalf of the condemned Sioux, launching an illustrious career as an Indian reformer. Indian Commissioner William Dole and Interior Secretary Caleb Smith likewise threw their support behind efforts to prevent the mass executions. After a review of the verdicts, Lincoln authorized the hanging of less than forty of the condemned Santee Sioux. All of the condemned had either participated in the massacre or raped women. Lincoln's goal, as he told the Senate, was neither to act "with so much clemency as to encourage another outbreak, on the one hand, nor with so much severity as to be real cruelty, on the other." A large gathering watched as thirty-eight Santees died on a single scaffold at Fort Mankato, Minnesota, on the day after Christmas, 1862.

Those Santees remaining in the state had little to hope for at the hands of Minnesotans. As the Civil War had provided a solution to the Indian question in the Indian Territory, the tragic events of 1862 served the same end in Minnesota. The state's representatives in Washington urged Congress to authorize the immediate expulsion of all Indians from Minnesota: not just the Santees, but also the Winnebagos, whose fertile land in Blue Earth County white settlers coveted. Congress acquiesced. On February 21, 1863, it authorized the eviction of the Winnebagos. The Santee removal bill of March 3, 1863, revoked the earlier treaties with the tribe and by "right of conquest" extinguished title to their land in Minnesota. The government ordered the two tribes removed to a desolate tract of land at Crow Creek near Fort Randall on the Missouri River, in the Dakota Territory. There the army could keep them under close scrutiny.

On May 4 and 5, 1863, 1,300 Santee Sioux, mainly women and children, boarded two steamboats that carried them into exile. While one of the vessels was docked at St. Paul to take on supplies, whites on shore, in a final act of reprisal, hurled rocks at the hated passengers. In addition to their banishment, Washington suspended the tribe's annuity payments for four years and converted the monies to reimburse the damage claims of citizens of Minnesota. Well before this four-year period ended, crop failures at Crow Creek, coupled with a severe shortage of essential supplies, reduced hundreds of Santees to death by starvation. Luckily for the Winnebagos, the Indian Bureau had relocated them from Crow Creek to the Omaha reserve in Nebraska in 1864.

As for Little Crow, his stature in the eyes of his followers diminished rapidly after his flight into the Dakotas, and his attempts to organize another attack on Minnesota from the land of the Teton Sioux failed. By July 1863, the discredited chief was back in Minnesota attempting to steal horses. On the afternoon of July 3, a farmer named Chauncey Lamson shot and killed Little Crow while the Santee was picking raspberries. The shooting took place to the south of Acton, where all the violence had begun the previous year. Little Crow's head was cut off and displayed at St. Paul. His body was disposed of in the refuse pit of a local slaughterhouse in Hutchinson. For his marksmanship, the state legislature awarded Lamson $500.

Fears of a widespread Indian war permeated the northern frontier in the aftermath of the Santee Sioux uprising. "From all indications and information, we are likely to have a general Indian war all along the frontier," predicted General Pope. Governor Samuel Kirkwood of Iowa notified Secretary of War Edwin Stanton, "I have reliable information that the . . . Indians on our western border, north of the Missouri River, have joined with the hostile Indians of Minnesota, and threaten our whole northwestern border." Already the Teton Sioux, after hearing tales of the events in Minnesota from the renegade Santees, made it known that no longer would whites be allowed to pass through their lands. "If you have no ears, we will give you ears," they warned those who refused to heed their admonition.

In the spring of 1863 General Pope, hoping to exert federal authority over the northern frontier, ordered two columns of troops into the Dakota Territory to deal with the Teton Sioux. The thrust was unsuccessful. The troops managed only to engage the Tetons in a few inconsequential battles. The Sioux, in turn, infuriated by what they judged as invasion of their country, lashed out at whites. They made good their threat to halt traffic on the Upper Missouri and on the overland roads across the Dakota Territory, and in the spring of 1864 Sioux raiding parties struck hard at settlers along the Minnesota-Iowa border. The fires of war on the upper plains, ignited in the aftermath of the Santee Sioux uprising, blazed throughout most of the next two decades, not to be extinguished until the battle at Wounded Knee. Meanwhile, farther west, another severe struggle had erupted in Colorado.

Colorado and Sand Creek

In 1858, gold was discovered in the Pike's Peak region of present-day Colorado, on the western edge of the Southern Cheyennes' country. As with all gold discoveries, it caused dramatic changes to the land and the Indian people near the strike. The Pike's Peak gold strike set in motion events that destroyed the Concentration measures implemented by the Lea and Manypenny Indian Bureau in the 1850s and led to all-out war on the central plains by the mid-1860s. That the discovery produced only meager amounts of the precious ore did not deter the swarms of gold hunters who cascaded across Cheyenne lands flaunting the slogan, "Pike's Peak or Bust." For all but the luckiest miner, Pike's Peak was a bust.

In 1859 a second find, near Clear Creek, sent even greater numbers rushing to make their fortunes. In that year alone over 100,000 people traveled to the fields along the new Smokey Hill Trail, which ran directly westward through the center of Cheyenne-Arapahoe territory as defined by their Concentration policy treaty. A decade earlier, when it implemented this policy with the Fort Laramie Treaty of 1851, the U.S. government had pledged the grasslands between the North Platte and Arkansas rivers to the Southern Cheyennes and Arapahoes. This trespassing was a source of irritation compounded by the multitude of Americans who actually spilled off the trail and squatted in the midst of Indian land, numbering over 34,000 by 1860. With the government's energies directed toward crushing the Confederacy, the United

States again proved unresponsive to the needs of Indians and undependable regarding its treaty obligations.

In the years 1860 and 1861, white population and business enterprises increased dramatically in this region. "We have substantially taken possession of the country and deprived [the Indians] of their accustomed means of support," assessed Indian Commissioner Alfred B. Greenwood. In response to such rapid growth, the United States organized the Southern Cheyenne–Arapahoe lands into the territory of Colorado in preparation for statehood. Again the government had to secure further land cessions from the Indians. By the terms of a new treaty concluded in 1861, the Treaty of Fort Wise, ten chiefs and delegates representing the Southern Cheyennes and Arapahoes relinquished all of their tribes' extensive landholdings except for a small, triangular tract along the Arkansas River in southeastern Colorado, designated the Sand Creek reservation. The treaty's civilization provision called for the land at Sand Creek to be allotted in severalty* to individual tribal members. With government assistance, the Southern Cheyennes and Arapahoes were expected to forsake the buffalo and horse culture and become self-supporting farmers. Most tribal members, however, had no interest in becoming farmers or abiding the new direction for them as outlined in the treaty. Instead they preferred to continue raiding, hunting the buffalo, and moving about freely on their former lands.

The same factors that had produced calamity and death in Minnesota quickly emerged in the Colorado Territory: the clash of convictions within the tribes between forsaking or maintaining the old ways, white demands for the Indians to stay off the land ceded by (a new) treaty, and mounting food shortages among the Southern Cheyennes and Arapahoes caused by the physical conditions of the reservation, a sandy, barren, agriculturally sterile piece of land. The scarcity of food at Sand Creek during 1862 made it inevitable that more men would secure food by hunting outside its

---

*Allottment in severalty refers to sole, separate, and exclusive possession without a joint interest in any other person or group, such as the tribe.

bounds, on their former ranges. There was even greater hunger in the following year. No buffalo, the staple of these people's diet, could be found within 200 miles of the reservation, reported their agent, Samuel G. Colley. Disease, brought in part by malnutrition, plagued the Southern Cheyennes and Arapahoes during that summer. Finally, out of desperation, the Indians reverted to raiding local farms and passing wagon trains; not necessarily to kill—there were remarkably few casualties as a result of the attacks—but to secure food. "Most of the depredations committed by them are from starvation," wrote agent Colley. "It is hard for them to understand that they have no right to take from them that have, when in a starving condition." William Gilpin, Colorado's first territorial governor and ex officio superintendent of Indian Affairs in the region, and his successor, John Evans, recognized that the Indians must be forced to remain at Sand Creek and convinced to adopt the government's civilization measures before a more dangerous situation arose.

Then, in April 1864, a small, rather typical, frontier incident turned into a crisis. It began with the arrival of a disturbing report at Camp Sanborn, Colorado. The report came from a rancher who charged that a party of Cheyennes had stolen horses and livestock from his land near Bijou Creek. Colonel John Chivington, Methodist minister, local politician, and militia commander of the District of Colorado, dispatched forty soldiers to disarm these Cheyennes and recover the allegedly stolen animals. North of Denver the militiamen encountered a group of Cheyennes herding horses and mules. The militia afforded them no opportunity to explain where they had obtained the animals, and violence quickly erupted. The Cheyennes drove the soldiers off, then unleashed their anger by conducting raids on ranches on the South Platte.

Governor Evans, outraged, decided that a swift and concentrated display of force was necessary to protect Colorado settlers and to drive the Cheyennes back to Sand Creek. He ordered a large force into the field under the command of Lieutenant George Eayre. Eayre's experience illustrates the difficulty plains commanders had in distinguishing peaceful from hostile Indians. In the spring of 1864 he assaulted a number of Cheyenne encamp-

ments in eastern Colorado and western Kansas, destroying clothing, food, weapons, and ammunition. Among Eayre's targets was
Chief Black Kettle's large camp, situated along the banks of the
Arkansas River. One of the leading chiefs of the Southern Cheyennes and a staunch advocate of peace and conciliation with the
Americans (as were nearly all of the Cheyenne leaders at this
time), Black Kettle had participated at the Fort Wise council in
1861 and, in March of 1863, had journeyed to Washington with a
delegation of plains chiefs to meet President Lincoln. It was natural, therefore, that Black Kettle did not expect violence at the
hands of the militiamen. The sight of soldiers approaching the
camp caused little alarm; Lean Bear, a lesser chief, rode out of the
camp with his son to greet the arrivals. On his chest Lean Bear
proudly displayed a large medal, a token of the friendship of Lincoln. As he neared the soldiers, his hand raised in a sign of peace,
he noticed too late that they had formed a skirmish line with artillery in position, facing the camp. When he was within twenty
yards of the soldiers, Lieutenant Eayre gave the command to fire
on him, his son, and the Cheyenne camp. The volley, immediately
killing Lean Bear and his son, rocked the camp. Swiftly, swarms
of Cheyenne warriors sprang to their horses and routed the aggres-
sors. The militiamen retreated westward to Fort Larned, Kansas.

The immediate effect of Eayre's raids was to escalate the violence. Cheyenne and Arapahoe war parties launched devastating
assaults against the major Colorado trails, the stagecoach lines
from Fort Kearny in Nebraska Territory on the Oregon Trail to
Denver, and the farms of settlers. The warriors burned ranches,
stole livestock, and took settlers as prisoners. In response, an
alarmed Governor Evans issued a proclamation on August 11,
1864, authorizing each citizen in the Colorado Territory:

either individually or in such parties as they may organize, to go in pursuit of all hostile Indians on the plains; [and] to kill and destroy as enemies of the country wherever they may be found, all such hostile Indians, and further, as the only reward I am authorized to offer for such
services, I hereby empower such citizens, or parties of citizens, to take
captive, and hold to their own private use and benefit, all the property of
said hostile Indians that they may capture, and to receive for all stolen

property recovered from said Indians such reward as may be deemed proper and just.

Chivington fully agreed with the stern measures authorized by the governor. As Lieutenant Joseph Cramer evaluated his superior: "He [Chivington] believed it to be right and honorable to use any means under God's heaven to kill Indians . . . and 'damn any man that was in sympathy with Indians.'"

Once the Coloradans attacked them, the Cheyennes and Arapahoes reciprocated, escalating their attacks on settlers and cutting telegraph lines between Colorado and the East. By late August other plains tribes had joined in attacking whites. "It will be the largest Indian war this country ever had," Governor Evans predicted, "extending from Texas to the British line involving nearly all the wild tribes of the plains." The Sioux, for example, besieged the area along the Oregon Trail in retaliation for raids directed against them by, among others, the Minnesota militia after the Santee Sioux affair in 1862. The Kiowas, Comanches, and Kiowa-Apaches vented their anger, frustration, and vengeance through raids against traffic on the Santa Fe Trail and against their hated enemies, the Texans. An observer described the volatile events in the West to the *New York Times,* which published the account on September 8. The report alluded to the widespread but incorrect belief that agents of the Confederacy provoked these Indian attacks:

Upon the overland route, devastation, terror, murder, has held a perfect carnival. From Denver to Fort Laramie to the Little Blue in Kansas, and to the Big Sandy in Nebraska, both within 150 miles of the Missouri, the Rebel Indians have swept like a hurricane. In a distance of four hundred miles along this great route they have captured at least 50 trains of merchandise or Government freight, driving stock, plundering and destroying to the value of a quarter of a million dollars. They have murdered two hundred white persons, among them many women and children. The stark bodies lie stripped and mutilated in the glaring sunlight, festering and rotting for want of burial, or half charred, are seen mouldering amid the ruins of ranches, cabins, and stage-stations.

As hostilities increased and the death toll mounted, some level-headed Americans, such as the influential trader George

Bent, attempted to reason with both sides, urging them to stop the warfare. Success seemed possible that fall at a council held at Camp Weld near Denver. There Black Kettle, tired of raiding, ready to camp for the winter, and still an advocate of conciliation with whites, acted as spokesman for the other six Cheyenne and Arapahoe chiefs present. He declared that he, the other chiefs, and their people desired peace above all else. Governor Evans, Colonel Chivington, and the other assembled officials doubted the Indians' sincerity and so offered no formal peace arrangements. The council failed, but with an odd twist. Black Kettle and the other chiefs, having misunderstood their interpreter, left Camp Weld believing in the success of their initiatives and confident that conflict with the Coloradans had ended.

Unaware of the misunderstanding, Black Kettle led some 500 Cheyennes toward the Sand Creek reservation to camp for the winter, where they thought they would be free from attack by the military. They knew nothing of the recent orders of Brigadier General Samuel R. Curtis, commander of the military Department of Kansas from Fort Leavenworth, to Colonel Chivington: "I want no peace until the Indians suffer more!" Curtis was not alone. In Denver, Evans prepared for further hostilities.

In the early morning hours of November 29, 1864, Chivington, leading the First Colorado Volunteer Cavalry and 100-day enlistees of the Third Colorado Cavalry, who carried with them four twelve-pound howitzers, attacked Black Kettle's sleeping encampment on the Sand Creek reservation without warning. The camp was virtually defenseless, filled with old men, women, and children. Most of the tribe's young men were miles away in Kansas that night hunting for food to bring back for the winter. On a pole over Black Kettle's lodge floated both a white flag and a flag of the United States. Near dawn, the assault began. First the militia ran off all Indian horses so that escape from the coming assault would be near impossible. Next a terrible volley of cannon and rifle shot ripped through the Cheyenne camp. Then the columns charged and encircled the camp, directing point-blank fire at its occupants. Any surviving Cheyennes who had not fled were subjected to the soldiers, who ravaged them with swords and knives. Men were castrated, and their organs, some soldiers promised each other, were to be saved as souvenirs and used as tobacco pouches. Pregnant women's abdomens were sliced open, with both mother and infant left to die. Children were dragged from their hiding places and murdered. Robert Bent, a local rancher who unwillingly accompanied Chivington, agonized, "There seemed to be indiscriminate slaughter of men, women and children." Some Cheyennes somehow managed to escape, Black Kettle being among the fortunate.

Sand Creek aroused few favorable responses. The most favorable was perhaps the ecstatic welcome of Chivington and his men upon their return to Denver. Cheyenne scalps were exhibited in the opera house, prompting wild enthusiasm. "All acquitted themselves well," proclaimed the *Rocky Mountain News.* "Colorado soldiers have again covered themselves with glory." Chivington's dictum, "nits make lice," allowed locals to feel justified about the slaughter of children. Outside of Colorado, people received the news with less ecstasy. Much of the nation recoiled in horror. The Commissioner of Indian Affairs castigated the Colorado militia, referring to its attack at Sand Creek as a massacre in which Cheyennes were "butchered in cold blood by troops in the service of the United States." As public condemnation swelled, calls rang out for a governmental inquiry into what was already being called the "Sand Creek massacre." Two federal committees eventually issued reports. The Joint Committee on the Conduct of the [Civil] War, following its investigation, vilified the Colorado militia and the conduct of Chivington:

Wearing the uniform of the United States, which should be the emblem of justice and humanity; holding the important position of commander of a military district, and therefore having the honor of the government to that extent in his keeping, he [Chivington] deliberately planned and executed a foul and dastardly massacre which would have disgraced the veriest savage among those who were the victims of his cruelty.

A joint congressional special committee agreed fully, concluding about Sand Creek: "The fact which gives such terrible force to the condemnation of the wholesale massacre of the Arapahoes and Cheyennes [was] that those Indians . . . believed themselves to be under the protection of our flag."

The Southern Cheyennes and Arapahoes kept on the move following the Sand Creek massacre. Some merely wandered the plains, avoiding all contact with whites. A number moved north into Sioux territory to reside with that tribe and their brethren, the Northern Cheyennes and Arapahoes. Still others, thirsting for revenge as word of Chivington's deed spread, organized huge war parties that scourged farms, trading posts, stagecoach stations, and wagon trains along the Platte River. Coloradans, anticipating they had "adjusted" one problem at Sand Creek, ignited a far more deadly one for themselves and other whites on the plains. By the spring of 1865 hostilities burned themselves out for the moment, but they had cost "many valuable lives and $40,000,000" the commissioner of Indian Affairs concluded.

In October 1865, Southern Cheyennes and Arapahoes, joined by Comanches, Kiowas, and Kiowa-Apaches, met in council with federal emissaries at the mouth of the Little Arkansas, where the United States offered all of them new treaties. The Little Arkansas Treaty required the Southern Cheyennes and Arapahoes to relinquish all claims to their Colorado lands, merely reiterating the Fort Wise Treaty of 1861. It also required that they forfeit the Sand Creek reserve and cede their cherished hunting grounds in western Kansas. In return the government promised the two tribes a new reserve south of the Arkansas along the Cimarron River. A minority of chiefs, including Black Kettle, signed the document. When other tribal members, especially those residing in the north with the Sioux, learned of this signing, they expressed consternation and great condemnation. Within a week of finalizing the Cheyenne-Arapahoe accord the government came to agreement with the Comanches, Kiowas, and Kiowa-Apaches, promising them reservations in the panhandle of northern Texas and the western part of the Indian Territory. None of the tribes received the land pledged at the Little Arkansas. The United States Senate amended the treaties in such a way as to make the clauses granting the new reservations virtually meaningless.

The Civil War proved as much a turning point for the trans-Mississippi West and its Indian population as it did for the nation as a whole. Federal officials solved the Indian question, as they defined it, with the Five Civilized Tribes, while opening half of the Indian Territory for further implementation of the policy of Concentration. And westerners, with the federal authority's attention focused on the Civil War, used the opportunity to open up more land in the trans-Mississippi West for white exploitation and settlement, expelling those tribes that stood in the way. But these actions heightened Indian hostility toward whites and galvanized among many the conviction not to yield further. Tribal leaders who still exhorted their people to follow the path of conciliation with whites found their arguments undermined by events of the Civil War years and their authority waning over younger warriors who would not retreat from confrontation. "Although wrongs have been done me I live in hopes [sic]," Black Kettle reflected. "But since they have come and cleaned out our lodges, horses, and everything else, it is hard for me to believe white men any more."

While the Civil War was in progress it had been the center of Washington's concern. Indian affairs, of necessity, had been made to wait in the wings. By the summer of 1865 the war had ended and Washington resumed its efforts to solve the Indian question. It had no choice. In the face of the turbulent atmosphere in the West in 1865 and the hardened sentiments of embittered Indians and aggressive whites, federal officials could not delay. The Indians were described as "a set of miserable, dirty, lousy, blanketed, thieving, lying, sneaking, murdering, graceless, faithless, gut-eating skunks as the Lord ever permitted to inflict the earth," in the *Topeka Weekly Leader,* and "whose immediate and final extermination all men . . . should pray for." The Great Plains was a tinder box, already ignited and about to explode. Although the federal bureaucracy disagreed about the best method of pursuing and fulfilling the goals of the policy of Concentration, none disputed that the Indian question must be solved immediately by that policy.

The country was made without lines of demarcation, and it is no man's business to divide it. . . . Perhaps you think the Creator sent you here to dispose of us as you see fit. If I thought you were sent by the Creator I might be induced to think you had a right to dispose of me. Do not misunderstand me, but understand me fully with reference to my affection for the land. I never said the land was mine to do with it as I chose. The one who has the right to dispose of it is the one who has created it. I claim a right to live on my land, and accord you the privilege to live on yours.

CHIEF JOSEPH, NEZ PERCÉ

The Plains Wars, Phase I: Realizing Concentration

The relentless westward push of humanity and enterprise that followed the Civil War rolled across the remaining Indian land like a tidal wave, with Americans clamoring for more and more of the republic's heartland. The middle of America seethed with activity. Ranchers moved in with growing herds of longhorns, launching great cattle empires. Pioneer families, lured by the Homestead Act of 1862, arrived to establish farms and attempt to bring forth bounty from the sod of the prairies. Miners continued to scour western rivers and mountains, driven by the irresistible dream that a fleck of gold or silver might open the door to untold personal fortune. The wagon trains of settlers, freight companies and stage-coach lines traversed the region in steadily growing numbers. Construction crews pushed to extend rail lines further onto the western plains. The Union Pacific and Central Pacific, with substantial financial assistance from the federal government, set to the massive task of laying a transcontinental railroad that would cut through the heart of the region connecting Chicago with San Francisco. Work crews, comprised largely of Irish and Chinese immigrants, labored for six years to join the two lines. In a lively ceremony at Promontory Point, Utah Territory, on May 10, 1869, dignitaries hammered a golden spike in place to complete the railroad. The news thrilled a nation. The settlement of the trans-Mississippi West in the years 1865 to 1900 was the largest migration of people in the history of the United States. Americans settled more land in those years than in any other period of their history. For the western Indians, the claiming of the "last frontier" by Americans became an episode of apocalyptic proportion.

The ever-increasing flood of humanity who moved into the West bred an intense resentment among tribes. As tribal holdings became more restricted, these feelings turned to violence as Indians fought to hold on to their homeland. The government in Washington, acutely aware of the potent, even dangerous, circumstances that expansion caused, could not have held back such overwhelming and burgeoning activity, even if it had wanted to, in order to assure peace with western Indians. "If the whole Army of the United States stood in the way," Senator John Sherman of Ohio concluded, "the wave of emigration would pass over it to seek the valley where gold was to be found." As a result, the years spanned by the Sand Creek massacre of 1864 and the Battle of the Little Bighorn twelve years later witnessed some of the bitterest conflicts in the history of Indian-white relations, with the prairies and plains of the West providing the setting for the climactic struggle.

Post–Civil War Indian Policy

The years after the Civil War confronted the United States government with an antagonistic situation on the Great Plains and elsewhere in the West. "What is to be done with the tribes of that region?" was an urgent question for Washington. Federal officials, by the latter half of the 1860s, envisioned a day not far in the future when the armed threat posed by western Indians to Americans would be eliminated. Only then could national objectives in the

West be fully realized. Both the civil and military arms of government recognized early that permanent peace could not be attained so long as tribes maintained their accustomed way of life, free of American hegemony. This realization guided Washington's Indian policy after the Civil War.

While much of the government's enterprise focused on reconstructing the states of the defeated South, federal officials also defined their program for terminating the Indian question. Three principal objectives ultimately characterized their efforts. The first called for Washington to pursue and enforce the policy of Concentration vigorously. This policy would solve the Indian question and further reduce tribal landholdings in the West, thus increasing opportunities for white settlement and enterprises in the region. The policy called for compulsory relocation of western tribes to federal land reserves, where permanent residency under strict government control would be obligatory. The government especially hoped to concentrate the plains tribes, the most formidable group of western Indians, on one of two large reservations: one south of Kansas in the Indian Territory and another north of Nebraska. When the United States cleared the central plains of free-roaming Indians, a wide east-west causeway would be available for white expansion and exploitation. Officials hoped to avoid conflict and the expense of Indian wars by methodically negotiating treaties with western tribes to consummate Concentration. Yet if they failed to yield peacefully, the government was fully prepared to employ the army to enforce the will of white society upon those Indians who resisted.

Loss of land would not be the full extent of the forfeiture. Under the second objective, Indians would be required to give up their accustomed way of life and, with the help of agents, reformers, missionaries, and educators, adopt the lifestyle of white society. Most Americans contended that Indians would live more satisfying lives by transforming themselves, to all intents and purposes, into whites. On their reserves Indians would learn the ways of civilized society, seek the whites' education, herd cattle and plow fields, wear the clothes of whites, speak their language, and practice the Christian religion. Federal officials and reformers acknowledged the near impossibility of achieving these cultural and economic objectives unless the United States circumscribed the Indians' fighting power and ended their capacity for armed resistance.

The third objective specified that absolute control of Indian affairs in the West must be assumed by the national government. Federal Indian officials would replace western governors, and regiments of the regular army would replace state and territorial militias. Although such a transfer of authority would make the region safer for white inhabitants, it angered some westerners. The increase in the role of federal troops meant that militiamen would no longer receive a bounty for fighting Indians. Others, while not adverse to a brief stint in the militia, did not want to serve in the regular army. Its personnel ("composed too largely of the scum of the great Cities," one westerner remarked), poor quality of food, low wages, and tough discipline was anathema to many westerners.

In September of 1865, the War Department appointed Lieutenant General William Tecumseh Sherman as commander of the Division of the Missouri. From headquarters at St. Louis he directed military affairs in that portion of the West roughly east of the continental divide. His responsibilities included restoring order and ending the troublesome meddling of western militias and governors, especially with regard to the Indian question, thus establishing the preeminence of federal direction and authority in the region. It was Sherman's conviction that if the West was to be made safe for Americans, the action of no agency but the United States Army would suffice. Western militias and governors, in the general's opinion based on the handling of Indian affairs during the Civil War years, were undisciplined, untrustworthy, and incompetent. "I think I comprehend the motives of some of the Governors," he told Ulysses S. Grant, commanding general of the army, but "I would not entrust [them] with a picket post of fifty men, much less with the discretionary power to call out troops at national cost."

General Sherman emerged from the Civil War a national hero, surpassed in stature only by Abraham Lincoln and Ulysses S.

Top: Tecumseh, Shawnee chieftain, warrior, orator and statesman, leader of the pan-Indian movement in the nineteenth century. Photo no. A93851, The Field Museum of Natural History, Chicago.

Bottom: The notorious "Trail of Tears" along which the Cherokees were forced to march to their new residence in the Indian Territory in 1838. Painting by Robert Lindneux. Woolaroc Museum, Bartlesville, Oklahoma.

Top: The United States government, locked in a struggle with a determined Southern Confederacy during the Civil War (1861–1865), of necessity was forced to give Indian affairs a low priority. Indians, who complained of many uncorrected injustices, now exacerbated by the absense of federal authority, took advantage of the recall of army regulars from frontier posts to adjust matters themselves. This resulted in two eruptions of violence. One involved the Santee Sioux, the other the Southern Cheyennes. Here, the execution of thirty-eight Sioux Indians at Mankato, Minnesota, December 26, 1862. #AV1989.44.365, Hayes Litho. Co., Minnesota Historical Society.

Bottom: The Sand Creek Massacre, 1864, by Robert Lindneux. In the early morning hours of November 29, 1864, John Chivington's Colorado militia attacked the sleeping Southern Cheyenne encampment of Black Kettle without warning. Robert Bent, a local rancher agonized, "There seemed to be indiscriminate slaughter of men, women, and children." #FC-40,342 (R72002 00872) Colorado Historical Society.

The U.S. government often dealt with the Plains Indians with a sword in one hand and an olive branch in the other.

Top: Custer's attack on the Cheyennes at the Washita River, 1868, an engraving that appeared in Harper's Weekly. *Kansas State Historical Society.*

Bottom: Fort Laramie Peace talks, 1868. Generals Harvey and Sherman appear in the middle. National Anthropological Archives, Smithsonian Institution, #3686.

Top: Joseph was one of the most able Indian leaders in the trans-Mississippi West. In 1877 he led several hundred Nez Percé over the northern Rockies in an incredible effort to escape the army and seek haven in Canada. Edward S. Curtis Collection, the Library of Congress.

Bottom: Red Cloud, Oglala Sioux, in old age. The only Plains Indian leader to defeat the United States in war. His role was critical in securing the Fort Laramie Treaty of 1868, which turned the western half of South Dakota into the Great Sioux Reservation. Edward S. Curtis Collection, the Library of Congress.

Top: A Crow (Apsaroke) camp on the Little Bighorn river in Montana, not far north of the location where the Sioux and Cheyenne defeated the U.S. Seventh Cavalry, commanded by George Custer, on June 25, 1876. Edward S. Curtis Collection, the Library of Congress.

Bottom: Two Moon, Cheyenne, was involved in numerous engagements during the Plains Wars, including the "Hayfield Fight" at Fort Smith along the Bozeman Trail in 1867 and "Custer's Last Stand" in 1876. His profile, combined with that of other men, was used to fashion the famous "Indian head–Buffalo" nickel. Denver Public Library, Western History Department–32029.

Top: New Chest, Blackfeet warrior. Once agrarians who lived north of the Yellowstone, by 1700 the Blackfeet, like some thirty other tribes, had adopted a new lifestyle based on the horse and moved to the Great Plains. Edward S. Curtis Collection, the Library of Congress.

Bottom: With the virtual end of the Indian wars in 1877, scenes such as these became increasingly rare. No longer permitted by the United States government to roam the western plains and prairies freely, American Indians were relegated to an immeasurably degraded life on federal reservations.

Gros Ventre warriors with their chief, who is in headdress. Edward S. Curtis Collection, the Library of Congress.

Top: The Carlisle Indian School, founded in 1879, was the prototype for government off-reservation boarding schools. At Carlisle, hundreds or even thousands of miles from the influences of family and tribe, Indian youths could be acculturated in the ways of the dominant American society. In March 1880 these Kiowa boys posed stiffly in their Carlisle uniforms. R.B. Hayes Presidential Center, Fremont, OH.

Bottom: Buffalo hunt (staged): near Rosebud Reservation, South Dakota, 1880. The Fred Hulstrand History in Pictures Collection, NDSU, Fargo, ND.

Top: Geronimo's Apache band on the way to military prison in Florida in 1886. U.S. Signal Corps, National Archives, photo no. 111-SC-82320.

Bottom: Drawing rations at the Agency, ca. 1881–1885. National Archives, photo no. 165-A1-2.

Top: "The Eyes of a Fawn." Mosa, a young Mohave girl. Her people's homeland was in the Great Basin of Utah and Nevada. Edward S. Curtis Collection, the Library of Congress.

Bottom: Two Indian women in front of teepees, likely North Dakota, early 1900s. The Fred Hulstrand History in Pictures Collection, NDSU, Fargo, ND.

Top: Cheyenne mother and child, c. 1900. LC-USZ62-112271. Edward S. Curtis Collection, the Library of Congress.

Bottom: The potter. Hopi woman painting a small pottery vessel, c. 1900. LC-USZ62-117704. Edward S. Curtis Collection, the Library of Congress.

Top: After the Plains Wars, some Indians resisted the United States by means of new spiritual directions that stressed regeneration, like the Ghost Dance. Sioux Chief Big Foot, a proponent of the Ghost Dance, lying dead in the snow, frozen, at the Wounded Knee (South Dakota) battle site, January 1891. National Anthropological Archives, Smithsonian Institution #55,018.

Bottom: Ghost Dance, women chanting with arms raised, ca. 1893. National Anthropological Archives, Smithsonian Institution #55,297.

Crow (Apsaroke) warriors during a winter campaign in a valley of the Pryor mountains in Montana. Edward S. Curtis Collection, the Library of Congress.

Grant. But recognition often is not the equivalent of acclaim, and the public vilified Sherman as well as idolized him. To Southerners in particular, he was much more than just another former Yankee. They called him a butcher, a despoiler, a man who gloried in war—not only gloried in it, but raised it to a higher plane of what some called martial creativity and others called ghastliness. Sherman's tactics in the Civil War presaged modern "Total War," a kind of war that spares no one and no thing. "You cannot glorify war in harsher terms than I will," Sherman warned. "War is cruelty, and you cannot refine it." He believed firmly that war must be waged relentlessly and unsparingly against the enemy's army *and* its civilian population and homeland. Many admired him and took him at his word when he protested that war was hell, and the only thing to do with it was to get it over as soon as possible. It is unlikely, however, that any observer of his pitiless application of scorched earth tactics as his army slashed across the Deep South during his March to the Sea in 1864 and 1865 would have endorsed Sherman's contention. This is the man who would oversee military operations on the Great Plains, and the cold fury he had directed against the Confederacy would now be unleashed on the tribes of the heartland, so General Sherman promised, if they spurned the policy of Concentration.

Clearly the government's objectives contained two divergent concepts of the federal authority's responsibility in resolving the Indian question. One viewed the government's civil arm, especially the Bureau of Indian Affairs of the Department of Interior, as the mediator with and the agent of acculturation for the Indians. The other saw its military arm, particularly the War Department, as the instrument for subduing western tribes and clearing the way for American settlement. Consequently, federal Indian policy from roughly 1865 to 1877 wavered between the two concepts: Acculturation or Subjugation—the "Peace Policy" or the "Force Policy"—as the most pragmatic and effective method of realizing the objectives of the policy of Concentration. A contemporary criticized this dichotomy in *The Nation* magazine: "Comprehensively speaking it may be said that hereto the Indian Bureau has *bribed* [tribes] into . . . peace, while the War Department has desired to *frighten* them into permanent quiet; and between the two they have been nearly exterminated."

This divergence between peace and force sparked heated debates in the executive and legislative branches over the attributes or ill-nature of one role or the other. The War Department and its supporters accused the Interior of softness, mismanagement, corruption, and ineffectualness in dealing with the Indian question. The Interior Department and its backers countered by charging the War Department with callous, even brutal treatment of Indians that exacerbated, rather than solved, the question. Nonetheless, both groups agreed that they pursued the same objectives: to place the Indians completely under federal authority and transform their way of life to make it acceptable to the American public. Each department, however, believed it alone held the solution, which stirred an intense jurisdictional dispute over control of Indian affairs. Known as the Transfer Issue, the problem centered on the War Department's attempt to assume jurisdiction over the Bureau of Indian Affairs of the Interior Department. Disagreement over control had been unrelenting since 1849, when the bureau was taken from the War Department and given to the newly created Department of the Interior—"for political reasons and to promote party interests," asserted General Nelson A. Miles, reflecting the overwhelming opinion of the military for the transfer.

Senator James R. Doolittle of Wisconsin, chairman of the Senate Committee on Indian Affairs, trying to resolve the heated question, inquired in a circular sent to military and civilian Indian affairs authorities in May 1865: "Under what department of the government, the War Department or the Interior, should the Bureau of Indian Affairs be placed, to secure the best and most economical administration of it?" Every army officer who replied favored transferring the Indian Office to the War Department. Not surprisingly, most of the civilians opposed transfer. William P. Dole, first Lincoln's, then briefly Andrew Johnson's, commissioner of Indian Affairs, adamantly fought transfer and strenuously advocated the treaty process as the only method of serving the interests of "humanity, economy, and efficiency." To him, no better system existed "for the management of the Indians" than the

Interior's Peace Policy, because the War Department's Force Policy would lead tribes to regard Americans as "merciless despots and tyrants, who have deprived them of their homes and liberties." This conclusion is "so apparent," Dole stressed, "that I can hardly realize that the former is seriously advocated." Such statements drew harsh criticism from transfer advocates such as General John Pope, who in a letter to General Ulysses S. Grant called the treaty process worthless. "It is a common saying with the Sioux," he protested, "that, whenever they are poor and need powder and lead, they have only to go down to the Overland route and murder a few white men, and they will have a treaty to supply their wants." Others in government suggested that to have the Concentration policy solve the Indian question, tribes "needed to feel the strong arm of the government." Senator Samuel Pomeroy of Kansas, who in a resolution introduced in 1865, suggested to colleagues:

The mild, conciliatory, and even magnanimous conduct of our government towards these savages not being understood or appreciated by them, but only construed to be weakness and cowardice, should now be followed by the most vigorous and decisive measures until those hostile tribes are effectually punished for their crimes, and whipped into a wholesome restraint and submission to the authority of the United States.

The transfer issue between the Interior and War Departments did not abate over the next decade. The troubled relations between the United States and some western Indians in those years only heightened the dispute.

Those Who Resisted Concentration

The goal of the Concentration policy was to place all western Indians on federal reservations without recourse to military coercion. Most tribes, all too aware that they could no longer successfully resist the demands of the United States government, accepted their fate. The Ponka, Osage, Snake, Ute, Navaho, Kansa, Shoshoni, Bannock, Arikara, Gros Ventre, Quapaw, and Mandan, among others, signed Concentration treaties and settled on their assigned lands. Except for efforts to avoid being converted into farmers and resistance to government programs to transform their culture, they generally caused Washington few problems. The nomadic buffalo-hunting societies of the plains and certain other western tribes, however, proved to be a markedly different case for one principal reason: still controlling vast domains in 1865, they possessed the strength of their convictions in combination with superb martial skills to defend their lands against the United States. Their resistance to the Concentration policy and Washington's absolute determination to impose it on them in order to end the Indian question resulted in over a decade of deadly confrontation called "the Plains Wars."

The Plains Indians strove to continue their accustomed way of life, the buffalo and horse culture, which was absolutely dependent on vast spaces, abundant game, and freedom of movement. They rejected the policy of Concentration because it required abandoning that way of life. Aside from motives such as revenge or retaliation, they fought to prevent American occupation of their lands and to defend their cultural lifestyle. Undoubtedly by this point in time many material goods of white society appealed to them as an enhancement of this lifestyle: cotton clothing, woolen blankets, buttons, thread and needles, metal pots and kettles, metal knives, rifles, revolvers, gunpowder, and a host of other items. But the culture of American society as a whole did not appeal to them. Federal officials recognized the plains tribes' attraction to and increasing dependence on the goods of white society, and they used this in the treaty process as an inducement to accept Concentration. For example, at the Medicine Lodge proceedings in the fall of 1867, a council to end recent belligerencies and concentrate the tribes of the southern plains in the Indian Territory, negotiators promised clothing, blankets, weapons, ammunition, and an assortment of trinkets. In return, the Americans required these tribes to restructure their lives by accepting concentration on a federal reserve, allotment of the land in severalty, abandonment of the buffalo and horse culture, and mandatory schooling for children.

The American public regarded those tribes that resisted as a dangerous impediment to expansion, enterprise, and settlement. End the Indian question, they demanded of Washington. The overwhelming majority of Americans refused to abide Indian intransigence, as they saw it, to the consummation of national purposes. Therein was the foremost source of the collision: the direct conflict of purposes, culturally and economically. Nor did either side—Indian or white—ever show itself willing or capable of understanding what the other wanted or how the other viewed the predicament. Many people suffered and died because of this virtually unbridgeable gulf of misunderstanding.

Inevitably, with the Peace Policy holding so little promise of success with the Plains Indians, the United States pursued the Concentration policy by force of arms. When these efforts were successful—and that too was inevitable—the government placed these tribes on reservations. No matter how hard the Indians resisted, their struggle was doomed to failure. Far too many factors worked against them. The flood of homesteaders to stake out farms, the growing interest of American and European investment capital in developing the West, the construction of a railroad system throughout the region moving not only people but supplies into the vast interior sustaining white population growth and providing the basis for a durable economy, the precipitous decline of the Indians' subsistence base—all combined to hasten the final outcome. Every advancement of settlement and business enterprise in the West came at the expense of resources, especially the buffalo, crucial to the continuance of the Plains Indians' way of life. Recognizing the role of the tribes' nomadic life in their resistance and the role of the buffalo in their nomadism, General William T. Sherman jested with earnestness to General Philip H. Sheridan that "it would be wise to invite all the sportsmen of England and America . . . for a Grand Buffalo hunt, and make one grand sweep of them all." In fact during the early 1870s, the federal government acquiesced in a measure not dissimilar to Sherman's idea. Officials permitted hunters to kill the remaining buffalo herds on the southern plains.

Yet, especially considering the disproportionate advantages apparently held by the United States, why did it take the United States Army over a decade to complete Concentration and accomplish the military subjugation of resisting Indians? The population of the United States in 1870 was almost 40 million. Americans in the tens of thousands plied the western mining frontier. Four hundred thousand homesteaders created a permanent farming population on the prairies, while a much larger number tried, then abandoned, this enterprise. By contrast, all Indians residing from the Great Plains westward to the Pacific numbered under 239,000 in 1872. Only a portion of the western Indian population offered armed resistance of any significant measure during the Plains Wars. Moreover, in the area of technology there was little contest. The United States Army had available rapid transportation and communication—railroads and the telegraph—as well as a modern industrial plant capable of mass producing vast quantities of items, particularly those needed to prosecute war. The Plains Indians, on the other hand, lacked the technology to make a wheel, much less the weapons of modern warfare. Additionally, during the Civil War the United States had developed perhaps the finest conventional military in the world. While the military did go into steep decline after that conflict, the War Department could still draw upon the experience and expertise of battle-tested commanders to direct operations against the Indians.

In light of these factors, and others, the anticipation of a quick victory by the army during the Plains Wars would seem reasonable. Nothing could be further from what transpired. Securing conclusive victory proved frustratingly difficult for many years. As Thomas W. Dunlay discussed in his perceptive essay "Fire and Sword: Ambiguity and the Plains Wars" (in *The American Indian Experience*), part of the paradox lies in the fact that those factors that seemed to favor quick victory for the United States were negated by others that aided the Indians and frustrated the U.S. Army.

The physical conditions of the western prairies and plains were one example. Summers on the Great Plains are extremely hot and exceedingly dry, with water often in short supply. Unless Indian scouts accompanied the troopers, directing them to water and other necessary resources, these conditions often took their toll on men and animals. The region's immensity made troop movements time-consuming and arduous, and for years the size of the war's theater decreased the impact and usefulness of railroads for the army. While the railroad could bring soldiers, horses, and supplies into the general vicinity of planned engagements, movement from that point was by foot or on horseback across hundreds of miles where terrain and climate were taxing, and often perilous, to the unaccustomed. The sheer size of the region made it difficult for the army to locate enemy positions, especially when the Plains Indians' nomadic lifestyle dictated nearly continuous movement, leaving no evidence of permanent villages. When soldiers finally located and engaged the Indians, warriors usually fought only a holding action against the army while the main tribal body escaped and dispersed. In their escapes, it often seemed to soldiers that the vastness of the plains simply swallowed them.

To the tribes of the region, however, this uncompromising land presented no such obstacle. The Plains Indians knew it intimately and used it fully to their advantage. They knew how to subsist on its meager resources; knew where to locate water in the dry season; knew the choice places to hide; knew the best locations for a successful attack or defense. Their nomadic life accustomed them to traverse the region's vast reaches expertly, changing camp sites readily and easily transporting their material possessions, all of which were designed for rapid, continuous maneuver.

The differences in military training and skills between Indians and soldiers of the U.S. Army played an important role, too. Indian males trained from youth to be warriors. Due to extensive instruction over many years, they were usually superior in horsemanship, endurance, tracking, scouting, and most martial skills when compared to their army counterparts. Soldiers, on the other hand, first encountered military life and training in early adulthood and simply did not have the time needed to master equally the skills needed to fight in the plains environment.

The Plains Indians esteemed courage and placed a high value on martial achievements and honors, and, especially for the latter reason, warfare was endemic to their culture. But they typically refused to involve themselves in massed engagements because of the inevitability of high casualties. When they did fight in this manner—such as Little Crow's assault on Fort Ridgley during the Santee Sioux uprising of 1862, or the Hayfield and Wagon-Box

Fights in 1867 during the Powder River War when Sioux and Cheyennes battled army regulars—their deficiency in tactical knowledge and ability often proved ruinous. Plains warriors preferred to engage enemies, Indian or white, in a "hit and run" style, or by using ambush or guerrilla tactics. Because of the relatively small size of the adult male population, they also selected those tactics that best preserved the lives of combatants on their side. The United States Army trained its personnel to obey a superior's orders and advance against an enemy, even if this carried the soldier directly into the line of fire and almost certain death. Such conduct puzzled the Indian fighter. An Indian war leader, employing a similar strategy, probably would have lost the confidence of his followers. Death in battle could bring glory, but managing to emerge from battle alive in order to care for your family and fight another day was usually judged the wiser course. Unless the chance of success was overwhelmingly in their favor, or if a village with women and children was threatened, plains warriors usually avoided massed, frontal engagements.

As Dunlay pointed out, "The real handicaps of the army were those inherent in its organization and doctrine. . . . An army organized on conventional, European lines, [intending] to fight similar enemies, was charged with police duties and with combating foes with a talent for guerrilla warfare in country giving them ample room to take full advantage of their mobility." Only when the army combined conventional tactics with more innovative ones that took advantage of vulnerable aspects of the Plains Indians' way of life—such as General Philip Sheridan's winter campaign with which he defeated the southern plains tribes in 1868–1869 and again in 1874–1875 during the Red River War, and then crushed the Sioux in 1876–1877 following Custer's Little Bighorn debacle—did the military arm of the government finalize Concentration, effectively enforce the policy, and successfully conclude the Plains Wars.

Olive Branch and Sword

The United States government, within a half year of the end of the Civil War, resumed implementation of the Concentration policy to end the Indian question. In October 1865, almost a year after the Sand Creek massacre, federal commissioners finalized an agreement with the Southern Cheyennes and Arapahoes, Kiowas, Comanches, and Kiowa-Comanches at the Little Arkansas. Following this council, the officials moved on to the northern plains planning to negotiate with the tribes in the upper reaches of the Missouri, Yellowstone, and Platte rivers. Concentrating these tribes would provide safe overland travel for those Americans involved in the region's burgeoning gold rush and secure a land corridor on the upper plains for future railroad construction. By the spring of 1866 they arranged accords with the Assiniboines and Crows, as well as with the Missouri River Sioux and a number of Northern Cheyenne and Arapahoe bands. General John Pope, an outspoken critic of the treaty system, expressed his opinion openly that these agreements would not bring lasting peace to the region. "I do not consider the treaties lately made with the Sioux, Cheyennes, and Arapahoes . . . worth the paper they are written on," he wrote General Sherman. "I have myself no doubt that hostilities will again break out on the Platte, the Smokey Hill, and the Arkansas rivers before the beginning of winter." Pope's assessment proved to be correct. The objective of post–Civil War Indian policy was to concentrate all western Indians. The circumstances surrounding the next council on the northern plains and the succession of events that followed assured the accuracy of the general's prediction and highlights the dichotomy within the government over the most pragmatic and effective means of achieving that objective and ending the Indian question: "Peace" or "Force."

In June 1866, a second commission traveled to Fort Laramie, situated along the Oregon Trail in southeastern Wyoming Territory. There they planned to meet and finalize crucial treaties with Sioux leaders of the Powder River country. The new accord would alter the terms of the Sioux's initial Concentration treaty, the Fort Laramie Treaty of 1851 (see Chapter Two). The Powder River country, bounded on the east by the Black Hills and the Bighorn Mountains to the west, was a hilly, bountiful land teeming with fish, game, and rich grazing areas. During the early decades of the nineteenth century the Sioux had wrested the Black Hills region from the Kiowas and the Powder River area from the Crows after nearly twenty years of warfare. Mainly Oglalas, Miniconjous, and Sans Arcs—tribal divisions of the Teton Sioux—lived and hunted there now. The commissioners knew that negotiations would be difficult, especially with the prickly Oglala Red Cloud, whose exploits and leadership in numerous campaigns against the Crows, Pawnees, and Shoshonis had earned him great respect and political influence among his people. Still, the commissioners confidently expected an agreement could be secured if they handled the meeting with the Sioux carefully. Their efforts would be severely impeded, however, by simultaneous developments in the region involving the military commander of the Great Plains, William Tecumseh Sherman.

The War Department charged General Sherman with safeguarding the Great Plains for Americans, as well as enforcing the reduction of tribal landholdings and moving the Plains Indians even farther north and south away from white travelers, homesteaders, settlements, and businesses. Insufficient troop strength forced Sherman to execute his responsibilities in a purely defensive manner. "I regret to say that . . . we do not now possess a force adequate to the wants of this extensive region of country," Sherman notified General D. B. Sackett, whom the War Department dispatched to assess western routes, posts, and settlements, "but you may assure the people . . . that their safety and the protection of their interests will command our attention as soon as Congress increases the regular army." High on General Sherman's list of priorities was protection of the lines of communication on the Great Plains: telegraph lines, railroads and their construction crews, and, above all, the overland trails. One of the newest and hence least secure trails was the Bozeman or Powder River Trail on the northern plains. Sherman, in the spring of 1866, therefore turned to building a chain of forts to protect the trail and the Americans who traveled over it.

The Bozeman Trail, originating seventy-five miles to the west of Fort Laramie, veered off the Oregon Trail and ran northwestwardly through the mining country of northern Wyoming and southern Montana, eventually ending at Virginia City, Montana. Bisecting the Powder River country, the Bozeman Trail proved a major source of irritation to the Sioux: partly because it violated the Fort Laramie Treaty of 1851, principally because it ran directly through some of their best buffalo-hunting lands. In the early 1860s the Sioux had made several half-hearted attempts to prevent the trail from going through their western lands. Later they made some equally half-hearted attacks on the early travelers—generally miners and hunters, not immigrants—who dared to use the risky route. In the middle of that decade, following the Sand Creek massacre, a number of Southern Cheyennes and Arapahoes arrived in the Powder River country to take refuge among the Sioux. Even more recently, the region had been the site of military action. A large army contingent under General Patrick Connor had been turned back in the spring of 1865 by the Sioux, with the aid of the Cheyennes and Arapahoes. Connor's defeat increased General Sherman's determination to complete construction of forts along the Bozeman Trail to secure the area.

In June 1866, the Powder River Sioux, many of whom had defeated Connor's force, received a request to come to Fort Laramie to meet with federal commissioners. Although he was not a chief, the esteemed war leader Red Cloud served as the principal spokesman. Always distrustful of whites, he was deeply suspicious of the negotiators and adamant against relinquishing any further territorial rights of the Sioux to the United States. The Americans reassured him that they respected both him and his convictions. They wished only to negotiate a treaty guaranteeing the Sioux their lands while allowing whites the right of passage through them, including use of the Bozeman. In payment the Sioux would receive presents and $70,000 a year in annuity issues. Red Cloud, believing that the Americans dealt with him honestly, did not dismiss their requests but decided to take council with other tribal leaders.

While the Sioux deliberated and the Americans waited, a substantial contingent of civilian workers and regular infantry and cavalry under the command of Colonel Henry B. Carrington arrived at Fort Laramie. Carrington traveled under orders to march to the Powder River country and erect three forts along the Bozeman Trail, with or without the permission of the Sioux. This action outraged the assembled Indians. They bitterly denounced the treachery and betrayal of the Americans. "The Great Fathers [the commissioners] sends us presents and wants [sic] us to sell him the road," Red Cloud decried, "but White Chief [Carrington] goes with soldiers to steal the road before Indians say Yes or No." The Powder River party stormed out of the fort, refusing to offer any guarantees of safety to either travelers or construction crews on the Bozeman Trail.

The troops and work crews soon left Fort Laramie, journeyed westward along the Oregon Trail, and then moved up the Boze- man Trail into the Powder River country. There they began their assignment of building three forts to guard the 545-mile trail from Bridger's Ferry, on the North Platte, to Virginia City, Montana. During July and August they enlarged Camp Connor, renaming it Fort Reno, and began erecting Fort Phil Kearny and Fort C. F. Smith. Throughout that summer Sioux warriors, resolved to stop construction of the forts, harassed the soldiers, suppliers, and builders. The Sioux realized that once the Bozeman Trail became a popular route for Americans, they would settle near it. The re- cent occurrences in Colorado buttressed their resolve. The Chey- ennes and Arapahoes living with them told of their people's expe- riences earlier in the decade: the gold rush and subsequent development of the Smokey Hill Trail through lands that the United States had guaranteed them in the 1850s; their displace- ment by Coloradans; the newest Concentration treaty at Fort Wise that ratified these acts; and the clashes with the Colorado militia. The Powder River Sioux agreed that they must ensure that the Bozeman Trail did not produce a similar outcome for them. Before the end of August they had killed thirty-three whites involved in work on the forts.

Soldiers and civilians worked desperately through the fall to complete construction of the forts before the bitter mountain win- ter set in. The Sioux worked with the same intensity to impede the work. In a skirmish on December 6, 1866, the Sioux discovered an especially effective tactic. If warriors fired upon soldiers as they went to and from the forts, the soldiers would give chase and could be led into ambush. Red Cloud decided that since the tactic had worked on a small scale, a large ambush might wipe out the garrison at each of the forts. He targeted the initial effort at the biggest fort along the trail, Fort Phil Kearny. High-Back-Bone, a Miniconjou, crafted the plan. Warriors would attack the wagons as the whites returned to Fort Kearny from cutting wood a half-dozen miles away. The assault on the wagons promised to bring reinforcements from the fort. Then, as the soldiers rode toward the besieged wagons, decoys would lure them away from the main fight and into deadly ambush.

The Sioux, accompanied by Cheyennes and Arapahoes, moved southward from their camps on the Tongue River ten miles north of the fort, and on December 19 they made the first attempt to execute the large-scale ambush. Their attack, however, failed to bring reinforcements from Fort Kearny. Snow postponed the ambush the following day. Then, one day later, the army's agenda for the Powder River Indians played into the hands of Red Cloud purely by accident. A month earlier Colonel Carrington had received orders from General Philip St. George Cooke, his departmental commander, to strike at the "hostiles." Although promising "to make the winter one of active operations," Carrington until now had tarried.

At about 10:00 in the morning on December 21, 1866, warriors led by the Oglala Crazy Horse, a young protégé of High-Back-Bone and soon to be the heir to Red Cloud's military leadership in the region, attacked the wagons of the fort's wood train and its military escort as it moved away from Fort Kearny. Whether Red Cloud participated in the engagement is undetermined. Between 1,500 and 2,000 warriors concealed themselves in nearby ravines. As quickly as he could, Colonel Carrington, seizing the opportunity to execute General Cooke's directive, ordered out a column of eighty men led by Captain William Fetterman. They anticipated inflicting heavy casualties on the Sioux. But on that cold December morning, the troopers rode behind Fetterman to their deaths. The Sioux could not have hoped for a better man for their designs. Recklessly disobeying Carrington's orders to relieve the train and battle the attackers, but not pursue them, Fetterman gave chase to the decoys and led his men straight into an immense ambush. After less than an hour of intense fighting, William

Fetterman and all of his command were dead. Post physician C. M. Hines, after seeing the scalped and mutilated bodies of the soldiers brought back to Fort Kearny, described them with horror as looking "like . . . hogs brought to market." Carrington's report graphically described how his troops' bodies had their eyes, noses, ears, arms, legs, fingers, genitals, entrails, teeth, brains, skulls, and chins cleaved; "eyes, ears, mouth, and arms penetrated with spearheads, sticks and arrows; ribs slashed to separation with knives; [and] muscles of calves, thighs, stomach, breast, back, arms, and cheek taken out."

The remaining soldiers and civilians inside Fort Kearny readied themselves for the impending Indian attack, but Red Cloud did not follow up the Fetterman ambush for the remainder of the winter. Since the men inside the fort could not have known this would happen, the level of anxiety ran extremely high throughout these months. That was exactly Red Cloud's objective—psychological warfare. No further Sioux assaults, either at Fort Kearny or on the other two Bozeman Trail forts, came until the following spring.

Word of the Sioux's victory in the Powder River country reached the East early in 1867, prompting mixed reactions from whites. Some Americans, surprisingly sympathetic to the Sioux, openly expressed indignation at the government's Concentration policy, which had brought about the catastrophe. They called for an immediate investigation into the government's conduct toward the Indians. The Indian Bureau agreed, placing blame for the recent difficulties in the army's lap. Commissioner Lewis V. Bogy's initial, albeit imaginative, explanation was that the Sioux were on a "friendly visit" to Fort Kearny when assaulted by Fetterman's troops. Bogy concluded that given this explanation, it was now the duty of the Interior Department, "with a view of putting the blame where it properly belongs, to have an investigation."

The War Department disagreed emphatically with both the Indian Bureau's charges and the proposed solution. General Cooke, Carrington's superior, whom General Grant relieved of his duties on January 9, 1867, laid the full blame on the Interior Department for failing to check the sale of weapons to the Sioux. Secretary of War Edwin Stanton minced no words in strenuously demanding immediate military retaliation. General Sherman, fully supporting Stanton's recommendation, thundered: "We must act with vindictive earnestness against the Sioux, even to their extermination, men, women, and children. Nothing else will reach the root of this case." Unhesitatingly most Americans, shocked and angered by Fetterman's defeat, concurred with Stanton and Sherman.

President Andrew Johnson, at the urging of Interior Secretary Orville H. Browning and most other members of the cabinet, reined in Stanton and Sherman. Still hoping to find some peaceful means for resolving problems with the Plains Indians, the president, in February 1867, appointed a fact-finding commission chaired by General Alfred Sully. Johnson wanted to know what method short of war would convince these tribes to accept Concentration. He charged the Sully commission with investigating the Fetterman incident and with assessing the mood of Indians on the northern plains, especially ascertaining whether they would still negotiate with the United States.

Hostilities in the Powder River country, and especially Fetterman's defeat, prompted Force Policy proponents in Congress to increase efforts to transfer Indian Affairs from the Interior Department to the War Department. Only the military could deal with the Indians effectively and realize the Concentration policy, they contended. Several senators, including Nevada's W. M. Stewart and Ohio's John Sherman, the general's brother, introduced transfer bills, arguing that the system of divided jurisdiction in administering Indian affairs caused the recent troubles. Wisconsin's Senator James R. Doolittle's Joint Special Committee on the Condition of the Indian Tribes countered these charges in its report of January 26, 1867. Chronicling the worsening state of western Indians' lives and stressing "the aggression of lawless whites" as the cause of recent interracial conflict, the report rebutted the transfer advocates:

The inconveniences arising from the occasional conflicts and jealousies between officers appointed under the Interior and War Departments are not without some benefits also; neither are slow to point to the mistakes and abuses of the other. It is therefore proper that they should be independent of each other, receive the appointments from and report to different heads of departments. Weighing this matter and all the arguments for and against the proposed change, your committee are unanimously of the opinion that the Indian Bureau should remain where it is.

After heated debate the transfer measure carried in the House but failed to pass in the Senate, due to the Doolittle Report. General Sherman, in correspondence with his brother Senator Sherman, expressed disappointment and reaffirmed his answer for ending the Indian question: Soldiers "must get among them, and must kill enough of them to inspire fear, and then conduct the remainder to places where Indian agents can and will reside among them, and be held responsible for their conduct."

Helping block the transfer of the Indian Bureau to the War Department was the immediate effect of the Doolittle Report. Its greater result was to prick the conscience of various groups of Americans, supportive of the Indians or at least concerned with their fate, agitating them to pressure the federal government into reevaluating its Indian policy. A good recounting of their attitudes and activities is Francis Paul Prucha's *American Indian Policy in Crisis: Christian Reformers and the Indian, 1865–1900.* As Americans of their time and place, these eastern humanitarians believed deeply in progress, and they especially believed in it for the Indian. They recognized that the nation was in a dynamic, rather than a static situation, and that Americans felt compelled to expand rapidly and continually. They conceded that the compulsion to engulf more and more land of the western Indians, with little regard to the consequences for these people, was a force that drove the United States government and the American people in this era as remorselessly as any other agent of modernization. These men and women who throughout the remaining decades of this century generously responded to the plight of the Indians, and who made strong appeal against specific iniquities, neither denigrated the steady march forward of progress nor denied an unshakable conviction in the necessity for the Indians to accept and adopt their vision of progress. Most individuals deeply concerned with the ultimate fate of the Indians could not acknowledge sufficient merit in the values, culture, and lifestyle of this minority not to press for acculturation as the best method of solving the Indian question.

That most Indians disagreed with their well-intentioned paternalism failed to sway them.

Meanwhile, the military, blocked by President Johnson from retaliatory measures against the Sioux, sought to redress the humiliation that Captain Fetterman brought upon them. By spring they had selected the target. These events rekindled warfare on the central and southern plains, strained relations between the War and Interior departments, and further fueled the disagreement between Force Policy and Peace Policy advocates.

By 1865 the Southern Cheyennes had experienced the depth of tragedy. Their lands had been forfeited to the United States. The bitter year-old memory of Sand Creek still burned deeply. It was hard for them to imagine that more could fall on them. After the fighting that followed the Sand Creek massacre, the Southern Cheyennes broke into two principal groups. The smaller band migrated to the Sioux's Powder River country, while the larger one, led by peace chiefs such as Black Kettle, moved southward in accordance with the terms of the Little Arkansas Treaty until they crossed the Arkansas River into southern Kansas, relocating near Fort Larned on the Santa Fe Trail. Here Colonel Edward W. Wynkoop, a welcome friend, joined them. "Tall Chief," as they called Wynkoop, had attempted to prevent the tragic events of the previous year in Colorado, especially by his heroic but unsuccessful effort to prevent Chivington's attack at Sand Creek. No longer in the army, Wynkoop now served as the Indian Affairs Office's civilian agent to the Southern Cheyennes and Arapahoes. He felt deeply the burden of the Sand Creek tragedy on his own conscience, although he was not to blame, and he vowed to help the remnants of these tribes to find peace. By 1866 Wynkoop was making progress in winning back their trust.

At the same time, more than a thousand Southern Cheyennes who had sought refuge in the Powder River area returned to Kansas. It was then that they learned of the Little Arkansas Treaty and of how Black Kettle and other tribal leaders had signed away their land in Colorado and their hunting grounds in western Kansas. Some bowed, albeit ungraciously, to the reality of the situation.

Others, embittered by the deed, rejected the peace chiefs and the treaty they had signed. They made a fateful decision to remain along the Republican and Smokey Hill rivers on their former Kansas hunting ranges, where they harassed settlers and commerce in the area.

Their decision was less an act of overt aggression than of laying claim to lands that they still considered rightfully theirs. It also underscored crucial differences in political organization between the plains tribes and the government of the United States. None of these tribes had the type of unitary state capable of coercing the obedience of its members. Plains Indians gave their overriding loyalty to the family first, followed by the war society, band, tribal division, and then, finally, the tribe itself. They gave little, if any, consideration to how a given action or strategy—such as remaining in Kansas—affected the interest of the tribe as a whole.

Another important difference was that tribal leaders served as the agents of their people and the executors of their wishes, not their unilateral rulers. Chiefs could not compel, nor would they have tried to compel, adherence by all tribal members to the terms of a treaty. Ultimately, only individuals could determine whether to bind themselves by the actions of their chiefs. Neither Black Kettle nor the other chiefs who signed the Little Arkansas Treaty could compel adherence from the tribe, unless, of course, all tribal members concurred with their actions. And in this instance they did not. Much of what whites considered inconsistent, even treacherous, conduct in Indians often could be explained by these differences. Thus military authorities viewed with the deepest suspicion the reports detailing how the tough warrior Roman Nose led his followers back to their hunting grounds in western Kansas in violation of the Little Arkansas Treaty.

Responding to complaints from settlers and military officers about the presence of armed Indians in the path of Kansas Pacific construction crews, General Sherman made his move in the late winter of 1867. He ordered General Winfield Scott Hancock to lead a large army expedition into Kansas to intimidate the Southern Cheyennes with a show of force. Hancock was not to attack the Indians, but merely march his command around their encampments as a demonstration of American martial superiority in the hope of convincing them to move below the Arkansas River. Yet Hancock made clear that if the Indians provided any cause, he would attack without mercy. He stated to his officer corps in his general field order: "We go prepared for war and will make it if a proper occasion presents. . . . No insolence will be tolerated."

Agent Wynkoop received advance notification of the operation. It alarmed him sufficiently to ride out to meet with Roman Nose and other recalcitrants. He tried to persuade them not to continue their provocative and potentially disastrous course. Wynkoop explained that Sherman, after hearing of Roman Nose's "occupation," was about to order the army out to bully them. Even more frightening to Wynkoop was the clear possibility that General Sherman might launch an indiscriminate attack on the peaceful Cheyennes, too. Wynkoop, well aware of what such an attack would mean, desperately hoped to prevent it. But Roman Nose firmly rejected all pleas to evacuate western Kansas. He was quite willing, he informed Wynkoop, to fight the whites if it came to that.

General Hancock left Fort Leavenworth and headed into central Kansas, picking up along the way the newly formed United States Seventh Cavalry led by Lieutenant Colonel George Armstrong Custer. The addition of the Seventh swelled Hancock's ranks to over 1,400 men. Their initial destination was a substantial Cheyenne and Sioux camp on Pawnee Fork, thirty-five miles upstream from Fort Larned. Wynkoop warned Hancock of the highly explosive situation he would run into if he persisted in marching on this camp. He reminded the general of Sand Creek, and of how warriors might be sent out to block him before the troops could come close enough to the camp to state their business. The likely result, as Wynkoop knew, would be another massacre. Hancock, dismissing the warnings, ordered his troops forward. The Indians, not waiting to see what the army wanted, abandoned camp, leaving behind most of their possessions, and put distance between themselves and the federal troops. The women and children left first while warriors covered their retreat. The following day the warriors also withdrew. The peace element eventually relocated further to the south below the Arkansas in the panhandle region of Indian Territory (present-day Oklahoma). The confrontational faction, led by Roman Nose, chose to strike back immediately. They remained north of the river and lashed out at whites, assaulting railroad work crews, stagecoach stations, settlers, and travelers on the overland routes. Soon they had halted all traffic in western Kansas.

Hancock, after arriving at the abandoned camp, hesitated to burn it. Three days later he received word of the attacks by those who remained in Kansas. Hancock concluded that it "was a nest of conspirators" and so, over Wynkoop's strong protests, ordered the camp, containing 111 Cheyenne lodges and 140 Sioux lodges and their contents, burned. Then he sent Custer to pursue the Indians, who led him on a frustrating and largely unsuccessful chase through western Kansas that summer.

Edward Wynkoop assessed General Hancock's actions a "disaster," and two days after the village burning bitterly wrote Indian Commissioner Nathaniel G. Taylor that "I know of no overt act that the Cheyennes had committed to cause them to be thus punished." General Sherman reacted initially to the news of Indian attacks in his accustomed style by calling for the destruction of all natives who might be found between the Arkansas and Platte rivers. Once he had calmed down, he asked civil authorities to define hostile from peaceful Indians so that the army might direct its efforts only at the guilty party, thus avoiding an assault on innocents. "We, the military," Sherman wrote Secretary of Interior Browning, "do not wish this result, because it would be a national disgrace." Officials in Washington realized they could little afford the bad publicity of another Sand Creek, especially as the national mood was one of general sympathy for the Indians because of the recent report by the Sully commission. General Sully's probe chronicled a string of flagrant violations of treaty guarantees by whites, accompanied by an unwillingness of the federal government to meet its treaty obligations to the Indians. The Sully commission called for direct action by the government to establish peace on equitable terms with the Plains Indians, particularly with Red Cloud and his Sioux as well as with the Cheyennes and other warring southern tribes. Secretary Browning conveyed the proposal to Congress for its approval. After intense debate, both houses consented on July 20, 1867.

Quickly, President Johnson ordered a federal peace commission to meet with the Indians. He charged them with removing the causes for further hostility, and, as far as possible, concentrating the western Indians on one of three reservations: the Plains tribes on either a large northern reserve west of the Missouri and north of Nebraska or a large southern reserve west of the Arkansas and south of Kansas; and those living west of the Rockies on one in the Southwest. General Sherman had offered the idea the previous year in his annual report. Indian Commissioner Nathaniel G. Taylor, Methodist minister, attorney, and close friend of the president, headed the United States Indian Peace Commission. "In my judgment," stated Taylor, assessing his mission, "the Indians can only be saved from extinction by consolidating them as rapidly as it can be peacefully done on larger reservations, from which all whites except Government employees shall be excluded." Taylor also boasted that his commission could achieve peace in 100 days at the cost of $250,000; far less than the $5 million expended on Hancock's recent efforts in Kansas. Civilian officials and high-ranking army officers rounded out the commission's membership: Kansas Senator Edmund G. Ross; Samuel F. Tappan, reformer and former abolitionist, and Generals William S. Harney, Alfred H. Terry, and William T. Sherman. Sherman, with his typical bluntness, commented about Commissioner Taylor's goals of securing peace, clearing the central plains of free-roaming Indians, and concentrating the tribes. "Get them out as soon as possible," the general remarked caustically, "and it makes little difference whether they be coaxed out by Indian commissioners or killed."

The Myth of Peace

Concurrently with events in Kansas and in Washington, Red Cloud resumed his assaults against the forts along the Bozeman Trail. That summer the Sioux and their Northern Cheyenne and Arapahoe allies terrorized whites along the Upper Missouri; assaulted their hereditary enemies, the Mandans, Gros Ventres, and Arikaras; and paralyzed travel in the Powder River country. In late July 1867, Red Cloud ordered two decisive actions. Unable to decide which fort to target first, the Indians divided their ranks and moved to strike two separate objectives. On August 1, a large force consisting mainly of Cheyennes, led by Two Moon, assaulted the Americans at Fort Smith. The battle, called the "Hayfield Fight," was fought to a stalemate, with each side sustaining heavy losses. Two days later on August 3, one thousand warriors under Red Cloud, chiefly Sioux, attacked Fort Kearny. However, the Sioux's deficiency in improvising tactics during the battle, coupled with the effectiveness of the soldiers' new breech-loading Springfield rifles in repelling the attackers, resulted in another indecisive battle, known as the "Wagon-Box Fight." Both sides sustained heavy losses, but casualties among Red Cloud's warriors were particularly high. He would later say that on that day he lost the flower of his young men. The army accepted its tenuous victory and applauded its success in holding onto the Bozeman Trail forts.

A month later, in September 1867, the United States Indian Peace Commission arrived on the Great Plains and initiated talks with tribes. Unfortunately, these councils failed to resolve many of the Indians' complaints about whites. A delegation of Brule and Oglala Sioux, along with some Cheyennes, met with the commissioners in mid-September at North Platte, Nebraska, to receive powder and lead and to complain about Americans in their Nebraska lands. They were particularly incensed by the white hunters who were working for railroad crews and destroying their buffalo supply by mass-kill methods. The commissioners only advised that the Sioux should as quickly as possible select a suitable area within their present territory as the site for a future reservation, before white settlers took it all. There, with the assistance of government agents and white missionaries and educators, the Sioux could convert to farming and learn the culture of the whites. "The President desires to see you prosperous and happy and has sent us here to devise means to secure this end," one commission member told the frustrated Indians. "We have exercised our best judgment and adopted the best plan to improve your condition and save your people. Accept it and be happy." This was hardly the solution the Sioux had expected from a federal commission charged with achieving an equitable peace settlement.

The commission hoped to talk next with Red Cloud, but scouts reported his refusal to come in for a conference. Promising to meet again with the Sioux in November, the commissioners headed for Kansas to meet with the tribes of the southern plains. The Southern Cheyennes were wary and required much coaxing before agreeing to meet in a peace council. In a further attempt to bring lasting peace to the southern Great Plains, the commissioners invited the Kiowas, Comanches, Southern Arapahoes, and Plains Apaches, as well. The council convened in October of 1867 at Medicine Lodge Creek, a popular Sun Dance* ground, seventy miles south of Fort Larned in southwestern Kansas and just north of the Indian Territory. Five thousand Indians arrived to observe the momentous discussions between their chiefs and the United States Indian Peace Commission.

The commissioners offered a plan of peace establishing two reserves in the western half of the Indian Territory. They would be fashioned from lands once belonging to the Five Civilized Tribes: the Cherokees, Chickasaws, Choctaws, Creeks, and Seminoles. Virtually charged with treason by the United States for their alliances with the Confederacy during the Civil War, these Indian republics—"Great Father's erring children"—were required to sign Reconstruction treaties in 1866, which, among other stipulations, drastically reduced the landholdings of each tribe. The commission proposed assigning the Cheyennes and Arapahoes to about 3 million acres between the thirty-seventh parallel and the Cimarron and Arkansas rivers in the Indian Territory. Directly to the south, the Kiowas and Comanches would be concentrated on a comparably large area between the Washita and Red rivers. The Plains Apaches would reside there, too. The commissioners promised honorable terms to the assembled chiefs: an assortment of trinkets, food, blankets, clothing, weapons and ammunition (for hunting), as well as farming tools, seeds, and other necessities to begin their new way of life, and, finally, peace with the United States. All would be theirs if they signed the treaty. War and the further de-

---

*Many of the Plains tribes observed this annual personal and tribal renewal rite, which included warrior self-torture.

struction of their people would be their lot if they refused. On October 21, 1867, the Kiowas, Comanches, and Plains Apaches signed the Medicine Lodge Creek Treaty. On October 28, the Cheyennes and Arapahoes resigned themselves to their fate and acquiesced.

But the Cheyenne warrior Roman Nose and the volatile Kiowa chief Satanta, two influential leaders, rejected the treaty. During the peace talks Satanta made his position on the Concentration policy absolutely clear to the commissioners:

All the land south of the Arkansas belongs to the Kiowas and the Comanches, and I don't want to give it away. I love the land and the buffalo and I will not part with any. . . . I have heard you intend to settle us on a reservation near the mountains. I don't want to settle there. I love to roam over the wide prairie, and when I do, I feel free and happy, but when we settle down we grow pale and die. . . . My heart feels like bursting with sorrow.

The peace commissioners granted permission to any of the five signatory tribes who preferred not to travel to their reserved land in Indian Territory until the following spring to stay near Fort Larned. While Black Kettle settled most of the Southern Cheyennes into their winter camp near that fort, and leaders of other southern plains tribes did the same, Roman Nose and his followers rode north into the forbidden central Kansas area and Satanta led his people away to Texas. The intransigence of two of the most aggressive Indian leaders boded ill for residents of the Great Plains, Indians and whites alike.

As for the commissioners, the treaty heartened them. Half of the Concentration policy's agenda for the plains tribes was in place. The Medicine Lodge Creek Treaty had reserved land below Kansas where the tribes of the southern plains would reside. The commission's next task was winning agreement from the northern plains tribes for a comparable arrangement above Nebraska. To complete the policy, the United States Indian Peace Commission moved on to Fort Laramie, sending messengers ahead into the Powder River country requesting that Red Cloud meet them at the fort for talks. Red Cloud again refused, explaining that he and his followers were too busy to come to the fort. They were preparing for their fall buffalo hunt. Red Cloud also sent a message back to the commissioners specifying his terms to end hostilities: the Bozeman forts had to be evacuated; only this would bring him down to Fort Laramie. During the winter of 1867–1868 the United States government reached the same conclusion. On March 2, 1868, General Grant wrote to General Sherman, "I think it will be well to prepare at once for the abandonment of the posts . . . and to make all the capital with the Indians that can be made out of the change."

The peace commissioners had to wait until the following spring before meeting with the dominant northern plains tribes. The result was a major federal treaty between these Indians and the United States. On April 29, 1868, chiefs of the Yanktonai Sioux and Brule, Miniconjou, and Oglala bands of the Teton Sioux signed the Fort Laramie Treaty. The agreement included important concessions and guarantees. The United States guaranteed the area comprising the western half of the present state of South Dakota to the signatory tribes as a permanent home to be designated "The Great Sioux Reservation." The United States also guaranteed these tribes the right to inhabit the Powder River country to the west of the Great Sioux Reservation. This land, defined as "north of the North Platte River and east of the summits of the Big Horn Mountains," was designated "unceded Indian territory," and it was closed to all whites henceforth. The Fort Laramie Treaty also secured for the Indians the right to hunt within this area "so long as buffalo may range there in numbers sufficient to justify the chase." Members of the signatory tribes could reside either on the reserve or in the unceded territory, or they could shuttle back and forth. The newest Fort Laramie Treaty also contained acculturation measures similar to those in the Medicine Lodge Creek Treaty. Finally, the United States agreed to abandon the three forts along the Bozeman Trail.

A week after the Sioux signing, the other major tribes came around. On May 7, 1868, the Crows met with the peace commissioners at Fort Laramie and accepted a reserve in Montana, relinquishing all claim to other territory in Montana and Wyoming guaranteed to them by their first Concentration treaty, the Fort Laramie Treaty of 1851. Three days later the Northern Cheyennes and Arapahoes also signed the accord. They agreed to live either on the Southern Cheyenne and Arapahoe reserve in Indian Territory or on the Great Sioux Reservation.

The following month negotiators in the Southwest realized another major goal of the Concentration policy, in this case with the Navajos. The previous five years had been traumatic for this tribe. During the Civil War, Union forces expelled the Confederate "Army of New Mexico" from the Territory of New Mexico (which included the present-day states of New Mexico, Arizona, and southern Nevada). With the Confederate threat to this area ended, they turned, in 1862, to ending the 250-year-old white struggle with the Navajos and the Apaches. Colonel James H. Carleton directed Colonel Christopher "Kit" Carson and the New Mexico volunteer militia to break the Indians' power in the area, ordering that there "be no council held with the Indians, nor any talks. The men are to be slain whenever and wherever they can be found. The women and children may be taken as prisoners, but, of course, they are not to be killed." A campaign without quarter during 1863 accomplished the objective of subjugation. Following capitulation, Carleton directed that the approximately 9,000 Navaho survivors be held along with the Apaches at Bosque Redondo near Fort Sumner, New Mexico Territory, on the Pecos River. Disease, coupled with lack of water, food, and the most basic essentials needed to sustain a minimal existence, caused the death of an estimated one-quarter of the Indians there. The government ended the disastrous Bosque Redondo experiment in 1868. On June 1 of that year the Navaho relinquished all claim to their territory and agreed to a 14-million-acre reserve encompassing parts of Utah, Arizona, and New Mexico.

Meanwhile, Red Cloud still refused to come to Fort Laramie and discuss signing the treaty. His refusal was not an objection to the treaty itself, but a determination not to sign anything until the United States evacuated the Bozeman Trail forts. "We are on the mountains looking down on the soldiers and the forts," he notified the commissioners through a messenger in May. "When we see the soldiers moving away and the forts abandoned, then I will come down and talk." On May 19, 1868, Washington issued orders to abandon the forts along the Bozeman Trail. During August the orders were executed. All soldiers and civilians at Forts Smith, then Phil Kearny, and finally Reno, vacated their posts. The Sioux then burned each installation to the ground. With these victories accomplished, and with meat stored for winter, Red Cloud and his followers journeyed to Fort Laramie. On November 6, 1868, he, too, signed the Fort Laramie Treaty.

Indian Commissioner Taylor had asserted in 1867 that peace could only be secured, and the extinction of Indians prevented, by realizing the policy of Concentration: "consolidating them as rapidly as it can be peacefully done on larger reservations." The United States Indian Peace Commission then labored throughout much of 1867 and 1868 to accomplish this goal. While the peace they secured at Fort Laramie for the northern plains lasted for almost a decade, the time of amity on the southern plains was short-lived. Civil and military officials disagreed about what caused it to shatter. Taylor suggested that a "spirit of revenge" over the failure of the government to supply the food, guns, and ammunition promised at Medicine Lodge Creek provided the cause. General Sherman was convinced that the government's concessions to the Sioux on the Bozeman Trail issue led some members of the southern tribes to emulate the Sioux in the hope that Washington would give in. There was truth in both explanations.

The southern tribes, throughout the winter of 1867–1868, had waited in vain for their provisions. During those months Commissioner Taylor had repeatedly warned of the "grave importance" of supplying the southern tribes "in order that the faith of the Government and the promises of the Indian Peace Commission, may be kept good." Congress, however, preoccupied with the impeachment of President Andrew Johnson, failed to appropriate funds to fulfill the commissioners' promises until July 1868, nine months after the peace council at Medicine Lodge Creek. As the Indians' disillusionment and frustration mounted, a growing number of the young men left camp to follow the trail north into the forbidden

Smokey Hill hunting grounds of Kansas, acknowledging they did not want to be restricted to living on lands dictated to them by the white man. Recalcitrants like Roman Nose and Medicine Arrows, who had resided in that region since repudiating the peace commission, seized the opportunity to persuade the newcomers to emulate the resistance of Red Cloud.

Hints of trouble came when the Cheyennes and Arapahoes in Kansas launched strikes against their old enemies, the Kaws and Pawnees. More serious trouble did not arise until August. On August 9, 1868, Agent Wynkoop finally delivered weapons and ammunition to the Southern Cheyennes in accordance with the Medicine Lodge Creek Treaty. The supplies were intended for use in securing winter meat. Before a week had elapsed, a party of about 200 Cheyennes, with a few Arapahoes and Sioux, rampaged against white settlers residing on the Saline and Solomon rivers in Kansas, killing fifteen men, raping women, capturing children, and looting and destroying property. More depredations followed in September. It is unlikely that these men intended to start a full-scale war. Revenge, anger, and the easy availability of liquor from white traders seems to have been at the root of their behavior. That starting a full-scale war was not their intent did not mitigate their actions, which precipitated one.

General Sherman, concluding that there was "open war, all the way from Fort Wallace to Denver," moved quickly. In early August 1868, he issued orders directing his field commanders to bring all Indians into their new reservations in the Indian Territory, peaceful and hostile factions alike. While most complied, some clung tenaciously to their old hunting grounds. Predictably, when the army moved in to round up the hostiles, violent clashes ensued. One of the more famous encounters occurred when troops commanded by Major George A. Forsyth moved against the Southern Cheyennes. The fight became known as "The Battle of Beecher's Island." On September 17, 1868, massed Cheyenne, accompanied by Sioux warriors, engaged Forsyth and his men, trapping them on an island of the Arickaree River, a fork of the Republican River, in northeastern Colorado just over the western border of Kansas. The Indians besieged the island for nine days, nearly eradicating the contingent of Americans. Only after the arrival of a column of the Tenth Cavalry were the survivors rescued. Realizing that more troops surely would be ordered out to subdue them, many Indians fled toward the Indian Territory to seek haven among the peaceful faction. The reaction of white authorities, however, was far greater than they ever anticipated.

General Sherman was furious when word reached him of Indian resistance to his orders to retire immediately to their reservations. "These Indians require to be soundly whipped," Sherman harangued, "and the ringleaders in the present trouble hung, their ponies killed, and such destruction of their property as will make them very poor." Now with treaties signed and the Concentration policy apparently realized, Sherman was more determined than ever to use military force to keep tribes on their reservations. All Indians, he now directed, who continued to reside off their reservations were to be considered "hostile" and, as such, could be attacked in whatever way military assessment dictated. "We have now selected and provided reservations for all," stormed Sherman. "All who cling to their old hunting grounds are hostile and will remain so till killed off."

Sherman's decision received the support of General of the Army Ulysses S. Grant, the Republican nominee for president and the man whom almost everyone expected would occupy the White House after the fall elections. Although Grant showed understanding of the problems of the Indians (he would later as president appoint the Seneca Ely Parker to head the Indian Bureau), in this case he supported his old comrade's determination to attack the hostiles without mercy. Grant, with uncharacteristic bombast, asserted to newspapermen: We must "clear the plains for the immigrants even if extermination of every Indian tribe is necessary." Wynkoop, the Southern Cheyennes' and Arapahoes' agent, vehemently disagreed with Sherman and Grant and the course they approved. He resigned his post and left for Philadelphia, declaring in a widely published letter condemning the army that he feared the military would use him as "a decoy to lure Indians into a trap."

The forthcoming campaign had three principal objectives, all aimed at enforcing the Concentration policy: first, to permanently remove the southern plains tribes from the land north of the Arkansas River; second, to confine the signatory tribes of the Medicine Lodge Creek Treaty to their reservations in the Indian Territory; and third, to punish those involved in the August and September 1868 outbreak of violence in Kansas. Responsibility for the campaign fell to General Philip H. Sheridan, a famous Civil War cavalry leader and now commander of the Department of the Missouri, which included Kansas, New Mexico, Colorado, and the Indian Territory. Soon he received instructions from Sherman: "Go ahead in your own way, and I will back you with my authority. If it results in the utter annihilation of these Indians, it is but the result of what they have been warned again and again."

Armed thus with specific approval from his superior, Sheridan readied plans for a war of extermination. He resolved to conduct it by means of a new strategy in fighting the Plains Indians: a winter campaign. The people of the plains had no experience with such warfare. Because theirs was largely a food-gathering economy, they obtained no profit from waging war during the winter, such an undertaking would greatly diminish their limited store of food. Sheridan concluded that the Indians' horses, extremely weakened from foraging on a few tufts of frozen grass during the winter months, could only poorly carry the fighting warriors and escaping tribespeople. He also realized that since the military had usually left Indians alone during the winter, their camps probably would be caught off guard by his troops. As he explained in a letter to William Sherman: "In taking the offensive, I have to select the season when I can catch the fiends." Sheridan also acknowledged the likelihood of casualties among the Indian women and children, and he rationalized, "If a village is attacked and women and children killed, the responsibility is not with the soldiers but with the people whose crimes necessitated the attack." Reminding Sherman of their tactics while campaigning in the Civil War, Philip Sheridan continued, "During the war did any one hesitate to attack a village or town occupied by the enemy because women and children were within its limits? Did we cease to throw shells into Vicksburg or Atlanta because women and children were there?"

Black Kettle, as always a believer in peace and compromise with the white men, had scrupulously obeyed the provisions of the Medicine Lodge Creek Treaty. In the spring of 1868 he had moved his people to the Indian Territory, settling them along the Washita River at the far western edge of the Cheyenne-Arapahoe reserve. In early November the renegades reached his encampment. As he listened to their tale of the recent fighting and learned that soldiers were still in pursuit, he could think of nothing but another assault like Sand Creek on his peaceful village. Black Kettle quickly resolved to journey southward to Fort Cobb on the northern perimeter of the Kiowa-Comanche reservation. There he would seek help from the military authorities. Upon his arrival, he explained his fear to the fort's commander, General William B. Hazen. Black Kettle asked Hazen for permission to move his people to this reservation where they would be under the general's protection. Black Kettle made clear that he spoke only for his band, who wanted peace, not for hostiles who were the target of Sheridan's campaign. Hazen, as he stated in his report of the incident, "followed the book" and suggested that Black Kettle return to his camp on the Washita, contact General Philip Sheridan, and surrender. Uneasy about his decision and worried about the fate of Black Kettle's band, he sent word of the meeting to General Sherman. Hazen was too late to help. Black Kettle, meanwhile, hurried back to his Washita River camp.

By November, Sheridan's scouts had informed him of the whereabouts of the hostile Cheyennes, Arapahoes, Comanches, and Kiowas in the Canadian and Washita valleys in western Indian Territory and northern Texas. With this information, he decided on a three-columned encircling movement to trap and destroy them. He ordered one column, commanded by Major Eugene A. Carr with seven companies of his Fifth Cavalry, to move southward from Fort Lyon, Colorado, toward those Indians wintering near Antelope Hill in western Indian Territory. A second column under Major Andrew W. Evans simultaneously would push eastward from Fort Bascum, New Mexico Territory, toward the Indians along the Canadian River in the Texas panhandle. The third column would be the main strike force, engaging those Indians pushed toward it by Carr's and Evans' troops. It would embark from Camp Supply along the North Canadian River in northwestern Indian Territory. Commanded by Sheridan himself and General Alfred Sully, it consisted of eleven companies of the Seventh Cavalry under Colonel George A. Custer, the Nineteenth Kansas Volunteer Cavalry under Colonel Samuel J. Crawford, and five companies of infantry under Captain J. H. Page. Together the three columns comprised 1,500 troops. Sheridan's orders to his commanders left no doubt about how the campaign should be conducted: "To destroy their villages and ponies, to kill and hang all warriors, and bring back all women and children."

The assaults began during the snowy days of late November 1868. The first took place in the early morning hours of November 27 against Black Kettle's village. The hostile Cheyennes had been successfully tracked as they fled across the snow-covered plains. Without a doubt, scouts reported, they presently resided at the peace chief's village along the Washita River on the Cheyenne-Arapahoe reservation. Only a few hours after Black Kettle returned from his unsuccessful trip to Fort Cobb, the Seventh Cavalry attacked his village. As the chief had feared, the scene was all too reminiscent of Sand Creek, almost four years ago to the day. The soldiers charged from all four sides while a military band, one of Colonel Custer's inspirations, enthusiastically thumped out the marching tune "Garry Owen." Custer reported that his men killed 103 warriors and captured fifty-three women and children. Almost incidentally, he also mentioned that "in the excitement of the fight, as well as in self-defense, it so happened that some of the squaws and a few children were killed and wounded." Additionally, his troops seized or destroyed 875 horses, ponies, and mules; a vast amount of robes, equipment and clothing; and a "whole supply" of meat and food.

Black Kettle, who had twice before missed death in similar circumstances, was killed as he tried to lead his people away from the rampaging soldiers. With a bullet in his back, he toppled from his horse into the cold waters of the Washita. Sheridan, in his official report to General Sherman, expressed jubilation that his troops finally had "wiped out old Black Kettle, . . . a worn-out and worthless old cypher." Far to the east in Philadelphia, Edward Wynkoop anguished over the accounts of the Battle of the Washita and of the death of his old friend. The Cheyennes' former agent bitterly denounced the betrayal by white authorities of this tribe, whom he had labored so diligently to protect from yet another catastrophe of this sort. Black Kettle "met his death at the hands of white men in whom he had too often fatally trusted," lamented Wynkoop, "and who triumphantly report the fact of his scalp in their possession."

Sheridan's campaign pressed ahead relentlessly throughout the winter of 1868–1869, crushing the Indians found off the reservation. A month after the Washita fight, on Christmas Day, 1868, Major Evans struck the Comanches and Kiowas hard at their village on Soldier Spring, routing them and destroying large stores of food and supplies. His victory broke their resistance and forced the two tribes back onto their reservation. Colonel Custer likewise remained in the field throughout the first months of 1869, searching the Texas panhandle and harrying back to the reservation those Cheyennes and Arapahoes who had yet to surrender. The great majority of those Indians who had not perished from the soldiers' onslaught were residing at their assigned reserve in the Indian Territory by spring. During the winter campaign of 1868–1869 one of America's most famous aphorisms was coined. Tosawi, the Comanche chief who brought in the first group of his people to surrender, confronted Philip Sheridan while on a stopover at Fort Cobb. Tosawi plaintively asked the general, "Why am I and my people being tormented by you? I am a good Indian." Sheridan replied with one of the Plains Wars' most infamous and most memorable statements: "The only good Indians I ever saw were dead." Lieutenant Charles Nordstrom, who was present, reported and retold the epigram, although General Sheridan, in his *Personal Memoirs,* denied ever uttering it.

By the spring of 1869, Sheridan had realized the three main objectives of his winter campaign. Indians had been evicted from the land north of the Arkansas River. The signatory tribes of the Medicine Lodge Creek Treaty had been confined to their reservations in the Indian Territory. And those who had been involved in the August and September 1868 outbreaks of violence in Kansas, and quite a few others as well, had been punished by the military.

Some Americans were heartsick over Sheridan's winter campaign. The Quakers, in a memorial to Congress, asked the government to alter its course toward the Indians and prayed "that the effusion of blood may cease, and that such just and humane measures may be pursued as will secure a lasting peace, and tend to the preservation and enlightenment of those afflicted people, whom we regard as the wards of the nation." Eastern humanitarians, stirred to action on behalf of the Indians, bitterly denounced the army's actions and declaimed the Washita River attack as another Sand Creek. Samuel Tappan, a member of the now defunct United States Indian Peace Commission that had secured the Medicine Lodge Creek Treaty in the hope of bringing peace to the southern plains, condemned the campaign as "stupid and criminal blundering." Tappan, Wynkoop, and reformers who promoted the Indians' welfare, such as John Beeson, Lydia Maria Child, and Peter Cooper, demanded that the federal government henceforth permit Christian denominations and humanitarian groups to assume a major role in guiding Indian policy. Indian Commissioner Nathaniel Taylor concurred with the reformers, recommending in his final annual report that "the government should invite the cooperation . . . of all Christian societies or individuals who may be disposed to take part in the work." The new Grant administration soon acted upon these calls.

On the other hand, many Americans, and most especially those residing in the West, were gratified by the winter campaign, and with Philip Sheridan in particular. "Shall we Williampennize or Sheridanize the Indians?" asked the Columbus, Nebraska, *Platte Journal.* The answer was no doubt obvious to the editor who posed the question and to many readers who paused to ponder it.

Federal officials hoped that the winter campaign of 1868–1869 would prove decisive, and that they had advanced far in solving the Indian question. Certainly peace in the West appeared to have come at last, secured by the policy of Concentration with the federal authority holding, as William Sherman pointed out to Philip Sheridan, "the olive branch with one hand and the sword in the other."

When I was a boy the Sioux owned the world; the sun rose and set on their land; they sent ten thousand men to battle. Where are the warriors today? Who slew them? Where are our lands? Who owns them? . . . Is it wrong for me to love my own? Is it wicked for me because my skin is red? Because I am a Sioux; because I was born where my father lived; because I would die for my people and my country?

SITTING BULL, HUNKPAPA SIOUX

CHAPTER FIVE

The Plains Wars, Phase II: Enforcing Concentration

Hostilities between the United States and the Plains Indians decreased sharply following Philip Sheridan's winter campaign of 1868–1869, as Washington realized the policy of Concentration. While the West enjoyed a period of relative calm, the East stirred with controversy over Indian affairs. The violent events of the preceding fall and winter had produced two immediate consequences. First, they revived the Transfer Issue and the controversy over the government's system of jurisdiction in Indian administration. Second, they heightened demands by humanitarian reformers for a greater role in shaping the government's Indian policy. President-elect Ulysses S. Grant, soon to face the task of enforcing the Concentration policy, had to decide which side he would support in each controversy to effectively administer the nation's Indian affairs.

Grant's "Peace Policy"

Captain William Fetterman's defeat in December 1866 during the Powder River War had infused the Transfer Issue. But Congress, following intense wrangling between proponents and opponents of transfer, early in 1867 voted against moving the Indian service to the War Department. With the Indian service remaining under the Interior Department, the military had little choice but to acquiesce, however grudgingly, in the conciliatory measures advanced by the civilians who oversaw the nation's Indian affairs. By late 1868, in light of almost a half decade of hostilities with the plains tribes and the seeming failure of the treaty system in securing peace with Indians, the nation's military leaders again openly expressed their disillusionment with civilian control of the Indian Bureau. "Does not this magnanimity verge on the borders of folly?" General William T. Sherman argued in a letter to his brother John, the senator from Ohio and a staunch supporter of transferring control to the War Department. "It is a waste of life and waste of money to hunt down nomadic Indians like the Sioux to be turned over to the Indian Bureau, and then turned loose well supplied with food and the means of renewing the war."

General Sherman sounded the clarion for change in his annual report of 1868, renewing the military's demand for transfer of jurisdiction over Indian affairs to the War Department. He strenuously suggested that the change was the "only hope" for concluding the "eternal" struggle with the Indians and for ending the Indian question. Ulysses S. Grant supported Sherman fully, and he threw his considerable prestige behind the calls for transfer of the Indian Bureau. "If the present practice is to be continued," concluded Grant, "I do not see that any course is left open to us but to withdraw our troops to the settlements and call upon Congress to provide means and troops to carry on the formidable hostilities against the Indians until all the Indians or all the whites on the great plains and between the settlements on the Missouri and the Pacific slope are exterminated."

The outgoing administrator of the Indian Bureau disagreed emphatically. Commissioner Nathaniel Taylor, in his final annual report, took exception to Sherman's and Grant's conclusions, offering a nine-page rebuttal of the generals. Asserting that his sole motive was to save the "unlettered children of the wilderness" from the "blighting scepter of military despotism," Taylor contended that transferring the Indian Bureau from the Interior Department would be "tantamount . . . to perpetual war." His superior, Interior Secretary Orville Browning, found little cause to judge the military's demands any more sympathetically. "Our experience during the period when the Indians were under military care and guardianship," he wrote, "affords no ground for hope that any benefit to them or to the treasury would be secured."

Philip Sheridan's winter campaign of 1868–1869 gave impetus to humanitarian reformers, and, understandably, they threw their support behind the civilian authorities during the transfer dispute. Appalled by the bloodshed on the western prairies in recent years, their calls for a more humane and enlightened Indian policy had mounted steadily during the Johnson presidency. They charged the military with brutal treatment and indiscriminate aggression against western tribes. They suggested that the Indians' well-being could only be safeguarded, and progress in civilizing the Indians would only be realized, through the efforts of conscientious, concerned, and benevolent civilians. The Religious Society of Friends, a Quaker group advocating a Christian approach to solving the Indian question, characterized the goals of the various and proliferating Indian reform groups: to "endeavor to treat them with kindness and justice; to guard them against the imposition and fraud to which their ignorance exposed them; to meliorate and improve their condition; and to commend the benign and heavenly principles of the Christian religion to their approval and acceptance by an upright example consistent therewith."

Congress soon undertook to resolve the controversy. In early December 1868, Congressman James A. Garfield of Ohio, chairman of the House Military Committee, introduced legislation to return the Indian Bureau to the War Department as of January 1, 1869. Garfield noted that "General Grant, General Sherman, and General Sheridan, and nearly all of the leading officers of the Army connected with the Indian service recommend this." Congressman William Windom of Minnesota, chairman of the House Committee on Indian Affairs, led opposition to the proposed legislation. Asserting that transfer would mean all-out war on the Indians, Windom argued that "if there is any Department of this government in which we find the great maelstrom of the treasury, where money is sunk by millions and never accounted for, it is the War Department." His argument failed to sway most colleagues, and the House passed the Garfield bill by a commanding margin of 116 to 33. The final determination of the Transfer Issue now rested with the Senate. "It has cost this government much more to fight the Indians than to feed them—very much more," Senator Thomas Hendricks of Indiana contended, summing up the position of the antitransfer forces in the upper house, "and I think this a question of whether they shall be . . . fed or fought." The Senate ended the debate by voting to refer the Garfield bill to the Indian Committee, where it died. Other attempts were made in the House that winter to effect transfer. The Senate rejected each effort. Still, those who advocated military control of Indian affairs were confident. General Grant would be inaugurated in March. With him in the White House, they anticipated changes in the administration of Indian affairs. The changes, however, shocked them at first.

Ulysses S. Grant's first inaugural address on March 4, 1869, heartened reformers and distressed many former comrades in the army. "The proper treatment of the original occupants of this land—the Indians—is one deserving of careful study," declared President Grant. "I will favor any course toward them which tends to their civilization and ultimate citizenship." William T. Sherman, whom Grant appointed general-in-chief of the army, a post he held for the next fourteen-and-a-half years, could not believe the turn of events. Sherman, six weeks after the inauguration, wrote General Philip Sheridan expressing dismay and complete disbelief that their old commander apparently had dramatically altered his approach to dealing with the Indian question.

In calling for the "civilization and ultimate citizenship" of the Indians, President Grant seemed to place his administration squarely on the side of the reformers, for they believed fervently that to civilize the Indians was to safeguard them—from the "deleterious" effects of the customs and values of their native cultures and, equally, from white aggression. Was it possible, reformers wondered, that of all people the former commanding general of the United States Army might eschew the sword for benevolent methods to manage Indian affairs and solve the Indian question? Certainly the president's statement seemed to affirm a conviction held by only a minority of his fellow citizens: that Indians were not hopeless unregenerate savages; not unchangeable impediments to American pioneer progress whose extinction was a tragic but inevitable fate. Perhaps Grant, after all, agreed with the reformers, that with time and diligent effort the Indians could be "civilized." Was a more humane administration beginning in the federal government's dealings with Indians? In 1869, many reformers thought so.

The genesis of the so-called "Grant Peace Policy" occurred roughly six weeks prior to the general's first inauguration. In late January of 1869 a delegation of Quakers, one of the most active sects in the field of Indian reform, called on the president-elect urging him to embrace an Indian policy grounded on Christian benevolence. "Gentlemen, your advice is good. I accept it," Grant replied to his visitors. "If you can make Quakers out of the Indians it will take the fight out of them. Let us have peace." The delegation was jubilant. After years of tortuous relations with tribes as the government attempted to solve the Indian question, here now was a national hero and the republic's next chief executive promising that "all Indians disposed to peace will find the new policy a peace-policy." Yet Grant, maybe as an instinctive afterthought, also made it clear to the Quakers that "those [Indians] who do not accept this policy will find the new administration ready for a sharp and severe war policy." Perhaps the delegation in its exaltation failed to weigh this statement as carefully as others made that day by Grant. Maybe their lack of apprehension sprang, too, from a supreme confidence in the ability of humanitarians to transform the hearts and ways of the Indians through philanthropic means, thus making enforcement of the Concentration policy through military means unnecessary.

Shortly after inauguration day, on March 20, 1869, Christian reformers met at Philadelphia. Led by William Welsh, Episcopal layman and Philadelphia businessman, the group appointed a committee to press further the humanitarians' demands with the new president. On March 24, President Grant and Interior Secretary Jacob D. Cox welcomed to the White House a delegation of prosperous and influential Pennsylvania reformers, including Welsh; William Strong, judge on the Pennsylvania Supreme Court; and George H. Stuart, Presbyterian layman and merchant from Philadelphia. Like the Quakers they stressed the need for a benevolent policy to solve the Indian question. They also requested that the president let Protestant denominations and humanitarian groups assume a major role in supervising the Indian service and in guiding federal Indian policy, stressing that "without the co-operation of Christian philanthropists the waste of money would be great, and the result unsatisfactory." The Philadelphia delegation urged Grant to establish an autonomous commission to achieve these ends. The president agreed that the idea had merit. On April 10, 1869, Congress passed legislation authorizing Grant to "organize a board of Commissioners, to consist of not more than ten persons, to be selected by him from men eminent for their intelligence and philanthropy, to serve without pecuniary compensation." Accordingly, on June 3, the president issued an executive order establishing the Board of Indian Commissioners. It was assigned a number of important duties: advising the secretary of the Interior and the commissioner of Indian Affairs regarding Indian policy and reform initiatives, serving as a watchdog over the disbursement of funds appropriated by Congress for the Indians and the Indian service's work among them, and supervising the appointment of all agency personnel by Protestant denominations.

President Grant, by creating the Board of Indian Commissioners and by relying on it and Protestant denominations to advise Indian administrators and nominate Indian agents, advocated major changes in the management of Indian affairs in the hope of maintaining peace with tribes and improving their conditions. Grant's agenda did not end here, though. In an effort to reduce fraud and fashion an efficient and honest management system by which to ensure Indian adherence to Concentration policy, the president, now acting more in character, wanted to involve the military heavily: first by appointing army officers to civil posts in the Indian service, and second by placing the Indian Bureau under the

War Department, thus striking doubly "at the heart of the old Indian system—the patronage prerogatives of members of Congress." To federal legislators, permitting sweeping denominational influence was one thing, but to relinquish this sizable share of the lucrative spoils system without a fight was a completely different matter. Consequently, Congress retaliated against Grant's military agenda by striking down another transfer bill and interdicting the appointment of army officers to civil posts within the Indian service. The furious president, thereafter throwing his support ever more behind Christian reformers, chided Congress: "Gentlemen, you have defeated my plan of Indian management; but you shall not succeed in *your* purpose, for I will divide these appointments up among the religious churches, with which you dare not contend."

While denominational control of the Indian service became the principal characteristic of Grant's Peace Policy, two additional provisions were eventually embodied in it as well. First, the United States would discontinue negotiating treaties with Indian tribes. The government under the Concentration policy would no longer regard them and deal with them legally as sovereign polities. To Grant, the Board of Indian Commissioners, and most reformers, treaties perpetuated a fiction. "We recognize a wandering tribe as an independent and sovereign nation. We send ambassadors to make a treaty as with our equals," criticized one principal reformer, Episcopal Bishop Henry B. Whipple. It is "impolitic for our Government to treat a heathen community living within our borders as an independent nation, instead of regarding them as wards." By an act of Congress in 1871 the United States government ended the treaty-making process with Indians. Second, the government would move to extinguish tribal identification among Indians, ending their reliance on that community for well-being and hopefully replacing it with the ethic of individual responsibility for personal welfare. Grant saw the reformers as the agents for realizing these changes.

To his credit, Ulysses S. Grant was willing to take a relatively open-minded position for that era regarding the Indians, an open-mindedness shaped in no small measure by his newly appointed commissioner of Indian Affairs, Brigadier General Ely S. Parker. Certainly the new commissioner influenced Grant's faith in the potential of civilizing the Indians. As William H. Armstrong skillfully described in *Warrior in Two Camps: Ely S. Parker, Union General and Seneca Chief,* Parker, or Ha-Sa-No-An-Da, an Americanized Seneca from New York State, had enjoyed prominence in both the Indian and white worlds. Not only was he chief of the Senecas and Grand Sachem of the Iroquois Confederation, Parker also was a lawyer, an engineer, a Worshipful Master in the Masons, and a Union Civil War veteran. Only with the greatest of difficulty had he secured a commission as captain of volunteers during the late war, but from that point onward his military career advanced rapidly. Parker joined General Grant's staff during the Vicksburg campaign of 1862 and 1863, and he served on it throughout the remainder of the war. General Parker was one among an intimate circle of trusted lieutenants who accompanied the commanding general to the parlor of Wilbur McLean's farmhouse at Appomattox, Virginia, where Robert E. Lee surrendered.

Following the war, Ely Parker remained as Grant's aide-de-camp until resigning to accept the post of Indian commissioner. Parker directed the Indian Bureau for two years, backing Grant on using the military to control the Indian service, fighting successfully for the abandonment of the treaty system, and supporting both increased denominational influence in the selection of Indian agents and the reforms recommended by humanitarians and by the Board of Indian Commissioners. Like those of an increasing number of Grant administration appointees, Parker's record was eventually called into question by a House investigating committee. Its report censored the Bureau's awarding of private contracts to some Sioux agencies, although Parker himself was exonerated of fraud or corruption. He resigned as commissioner in July 1871, declaring angrily that it was "no longer a pleasure to discharge patriotic duties." Parker returned to New York, where he suffered a series of major financial, professional, and physical difficulties. He died in 1895. At that time Ely Parker held a minor position on the New York police force.

To Grant, Ely Parker personified all that Indians might become in the United States. The president, in his own way, stood ready to help and support the struggle to bring all Indians into the American societal and economic mainstream. Yet Grant's Indian policy, as expressed to the Quakers, other reform groups, and in his first inaugural, actually deviated little from the guideline set by the Concentration policy of the post–Civil War period: force should be employed only after peaceful means had failed. The Grant administration demanded the absolute concentration of Indians* in reservations, where missionaries of various religious denominations could then labor at transforming them into Americans—culturally, not into U.S. citizens. Peace could indeed be secured by tribes and the Indian question solved, but *only* in this manner. This administration, as Grant himself had promised bluntly, was fully prepared to employ the military to ensure that the Indians obeyed its first dictum absolutely. The occasion to do so arose twice, as the Plains Wars would erupt again in the course of the Grant presidency. And unlike the campaigns of 1866–1869, these operations were decisive. The Red River War of 1874–1875 brought significant conflict on the southern plains to an end, while the Great Sioux War of 1876–1877 closed belligerencies on the northern plains.

At the Watershed

By 1870 relative peace reigned on the lower Great Plains, less a peace of reconciliation than of exhaustion. The Kiowas, Comanches, Southern Cheyennes, and Arapahoes for the most part remained on their reserves in the Indian Territory. Although the hostilities of the preceding years had mentally and physically worn tribal members, they did not view themselves as conquered peoples, nor did they regard residency on their reservation as a permanent badge of subjugation by the United States' Concentration policy or as final defeat. Among many, the desire to follow their accustomed ways and to eschew the ways of white society burned strong. They were not yet ready to accept the fate befalling them. What was natural, indeed inevitable, was that they would

---

*After 1871, they were no longer officially dealt with as members of sovereign nations or tribes, but as wards of the United States government.

cling to their old ways and long to find the means of throwing off the restraints and thwarting the plans of those who would lead them to a new way of life. The young men in particular were unable to accept that their people's days of freedom on the plains had ended, and especially that they would be deprived of opportunities to achieve cherished societal honors through raiding and warfare.

The attractions that lured the Indians out of the Indian Territory reservations in the early 1870s were simple. Among them was the desire to delay the transformation that required them to abandon the life of migratory hunters and to take up that of farmers. Few if any of them, at least among the males, could even imagine their new status as anything but odious. There is nothing surprising in this attitude, yet much of the white population seemed to have found it puzzling that the Indians did not like or welcome what was happening to them. White males, who argued quite clearly about the division between men's and women's work, apparently took it for granted there could be no such divisions among "savages." Forcing Indian males to take up farming, traditionally the job of women, was tantamount to stripping them of their masculinity.

With their background and cultural beliefs, the men readily took advantage of the provisions in the Medicine Lodge Creek Treaty that permitted them to leave the reservations to hunt the buffalo. It seemed to them that from time immemorial this had been the traditional and manly way to secure food. Although the federal government required the four tribes to live on their reservations in the Indian Territory, it granted them the right to supplement food allotments by hunting those buffalo grazing on the lands to the south of the Arkansas River, so long as the "buffalo may range thereon in such numbers as to justify the chase." Contained in this seemingly benevolent clause was the legal justification for restraining the southern tribes from all activity on the white settlers' lands and ultimately for permanently restricting them to their reservations. White authorities and Indian leaders alike recognized the implication, and each side manipulated it to their own advantage. Both sides realized the pronounced and obvious potential for violence in this strategy. Yet in light of what was at stake—for the Indians, remaining free of total confinement on the reservations; for the whites, enforcing the Concentration policy, permanently restricting the Indians to the reservation, and ending the Indian question—probably little could have been done to prevent the conflict known as the Red River War. Fought in 1874 and 1875, it represented the last significant armed encounter between the United States and the southern plains tribes.

In 1870 buffalo on the southern plains still roamed in plentiful numbers, although nowhere near the size of the herds that covered this region before the 1840s and the onset of American migration across the West. But the situation in 1870 would soon change, paralleling the recent demise of the buffalo on the central plains. In the late 1860s, white buffalo hunters killed the remaining herds on the central plains in overwhelming numbers. Hunters with new high-powered buffalo rifles spent most of each year in the wholesale slaughter of the lumbering beasts. The skinners, who took only the buffalos' hides, and sometimes just their tongues, followed these men. The remains of the carcasses were left to rot. White men killed tens of thousands of buffalo per week in this manner. In the face of such slaughter, the central plains became a great charnel house: a buffalo graveyard of decaying, putrid, stinking remains. By 1870 no buffalo could be found on the central plains, a striking testimony to the power of the modern rifle to wipe out animals in numbers now incalculable. In that same year federal officials gave the hunters and hidesmen permission to hunt buffalo on the upper southern plains. The hunters moved to the south and east, nearing the southern plains tribes who resided in western Indian Territory and who continued to journey north and west from their reservation. Since they too were on the move to hunt buffalo, a confrontation became increasingly possible.

There was rising discontent on the reservations in western Indian Territory by the early 1870s. The diminishing buffalo herd provided one source of antagonism, but there were others as well. One was a combustible group of youthful warriors and older, recalcitrant war leaders. Young Kiowas and Comanches, chafing at the restraints of reservation life and longing to secure war trophies to enhance warrior status on which their culture put such a high premium, in increasing numbers followed firebrands like Satanta, Big Tree, Eagle Heart, and Satank into Texas and Mexico to raid white settlements. They sent overtures to the Cheyennes, many of whom accepted the tempting offer to join them. In an effort to halt the raids in the summer of 1871, General Sherman ordered the arrest of Satanta and Big Tree after learning that they were openly boasting of killing and robbing whites. The two men were imprisoned at the Texas state penitentiary. The government now hoped that the younger warriors, deprived of these influential leaders, would be discouraged from raiding south of the Indian Territory and thus remain on the reservation, but they were not so disposed. Under pressure from humanitarian groups to release the Kiowa prisoners, the government freed Satanta and Big Tree in October 1873 on the conditions that they remain peaceful and that they convince the young men to end the war against Texas and return to the reservation. An exasperated General Sherman strongly opposed the move and predicted that the raids would not only continue, but would mount. "I have no more faith in their sincerity than I have in the prarie [sic] wolves," he told General Philip Sheridan, "and as I once risked my life to test their sincerity, I do not propose again to expose others to a like danger." As Sherman predicted, Kiowa and Comanche depredations against the Texas frontier escalated.

In those same years white horse thieves, mainly from Kansas, roamed the Indian Territory unchecked, plundering the Indians' herds and antagonizing the southern plains tribes. Cheap whiskey plied by white traders was also plentiful on the Indian Territory reservations, fueling resistance, fraying tempers, and turning more men into besotted, indolent drunks unable to provide minimal food for hungry families. In February 1873 a local observer apprised John D. Miles, the Southern Cheyennes' agent, of the dangerous situation: "The Indians will be hungry and mad very soon and . . . whiskey is more plentiful than good water and all hands in the vicinity are nearly continually drunk." A lack of rations added to the mounting problems. Food allotments that the Medicine Lodge Creek Treaty promised, small as they would have been, were often late, and sometimes never arrived. At times white authorities withheld rations, hoping to force Indians to return captives or stock taken from Texas. And for those Indians who attempted farming, the poor soil of the reservations made it impossible for residents to supplement diets satisfactorily by their own efforts.

These misfortunes came at a time when the mass slaughter of the southern buffalo herd by white hunters drastically decreased the availability of food from that source. Men brought back less and less to their hungry people on the reservation, as their hunting efforts became increasingly ineffective. The killing of the buffalo herds constituted the deadliest threat to these people. The eradication of the southern herd would also mean, technically, that the Indians would no longer be allowed to leave the reservation. Per the federal government's latest mandate, when the buffalo were insufficient to justify "the chase," the government would confine the Indians to their reserves permanently.

During the early 1870s white hunters continually moved their operations southward. In 1872–1873 they shipped 1,250,000 hides eastward by rail. By the winter of 1873–1874, so many buffalo had been killed on the lands north of the Cimarron River (estimated at 7.5 million) that a new source had to be secured. If other herds were to be exploited, it could only be those in the Texas panhandle between the Cimarron and South Canadian rivers. Lying just to the west of the Cheyenne-Arapahoe reservation, this locale was the Indians' primary buffalo-hunting ground.

With the arrival of spring in 1874, the buffalo hunters moved into northern Texas. There they made their primitive headquarters in the small town of Adobe Walls on the South Canadian River. From this base they fanned out over the prairie, where the Indians soon learned of their deeds and became deeply resentful. But among many bands the response remained only resentment. The quick instinctive response to retaliate was no longer unanimous among all Indians. While some tribesmen were as ready as ever to defend their hunting grounds, others saw this response as merely futile and only likely to bring in soldiers to mete out ever more repressive punishments. Still, a number of young Kiowas, Comanches, and Southern Cheyennes (the Arapahoes by this time no longer wanted any part in war against the whites) agreed to join in attacking the white buffalo hunters. As historian Donald J. Berthrong summarized in *The Southern Cheyennes*: "Horse thieves, buffalo hunters, poisonous whiskey, lack of rations, restless young men needing trophies and coups for warrior status, and inadequate law enforcement had finally taken their toll." Just before dawn on June 27, 1874, 300 Cheyenne and Comanche warriors led by Isatai, a Comanche medicine man, assaulted Adobe Walls and the buffalo hunters within. Although repulsed, the warriors sufficiently alarmed the hunters so as to cause them to abandon Adobe Walls and retire to safer lands above the North Canadian River. A number of officials in the Indian Territory urged the army to take action in response to the attack. General John Pope, military commander for the southern Great Plains district, did not agree. Characterizing the white hunters as the basest frontier element who plundered the Indian country in violation of the law while committing "violent and inexcusable outrages upon the Indians," Pope wrote Kansas Governor Thomas A. Osborn: the hunters "have justly earned all that may befall them, and if I were to send troops to the locality of these unlawful establishments, it would be to break them up and not to protect them."

The battle at Adobe Walls stirred the martial ardor of other warriors who had remained in the Indian Territory. With spirits heightened, warriors in mounting numbers poured from the reservation to join the fighting. Punitive raids erupted against settlers, travelers, and even army parties within a 200-mile radius of the reservations. Making their base in the Staked Plains region of northern Texas, raiders swept into Texas, New Mexico, Kansas, and even faraway Colorado. Yet the Indians' security was to last only briefly before disaster overwhelmed them, once again in the form of Philip H. Sheridan. "This outbreak," Sheridan concluded, "does not look to me, as being originated by the actions of bad white men, or the sale of whiskey to Indians by traders. It is the result of the restless nature of the Indians who has [sic] no profession but arms and naturally seeks for war and plunder when the grazing gets high enough to feed his ponies." By mid-summer hostilities were so widespread that civil authorities felt compelled to turn matters over to the military. In July 1874, Interior Secretary Columbus Delano and Indian Commissioner Edward P. Smith gave Secretary of War William W. Belknap full authority to control Indian affairs in and around the Indian Territory. Accordingly, on July 20, General William T. Sherman ordered General Sheridan to enforce the Concentration policy and crush the hostiles.

While the army prepared for this newest mission, several nasty incidents occurred on the Indian Territory reservations. On August 22, for example, troops of the Tenth Cavalry under Lieutenant Colonel John W. Davidson tried to disarm the Comanches and force them to relinquish their white prisoners of war. Gunfire erupted and the two sides battled each other from long-range for two days. The melee produced few casualties, but as a result scores of previously peaceful Indians moved into northern Texas to join the hostiles. By late August thousands of men, women, and children had bolted from the reservations: 1,800 Southern Cheyennes, 2,000 Comanches, and 1,000 Kiowas. Of these, according to historian Robert M. Utley, perhaps 1,200 were warriors.

Meanwhile, Sheridan readied his commanders. The general sympathized with the tribes' plight, and he understood clearly the principal source of the Indians' hostility and their resistance to the Concentration policy: "We took away their country and their means of support," he reflected, "broke up their mode of living, their habits of life, introduced disease and decay among them, and it was for this and against this they made war. Could any one expect less?" Sheridan also was convinced that they had "only one profession, that of arms, and every one of them belongs to it, and they never resist the natural desire to join in a fight if it happens to be in their vicinity." Therefore, stamping out this "natural inclination" required that the Indians be punished severely for each breach of the peace.

And so Sheridan again chose a tactic approximating a war of attrition: a total war against the entire population residing off the reservations. Only such a war would convince the hostiles they could not win. It would force proud warriors to consider the welfare of their families and war leaders to think of their bands, however crushing the blows to their pride. Employing the same strategy of convergence used to destroy Indian resistance during the winter campaign of 1868–1869, Sheridan ordered a five-pronged drive aimed at encircling the hostiles in Texas. Although brutal, the strategy was overwhelmingly successful. Wherever the soldiers discovered camps, they put them to the torch. Food, animals, weapons, vast quantities of supplies—all were destroyed, leaving survivors thus impoverished to face the bitter winter on the plains. Deprivation and want became the Indians' lot as they struggled against the elements. And even as the cold and hunger weakened them, troopers relentlessly pursued. The Indians hid or were in constant flight. Sheridan's tactics wore down Chief Lone Wolf and his Kiowas first. The plains were still frozen as the remnants of his band came into Fort Sill in February of 1875. A month later most Southern Cheyennes gave themselves up. Hundreds, however, tried to escape and join the Northern Cheyennes on the upper plains. For some, their efforts were thwarted in a manner that had become all too commonplace. Troops of the Sixth Cavalry under Lieutenant Austin Henely tracked down one group of about sixty and attacked them in their camp on the Sappa River in northwest Kansas. Henely took no prisoners. Other Southern Cheyennes successfully avoided pursuing patrols and in mid-May 1875 joined the Northern Cheyennes at the Red Cloud agency. By June 1875 the Comanches too faced the reality that further resistance would only result in complete annihilation and so came into Fort Sill and surrendered.

With the Red River War over, military authorities were more determined than ever to prevent a future outbreak. They imprisoned a number of the leading war chiefs. As Philip Sheridan suggested: "To turn them loose to renew the same old game in the spring seems folly." Among them was the famous—most whites thought infamous—Kiowa war chief Satanta, who was returned to the Texas state penitentiary to serve a life sentence. The absolute confinement proved so loathsome to him that he jumped to his death from an upper window of the prison on March 11, 1878.

A new military policy, proposed by President Grant on March 13, 1875, was implemented. Designed to destroy the southern plains tribes' leadership, and with it those peoples' ability to resist the Concentration policy further, the plan called for exiling the leading warriors and war chiefs from their families and tribes. The government selected seventy-four men, chained and shackled them, and then shipped them under heavy guard to the old Spanish fortress Castillo de San Marcos at St. Augustine, Florida, an installation renamed Fort Marion by the United States. There the men remained imprisoned for three years under the supervision of Lieutenant Richard H. Pratt. A number of the prisoners died— some from disease, others because they could not adjust to the sultry Florida climate, still others from loneliness. The survivors, characterized by reformer Henry B. Whipple as "desperate warriors as ever carried the tomahawk or knife," were treated with kindness and consideration by Pratt, who used the opportunity to educate the captives. Whipple, following a visit to the fortress, tried to meet the familiar charge that Indians could not be "tamed or humanized." From Savannah, Georgia, on March 24, 1876, he wrote of the prisoners:

Their faces are changed. They have all lost that look of savage hate, and the light of a new life is dawning in their hearts. It was my privilege to preach to them every Sunday and upon week-days I told them stories from the Bible. I have never had a more attentive congregation. Captain Pratt's success is due to the fact that he has taught them to labor: he has given them, in the best sense, a Christian school.

The remaining Indians were released on good behavior from Fort Marion in April 1878. Pratt was so exhilarated with this pedagogic calling that in 1879 he founded Carlisle Indian Industrial School in Pennsylvania to educate reservation youths. Carlisle became the model for the government's off-reservation school system, and Pratt himself dominated the Indian education system for nearly two decades.

The Red River War was a watershed for the southern plains tribes. On the one side they had the harsh but satisfying life of freedom on the plains. On the other side they faced adjustment to a life that denied all that they had cherished. No member of these tribes ever again freely roamed the region below the Platte River. Never again did they challenge the policy of Concentration with armed force. With these tribes effectively restricted to their reservations, the army gave full permission to white buffalo hunters to move onto the southern Great Plains. The vast area of New Mexico, Texas, and southern Kansas was open for whatever slaughter the hunters and skinners could commit. Only three years later they had all but eradicated the remaining millions of buffalo there. With the extermination of the last of the great herds, a way of life passed into darkness.

The Peace That Slipped Away

The Fort Laramie Treaty of 1868 led the dominant tribes of the northern plains to believe they had secured for themselves a right of self-determination under the Concentration policy and the possession of extensive tracts of land in the Dakotas, Montana, and Wyoming. In particular, the Sioux and their Northern Cheyenne and Arapahoe allies had fought grimly for these objectives in the Powder River War. The Fort Laramie Treaty, no scrap of paper but the pledged word of the United States, testified they had won these rights.

After signing the treaty, most of the Sioux moved onto the Great Sioux Reservation, essentially present-day South Dakota west of the Missouri River. There Red Cloud and his rival Spotted Tail continued as the principal sources of authority. In 1868, General William S. Harney, under orders from General Sherman, established a series of agencies along the Missouri where rations and supplies would be distributed to the Indians. Neither of the two Sioux leaders liked the locations. Preferring that their agencies be located closer to Fort Laramie and the Sioux's Powder River hunting grounds, for five years both men stubbornly pressed the government to relocate them. Finally the federal government, tired of the diplomatic wrangling with Red Cloud and Spotted Tail, gave in and in 1873 established agencies off the reservation in northwestern Nebraska along the White River. According to statistics published by the Bureau of Indian Affairs in 1875, the government supplied approximately 8,000 Brules at Spotted Tail agency, while about 9,000 Oglalas and 3,500 Northern Cheyennes and Arapa-

Northern Great Plains, ca. 1875-1890

hoes were served at Red Cloud agency. The Indian Bureau supplied the other reservation Sioux through its Missouri River agencies.

The remaining Sioux, who rejected the reservation and preferred to keep away from the whites and live in the more traditional way, continued to hunt the buffalo. They stayed on the lands of the Powder River and Bighorn Mountain region, "unceded Indian territory" as the Fort Laramie Treaty designated it, where they were entitled to hunt "so long as the buffalo range thereon in sufficient numbers as to justify the chase." Here the Hunkpapa Sitting Bull and the Oglala Crazy Horse emerged as the dominant leaders. Sitting Bull had nothing but disdain for the Concentration policy and the agency Sioux who adhered to it. "Look at me—see if I am poor, or my people either," he taunted. "You are fools to make yourselves slaves to a piece of fat bacon, some hard-tack, and a little sugar and coffee." Yet, many off-reservation Sioux were not above seeking free rations at the agencies, and so shuttled back and forth between the Great Sioux Reservation and the unceded territory. Colonel David S. Stanley in 1869 noted that this group spent "half their time at these agencies and half in the hostile camps. They abuse the agents, threaten their lives, kill their cattle at night, and do anything they can to oppose the civilizing movement, but eat all the provisions they can get." By 1871 pressure was mounting from settlers in Kansas and Nebraska and from the War Department for the Interior Department to expunge the buffalo-hunting clause. They argued that this right was the principal source of ongoing friction and possible hostilities. Reformers, such as William Welsh, concurred that the clause should be repealed, but for the reason that continued buffalo hunting by the Sioux promoted "vagrancy" and retarded detribalization efforts.

For four years following the signing of the Fort Laramie Treaty of 1868 relations between the United States and the Sioux and their Cheyenne and Arapahoe allies remained generally harmonious. But the circumstances were changing. New tensions on the upper plains would push the government's commitment to its treaty obligations to the limit. The first tremors of disruption occurred in 1872. In that year the Northern Pacific Railroad announced its intention to lay another section of its line across the northern Great Plains.

The Northern Pacific was in the last stages of constructing a rail line from Duluth, Minnesota, to Bismarck on the Missouri River in the Dakota Territory, lying just to the northeast of the Great Sioux Reservation. It then planned to run the new extension from Bismarck westward, passing above the Great Sioux Reservation until it reached the Yellowstone River valley. There the railroad intended to build along the Yellowstone. Because of the vague clauses in the Fort Laramie Treaty, it was unclear whether the planned route encroached on the Sioux's unceded western lands in violation of terms. One thing, however, was clear: the off-reservation Sioux adamantly opposed the building of the railroad. Not only would the proposed line pass through their buffalo-hunting range and disrupt the remaining herds, it would soon bring white settlers into the region, people who would surely demand that the Sioux be confined to their reservation.

The railroad, realizing its action could shatter the fragile peace of recent years, requested the assistance of the federal government. Officials in Washington, equally aware of the possibilities, sent two emissaries to discuss the problem with the Sioux in 1873. They asked for concessions under which the Sioux and their allies would grant the Northern Pacific Railroad a right-of-way through their lands in the Yellowstone Valley. The Sioux answered quickly and firmly. They wanted no whites on their lands. Experience had shown them that beginning any white enterprise would cause more whites to follow. They refused to amend the Fort Laramie Treaty. If they did, they reasoned, it would provide a precedent for other reductions of their promised rights. In the end, any bending would only hurt them.

The Sioux argued persuasively. Still, the Northern Pacific went ahead with its plan to build on the south side of the Yellowstone River. Surveyors for the railroad arrived in June to map the route. Federal officials made no attempt to stop such activity, nor did the army. In fact General Sherman, while acknowledging that the Sioux's arguments were correct, assigned a force of over 1,500 men under Colonel David S. Stanley to accompany and protect the surveyors. Had they not done so, the Sioux, who knew very well that their rights were being eroded, would certainly have attacked the surveyors. Protected by the army, the surveyors remained in the Sioux's western territory through the fall. By the time winter arrived, Stanley had quartered his units at Fort Abraham Lincoln, three miles to the south of Bismarck. Meanwhile at Sherman's headquarters in Chicago, plans were drawn for the Indian war that the military confidently expected to erupt in the spring when the railroad began construction. However, the army jettisoned its plans when the financial panic of 1873 threw the Northern Pacific into bankruptcy, obliging it to forego further construction. The Sioux were reprieved, but not for long. Although the thrust of the railroad subsided temporarily, an even more serious situation soon convulsed the Sioux country.

General Sheridan had decided that a new military post must be constructed in the heart of the Great Sioux Reservation to provide protection for future railroad construction and to counter potential Sioux raids along the frontier. He reasoned, "By holding an interior point in the heart of the Indian country we could threaten the villages and stock of the Indians, if they made raids on our settlements." The military selected the Black Hills as the location for the proposed fort, a place of deep religious significance to the Indians. Even if the Sioux had consented to an army installation somewhere on their reservation, they most certainly would not have consented to locating it squarely on the land most sacred to them. In the spring of 1874 Sheridan, with the permission of President Grant and the secretaries of the Interior and War, ordered Lieutenant Colonel George A. Custer to prepare an expedition into the Black Hills to survey for the new fort. Custer, at the head of ten companies of the Seventh Cavalry plus two companies of infantry, left Fort Abraham Lincoln in July and headed southwest across the Great Sioux Reservation toward his destination, the Black Hills. There he spent the summer conducting the survey for General Sheridan. Red Cloud protested the presence of over a thousand soldiers: "I do not like General Custer and all his soldiers going into the Black Hills, as that is the country of the Oglala Sioux." While there, Custer and his men also made a discovery that produced far wider and deeper tremors than Sheridan's fort ever could have. The Custer expedition confirmed speculations that the Black Hills held gold.

Returning to Fort Abraham Lincoln in September 1874, Custer telegraphed word to Denver and Chicago that veins of gold lay in the Black Hills. According to his report, gold was plentiful—veins of it could be found in every hill "from the grass roots down." Exaggerated as it was, his description prompted a resurgence of gold fever. By October the rush to the Black Hills was a stampede. As one miner expressed: "This wealth is hidden away in gorges and is doing the Red Man no good." The Sioux, already provoked by the recent surveying expedition, were enraged when they learned of the large number of prospectors digging in their sacred hills. The Sioux dealt with those they caught personally in a harsh and sometimes deadly manner.

The federal government, faced with a threatening state of affairs on the Great Sioux Reservation, acted quickly. President Grant, by executive proclamation, emphatically directed all miners to leave the reservation. General Sheridan issued orders for troops to intercept and remove, by force if necessary, all whites on the reservation illegally. Commanders promptly dispatched patrols to carry out these orders, but with the lure of gold, however exaggerated, leading them on, violators were not easily deterred. No sooner had the army escorted prospectors off the reservation than they found a different route by which to sneak back to the Black Hills to hunt for gold. The *New York Tribune* summarized the difficulty: "If there is gold in the Black Hills, no army on earth can keep the adventurous men of the west out of them."

Only the onset of winter ended this escapade. But as soon as spring arrived, whites were back again to find gold, dodging army patrols and Indian scouts. The number of prospectors who crossed the Great Sioux Reservation to the Black Hills mounted steadily as spring turned to summer, with no hint that the human flow would diminish. The angry Sioux demanded that the federal government enforce its treaty, remove the white gold hunters, and reimburse them for damage done to their land. "The white man is in the Black Hills just like maggots and I want you to get them out just as quick as you can," the Sioux leader Baptiste Good protested vigorously. "The chief of all thieves [George Custer] made a road into the Black Hills last summer, and I want the Great Father to pay the damages for what Custer has done."

It became evident to officials in Washington that they faced a crisis. Army patrols had been ineffective in keeping Americans out of the reservation. On the other hand, the Sioux, Cheyennes, and Arapahoes were becoming increasingly bitter at repeated treaty violations. It appeared only a matter of time before the Indians would take matters into their own hands and eradicate the prospectors on their land. As Secretary of War William W. Belknap assessed: Recent reports "fore-shadow trouble between the miners and the Indians of the country known as the Black Hills, unless something be done to obtain possession of that section; for the white miners have been strongly attracted there by the reports of rich deposits of the precious metal." The United States government concluded that it could not successfully defend the treaty and territorial rights of the Sioux. Indian Bureau, military, and congressional officials all now agreed that the way to defuse the crisis was to purchase the Black Hills from the Sioux.

In September 1875, a delegation of key congressional and military officials journeyed to the Red Cloud agency to discuss the hoped-for purchase. They also dispatched messengers to request the attendance of Sitting Bull and Crazy Horse, the off-reservation leaders. Sitting Bull and Crazy Horse replied that they would not come to the meeting nor would they authorize the sale of a foot of their land to the United States. "I want you to go and tell the Great Father that I do not want to sell any land to the government," Sitting Bull told the hapless messenger. "Not even this much," he added defiantly, waving a pinch of earth in the man's face. In spite of his intractability, the commissioners confidently believed they could persuade Red Cloud, whom they realized was losing touch with and authority over the younger warriors, to sell the Black Hills. After some preliminary discussions, the proposal was placed before the Sioux. The government offered to lease the Black Hills for $400,000 a year or buy the area for $6 million. The Sioux pondered the matter carefully before offering an opinion. Finally they declared the Americans' offer unacceptable. Government officials and Indians alike realized the futility of further conversation. There was nothing either could do but accept an impasse.

The commissioners, as much embarrassed as enraged, since they had been confident of getting their own way, returned to Washington in a vindictive mood. The United States government had no legal right to chastise the Sioux for refusing to sell the Black Hills. The Fort Laramie Treaty as well as general law made that clear. Yet officials strongly believed that the Sioux, especially those residing off the reservation, must be dealt with sternly and brought fully under the Concentration policy. A meeting of key officials convened at the White House on November 3, 1875. It included President Grant, Interior Secretary Zachariah Chandler, Indian Commissioner Edward Smith, Secretary of War William Belknap, and Generals Philip Sheridan and George Crook. The group approved the withdrawal of all troops from the Black Hills, thus effectively recognizing the possessory rights of the 15,000 miners squatting there. It also decided to take the necessary steps to break the power of the off-reservation Sioux, forcing them from the unceded territory and onto the reservation. The receipt, within a week, of a report by Inspector E. C. Watkins seemed to verify the wisdom of the group's decisions. Watkins, after scrutinizing the Sioux country, noted that off-reservation warriors under Sitting Bull and Crazy Horse terrorized white settlers and Indian tribes along the frontier and now seemed on the verge of a major outbreak of violence. "The true policy, in my judgment," Watkins stated, "is to send troops against them in the winter, the sooner the better, and *whip* them into subjection." The Interior Department agreed and acted immediately. Commissioner Smith issued an ultimatum to all Indians residing in the Sioux's western territory. It required them to come into the Great Sioux Reservation and report to their assigned agency by January 31, 1876. To fail to do so would expose them to military retaliation.

The commissioner's ultimatum was not only illegal, it was also impossible to comply with. By the terms of the Fort Laramie Treaty, neither the Sioux nor the Northern Cheyennes and Arapahoes were confined to the Great Sioux Reservation. Since all the unceded territory was unqualifiedly theirs, they could reside without restriction in any part of it. The demand to come into the reservation was, moreover, a near impossibility because of the desperately harsh winters in the area. Even if the off-reservation bands had desired to comply with the ultimatum, which none did, only the most foolhardy would have braved the elements to make the journey at that time of year. The deadline of January 31, 1876, came and went without compliance. No one in the unceded territory moved. Some consciously refused, others never heard of the ultimatum until the deadline had passed, still others never received word of it at all. On February 1, 1876, the War Department, upon the recommendation of the Interior Department, proclaimed that henceforth they considered all Sioux, Northern Cheyennes, and Northern Arapahoes not residing on the Great Sioux Reservation as hostile and in a state of war against the United States. It thus turned matters over to General Philip Sheridan and the United States Army on February 7. The "Great Sioux War," the final major engagement of the Plains Wars, was underway.

The Last Great Struggle

To defeat the Sioux and concentrate them permanently on the Great Sioux Reservation, General Sheridan again elected the tactic of convergence. William T. Sherman summarized the operation: "General Sheridan determined to proceed . . . systematically, by concentric movements, similar to those which in 1874–1875 [in the Red River War] had proved so successful at the south against the hostile Comanches, Kiowas, and Cheyennes." Sheridan planned a three-pronged encircling offensive against the people residing in the Bighorn Mountain area. General Alfred Terry was to move west from Fort Abraham Lincoln along the Yellowstone River, continuing through the northern part of the Sioux's western territory until reaching Rosebud Creek. Colonel John Gibbon at the same time was to move southward from Fort Ellis, Montana. His march would intercept the Yellowstone, and from there he was to push eastward along that river until his forces met Terry's at the mouth of Rosebud Creek. Finally, General George Crook was to start at Fort Fetterman on the North Platte River and thrust northward up the old Bozeman Trail until his troops joined with the other two wings of the assault. If Sheridan's strategy succeeded, all the "hostiles" would be trapped among the converging prongs and systematically destroyed.

Sheridan hoped to invade the Sioux country immediately, again using winter as his ally. "Unless they are caught before early spring," he assessed, "they cannot be caught at all." But his winter campaign failed to develop satisfactorily. Of the three columns of the invasion force, only Crook's engaged the off-reservation Indians before spring. Deep snows prevented Terry's forces from leaving Fort Lincoln on schedule, while it took Gibbon until early April to establish a supply depot at the junction of the Bighorn and Yellowstone rivers, and then his troops were unable to find any Indians in the vicinity.

In March, General George Crook led a large expedition into the Powder River country. On March 17, three companies of cavalry under Colonel Joseph J. Reynolds assaulted a Cheyenne and Sioux camp of 100 lodges, situated on the Powder River directly east of the Bighorn Mountains and just to the northeast of the former Fort Phil Kearny. Two Moon, Old Bear, Little Wolf, Maple Tree, and White Bull were the Cheyenne leaders. The Oglala chief He Dog led the Sioux. Reynolds's onslaught took the camp absolutely by surprise. As one old man sounded the alarm, "The soldiers are right here! The soldiers are right here!" Reynolds's men charged through the line of tepees. Warriors frantically grabbed their weapons and rallied to defend the women, children, and elders. Although driven from their camp, the Indians counterattacked and after a pitched battle repelled the soldiers. Nonetheless, the fight had destroyed the camp and left its inhabitants with little else than what they had on their backs. "Our tepees were burned with everything in them," Wooden Leg lamented, describing the plight he shared with all others of the camp. "I had nothing left but the clothing I had on." With the temperature well below freezing, Two Moon and the other chiefs sought refuge with Crazy Horse and his Sioux, encamped three days ride to the northeast. "I'm glad you are come," Crazy Horse declared, welcoming Two Moon upon his arrival. "We are going to fight the white men again." "All right, I am ready to fight," the Cheyenne chief replied. "I have fought already. My people have been killed, my horses stolen. I am satisfied to fight." An acute uneasiness over another attack by the army prompted Crazy Horse, within a week, to move the group farther north to Sitting Bull's camp alongside the Little Bighorn River, where they were generously received.

News of Reynolds's attack spread quickly throughout the Big-horn Mountain region, and from there to the Great Sioux Reservation where the Sioux greeted it with an increased resolve to defend their territory against American incursion. The events of the past months had renewed old fears and old animosities. The United States government was acting with such obvious duplicity that even those who had wanted to believe peace possible now joined the off-reservation Indians. Meanwhile, Sheridan ordered his forces into the field for a summer campaign, permitting his department commanders wide discretionary powers in developing field strategy for the operation. "I have given no instructions to Gens. Crook or Terry," Sheridan reported to Sherman, "as I think it would be unwise to make any combinations in such a country as they will have to operate in. As hostile Indians, in any great number, cannot keep the field as a body for a week or at most ten days, I therefore consider—and so do Terry and Crook—that each column will be able to take care of itself, and of chastising the Indians should it have the opportunity." General Alfred Terry and his 1,200 soldiers set out on May 17 from Fort Abraham Lincoln, Dakota Territory. The main attack force consisted of the Seventh Cavalry under George Armstrong Custer. At the same time, Colonel John Gibbon's columns, equal in size to Terry's, were patrolling the Yellowstone River waiting to rendezvous with Terry. By early June the two columns met according to plan at the mouth of Rose-bud Creek on the Yellowstone. Their responsibility was to intercept the fleeing Indians whom General Crook pressured northward.

Crook moved first. Since the battle at the Powder River he had remained immobilized for almost two months at his supply base in northern Wyoming. In May the general again ordered his troops up the old Bozeman Trail to engage the Sioux and their allies. Arriving in the Bighorn Mountain country, Crook sent out Crow and Shoshoni scouts to locate the camp of the "hostiles." The Crows and Shoshonis were willing to assist the army in this operation against the Sioux, their long-standing enemy. Unable to retaliate successfully against the powerful Sioux for conquering their lands in the Bighorn region and elsewhere earlier in the century, the Crows and Shoshonis eagerly looked forward to the Americans exacting the measure of revenge that the two tribes could not inflict. The scouts brought back a report in early June. A large camp of Sioux and Cheyennes lay a day and a half to the north. Crook made immediate plans to attack. On the morning of June 16 he moved his troops forward, anticipating an assault on the camp within two days.

If Crook expected to profit by surprise, he was to be disappointed—Sitting Bull's scouts had the troops under continuous surveillance. The Hunkpapa chief and spiritual leader was determined to keep the soldiers far enough away to preclude an attack on his camp. When Crook reached the Rosebud, Crazy Horse took the offensive. Just after dawn on June 17, 1876, Sioux and Cheyenne warriors directed a massive assault against Crook. A savage fight raged throughout the entire day. At times the fighting was in scattered areas where hand-to-hand combat prevailed; at other times the adversaries locked together in frontal assaults. Neither side obtained a decisive advantage. Many times Crazy Horse rushed to the front of his warriors, exhorting them with the cry, "Come on Lakota [Teton Sioux], it's a good day to die!" At one critical juncture in the fight, Crow and Shoshoni auxiliaries of the U.S. Army prevented Crook's troops from being overrun by the Sioux and Cheyenne warriors. By dusk, the combatants ceased fighting. Although Crook possessed the battlefield and would claim victory in the engagement, the Sioux and the Cheyennes emerged as the emotional victors of the Battle of the Rosebud by having prevented an American assault on their camp. The next morning General Crook, recognizing that he needed reinforcements before again engaging the determined Indians, retreated to his supply base. The Indians, meanwhile, returned to their camp on the Little Bighorn to celebrate their victory, unaware of an even stronger American force massed to the north at the mouth of Rosebud Creek.

General Terry, unaware of Crook's setback, sent Major Marcus A. Reno, second in command of the Seventh Cavalry, with six companies to scout for the hostiles. Eight days later they returned with news that Sitting Bull's camp appeared to be located between the Bighorn and Little Bighorn rivers, about fifty miles to the southwest of the army's position. With this information, Terry decided upon a circling tactic to trap the Indians. He and Gibbon would move thirty miles west until they reached the mouth of the Bighorn, then they would march southward down that river to Sitting Bull's camp. At the same time, Colonel Custer would move the Seventh Cavalry in a parallel line along Rosebud Creek before swinging westward around the southern edge of the Wolf Mountains. From there he was to follow the Bighorn River northward until he too reached Sitting Bull's camp. Terry ordered both columns to time their movements to reach their destinations simultaneously and thus assault the Sioux and Cheyennes in force. Custer, after receiving his orders, sent a note to his wife, Elizabeth. "Do not be anxious about me," he comforted, trying to reassure her that he soon would return home to her. "A success will start us all toward [Fort Abraham] Lincoln" (where the Custers resided).

On the evening of June 24, after two days of marching up Rosebud Creek, the Seventh Cavalry made camp. The troopers were at ease, confident in their belief that it would still be a couple of days before they linked up with Terry and Gibbon to initiate the assault aimed at destroying the hostiles. Their repose was cut short. After dusk, Crow and Arikara scouts came to Custer's tent and informed him that a large encampment lay fifteen miles almost directly west of them in the valley of the Little Bighorn. This could only be Sitting Bull's camp, the Seventh Cavalry's target, thought Custer. Fearing that Sioux scouts might already have detected his approach and sounded the warning for the camp's inhabitants to flee, Custer decided to attack his target without delay. Quickly he roused his weary troops for a night march. The cavalry marched half the night until exhaustion and poor visibility forced a halt until daybreak. But the men were up again and on the move as the sun rose on Sunday, June 25, 1876.

George Custer, never lacking in boldness, did not attempt to disguise his movement as the Seventh Cavalry steadily approached Sitting Bull's substantial camp. Instead of approximately 1,000 warriors expected by the army, at least double that number, with their families, resided in the camp, which stretched for nearly three miles along the west bank of the Little Bighorn. Within it were the Cheyennes of Two Moon, Lame White Man, Dirty Moccasins, and other chiefs, as well as more than a half dozen bands of Sioux under the direction of hardened and skilled war leaders, including Gall, Lame Deer, Hump, Sitting Bull, and Crazy Horse. A few Arapahoes also were present.

Crossing the Wolf Mountains about noon, the cavalry followed a stream (now named Reno Creek) westward that led directly to Sitting Bull's camp. Custer's next move, from a military point of view, was questionable: he divided his forces into four parts. Custer's unit of 225 soliders and Reno's of 112 soldiers with twenty-five Indian scouts and three white scouts constituted the first two battalions. They would strike the encampment. Custer ordered a third battalion of 125 men, under the command of Captain Frederick Benteen, to scout to the south and intercept all fleeing Indians. A fourth group, with the pack train and its accompanying 130 soldiers, bore the extra ammunition and supplies. That day it lagged several miles behind Custer's and Reno's columns.

In the early afternoon, Custer ordered Reno and his men forward to invade the southern end of the camp where the Hunkpapa lodges were located. Marcus Reno, after the attack began, was overcome by intense anxiety, a foreboding shared by his troops and the Indian scouts, many of whom now deserted the Americans. Their forebodings were justified as a massive wave of Sioux warriors counterattacked from the front and both flanks. The Sioux leader Gall, who had lost two of his wives and three of his children to Reno's assault, led the attack with vengeance. "It [the loss of his family] made my heart bad," he recounted a decade later. "After that I killed all my enemies with the hatchet." The soldiers dismounted and took cover as best they could in the nearby trees and sagebrush. From this position they tried desperately to fend off the onslaught. For over an hour the battle raged; half of Reno's men became casualties. Finally the Sioux routed the soldiers, chasing them south and east to the bluffs above the Little Bighorn where they frantically dug in using knives, cups, and spoons. Most of the shovels were with the pack train, an hour's ride behind them. Then suddenly, to the soldiers' amazement, most of the Sioux hurried off toward the north, where the sound of heavy gunfire could be heard. Major Reno realized that Custer's forces were in that general direction, but he did not know that they faced a situation worse than his own. Soon Captain Benteen arrived, after having scouted to the south, to reinforce Reno. At the sound of intense fighting Benteen and his men had returned to the area. "For God's sake help me, Benteen," the frantic Reno screamed as the reinforcements arrived, "I've lost half my men!" The two groups, unable to withdraw because of continuing enemy fire, remained trapped on the hill the rest of the afternoon and night.

At the same time that Major Reno launched his invasion against the southern end of Sitting Bull's camp, Custer led his men into battle. After ordering Reno forward, Custer and his command trailed behind him for about two miles before turning off to head northward along the towering bluffs overlooking the east bank of the Little Bighorn. On their left and down the steep escarpment they saw ravines leading to the wooded banks of the river. Across it they spied the camp of Sitting Bull, obviously a very large one. As they marched, Custer's units were under careful scrutiny: from the people in the camp, from Cheyenne warriors lying in wait beyond their lodges at the camp's north end, and from Sioux warriors hidden in the ravines past which the Seventh Cavalry rode.

As the soldiers neared a point directly across the river from the camp's northern end, Custer moved his troops into the formation from which they would charge. But before the Seventh Cavalry could advance, the Sioux hidden in the ravines broke over the ridge and attacked from the rear. As the soldiers wheeled to defend themselves, Sioux and Cheyenne led by Crazy Horse and Two Moon swooped in from the north, overwhelming them. Now, with the stunned Americans turned to face both assaults, a third wave of Sioux, recently freed from the engagement at the southern end of the camp, poured into the fight. Gall, who had led the mauling of Reno, was at their head. On that scorching afternoon, as warriors swarmed over Custer's defenses—"like a hurricane," remembered the Sioux chief Kill Eagle, "like bees swarming out of a hive"— the outcome could only be disastrous. Custer and all of his men perished after perhaps an hour of fighting in a dusty, choking cloud. "Where the last stand was made," said Sitting Bull in an interview given in Canada the following year detailing Custer's final moments, "the Long Hair stood like a sheaf of corn with all the ears fallen around him." Black Elk, the Oglala Sioux holy man, recalled how he felt as a thirteen-year-old boy witnessing the defeat of the Seventh Cavalry at the Battle of the Little Bighorn. "I was not sorry at all. I was a happy boy. Those Wasichus [white men] had come to kill our mothers and fathers and us, and it was our country."

Early the next morning the Sioux and Cheyennes pursued their attack against Reno's and Benteen's position; but by noon their assault slackened and, much to the soldiers' relief, the Indians began to dismantle their camp and move off toward the south. By dusk they had completely withdrawn from the area. The reason for their withdrawal soon became clear. Earlier in the day, Sioux scouts had detected a large body of soldiers to the north, moving toward Sitting Bull's camp. The troops spotted were those of Terry and Gibbon, who had waited only nine miles away throughout the Battle of the Little Bighorn for Custer's message telling them of his location and the speed of his movement. When no word arrived by June 26, the columns continued the march toward Sitting Bull's camp, reaching their destination the following morning, Tuesday, June 27. They rescued Reno, Benteen, and the survivors of their companies and found the battlefield where Custer and his command perished. "It is marked by the remains of his officers and men and the bodies of his horses, some of them strewed along the path, others heaped where halts appear to have been made," General Terry recorded that day. The sight appalled both the troops and their commanders: "a scene of sickening, ghastly horror," one soldier recalled after viewing the corpses littering the battlefield, some of whom were stripped and mutilated. Within several days, the entire nation shared their feelings.

"To Conquer a Lasting Peace"

News of "Custer's Last Stand" shocked a disbelieving American public on July 6, 1876, in the midst of the republic's jubilant celebration of its centennial. Philip Sheridan and many of the military's senior hierarchy learned of the Battle of the Little Bighorn while in Philadelphia attending the centennial exposition dedicated to the theme "A Century of Progress." At first Sheridan refused to believe the initial Associated Press wire story. The arrival of General Alfred Terry's confidential report left no doubt about the annihilation of Custer and his five companies. The nation clamored for revenge against the Indians.

But not everyone exonerated Custer. "We admire the gallantry of General Custer and his men," a commentator editorialized in *The Nation* magazine, "but who shall blame the Sioux for defending themselves?" General Terry's report clearly attributed the fiasco at the Little Bighorn to Custer's egregious conduct. "Custer's action is inexplicable in the case," Terry asserted. That his analysis was overwhelmingly correct was the least of the public's concern. The legend and the mystique of George Armstrong Custer—the martyred American hero, immortality secured through utter defeat—had already been born. "Victory that day on the Little Bighorn would have made Custer the historical equivalent of a Nelson A. Miles: an important frontier officer, certainly, but not a figure to command the popular imagination," wrote scholar Brian W. Dippie about the myth-making process surrounding the Custer legend. The legend is laced with irony, too, as Dippie further noted: "Defeat brought immortality. Custer's Last Stand: the very words still conjure up an unforgettable image of a soldier at bay, surrounded and doomed, winning lasting fame by failing to win a battle."

Tributes were fast in coming. *The New York Tribune,* for example, published Walt Whitman's "A Death Sonnet for Custer" on July 10, four days after news of the battle reached the American public:

> There in the far northwest, in struggle, charge, and sabre-smite,
> Desperate and glorious—aye, in defeat most desperate,
>   most glorious,
> After thy many battles, in which, never yielding up a gun or a color,
> Leaving behind thee a memory sweet to soldiers, Thou yieldest up
>   thyself.

The Custer legend continued to grow in the years following his death. Elizabeth Custer, widow of the fallen commander of the Seventh Cavalry, became a key person responsible for molding and defending it. Outliving George Custer by almost fifty-seven years, she published a popular three-volume reminiscence depicting the "Boy General" in the most positive terms: a gallant and courageous soldier, a caring, faithful, and sensitive spouse. *Boots and Saddles, or Life in Dakota with General Custer* appeared in 1885; *Following the Guidon* in 1890; and her third and concluding volume *Tenting on the Plains, or Gen'l Custer in Kansas and Texas* in 1893. If popular acceptance is any measure, Elizabeth Custer succeeded in nurturing and enlarging her husband's legend, as well as defending it against critics both in and out of the military, who characterized George Custer as an impetuous, ambitious, vainglorious officer who recklessly led his troops to annihilation.

Humiliated by the Battle of the Little Bighorn, the army clamored for swift retaliation. Stunned by the death of his young protégé, General Sheridan immediately prepared to invade the Sioux country again. First he ordered his soldiers to dismount and disarm all Indians at the Cheyenne River, Red Cloud, and Standing Rock agencies. Then dispatching substantial reinforcements to Montana, Sheridan ordered Terry and Crook into the Bighorn Mountain country to crush the Indians between their columns. Much to the chagrin of the invading forces, they were unable to find many Indians to crush. The army spent the remainder of the fall searching with little success for the vanished hostiles. The Sioux and Cheyennes, moving in small bands, successfully eluded the soldiers, anticipating that if they could sustain themselves until winter, the army might give up its hunt. They had not counted on the unwavering resolve of Philip Sheridan. The general, a man not easily deterred from his goals nor discouraged by the military's recent lack of success, merely changed his strategy. He selected another of his time-tested tactics: a winter campaign. Two years earlier, in the Red River War, Sheridan had destroyed the southern plains tribes' resistance to the Concentration policy with this strategy. He saw no reason why it should not succeed against the northern plains tribes, too. He realized the campaign would not result in one decisive battlefield victory as much as it would wear down the enemies through relentless pursuit and force them to surrender. "I have never looked on any decisive battle with these Indians as a settlement of the trouble," Sheridan informed Sherman. "Indians do not fight such battles; they only fight boldly when they have the advantage, as in the Custer case, or to cover the movement of their women and children as in the case of Crook on June 17 [the Battle of the Rosebud], but Indians have scarcely ever been severely punished unless by their own mode of warfare or tactics."

The winter campaign began in November of 1876, and it caught the Indians off guard. Conditions were excruciating for Indians and federal troops, in part because of blizzards, piles of drifting snow, and sub-zero temperatures. One soldier recalled the depravations: "Beards, moustaches, eye-lashes and eye-brows were frozen masses of ice. The keen air was filled with minute crystals, each cutting the tender skin like a razor, while feet and hands ached as if beaten with clubs. Horses and mules shivered while they stood in column, their flanks white with crystals of perspiration congealed on their bodies, and their nostrils bristling with icicles." The winter campaign of 1876–1877 completely wore down the Indians, as Sheridan had anticipated. "What have we done that the white people want us to stop?" Sitting Bull asked in the face of the troops who pursued relentlessly. "We have been running up and down this country, but they follow us from one place to another." The army engaged the Cheyennes, first and, as might have been expected, the soldiers were completely victorious. The government sent many of the survivors who turned themselves in south to the Indian Territory and placed them on the Cheyenne-Arapahoe reservation. The army engaged the Sioux next. Those who escaped the soldiers returned to their reserve by the spring. However, Sitting Bull and Gall avoided capture, and, with a small group of followers, fled to Canada in February 1877. Over the next few years, hunger and loneliness convinced many Sioux to slip back to the reservation and surrender. Sitting Bull did not return to the United States until 1881. On July 19 of that year he surrendered at Fort Buford, Montana. "I wish it to be remembered that I was the last man of my tribe to surrender my rifle," Sitting Bull declared to Major David H. Brotherton, as the Sioux chief handed his Winchester to his son, asking him to present it to the officer, "and this day have given it to you."

Only Crazy Horse escaped defeat in the winter campaign. Starving but proud and unbeaten, he brought his 800 followers into Fort Robinson, Nebraska, in May 1877. He perhaps best exemplified those Indians absolutely dedicated to resisting the United States' Concentration policy. Besides being alarmed, even frightened, by the depth and vehemence of his convictions, most whites found his strident demeanor offensive. "This incorrigible wild man," as one agent described Crazy Horse during his tenure at Fort Robinson, was "silent, sullen, lordly and dictatorial." He and his band finally submitted because General George Crook promised to secure them an agency on the Tongue River if they laid down their arms. But again they were to be frustrated. Officials in Washington refused to sanction the agreement. After learning that Washington had backed off of the agreement, Crazy Horse prepared to leave Fort Robinson for the Powder River country. Before he could leave, however, Crook ordered troops from the fort and Indian police to place Crazy Horse under arrest. Protesting their efforts to disarm him and take him into custody, Crazy Horse, true to form, resisted. In doing so, he received a mortal stab wound. It remains a matter of contention whether the perpetrator was a soldier or an Indian. Major H. R. Lemly, witness to the chief's final hours, recorded the scene:

In a weak and tremulous voice, he broke into the weird and now-famous death song of the Sioux. Instantly there were two answering calls from beyond the line of pickets, and Big Bat told me they were from Crazy Horse's old father and mother, who begged to see their dying son. I had no authority to admit them, and resisted their appeal, piteous as it was, until Crazy Horse fell back with the death-gurgle in his throat.

Crazy Horse died that evening, September 5, 1877. "It is good," one Miniconjou chief remarked at the Oglala's passing, "he has looked for death, and it has come." The following day soldiers released the remains to his parents. A horse-drawn travois transported Crazy Horse's body, placed in a wooden box, to Spotted Tail agency where, in the traditional fashion, the Sioux set it upon a burial scaffold.

With the fall of Crazy Horse, the self-imposed exile of Sitting Bull, and the crushing defeat sustained by the Sioux and the Cheyennes, the last possibility for armed resistance to the policy of Concentration by Indians on the northern plains ended. Sheridan's winter campaign had been overwhelmingly successful. One of the first actions of the United States shortly after the defeat of Custer at the Little Bighorn was to seize large portions of the landholdings that the Fort Laramie Treaty of 1868 had safeguarded to the Sioux and Cheyennes. First the government confiscated the Black Hills, with its billions of dollars in mineral wealth, then the Indians' unceded territory: the Bighorn Mountain and Powder River regions. Following the Sioux War and the shattering of the Sioux and Northern Cheyenne nations, the United States altered the western boundary of the Great Sioux Reservation from the 104th to the 103rd meridian and appropriated rich reservation land between the forks of the Cheyenne River, thus reducing the reserve by roughly a third. The United States also evicted the Sioux from Nebraska. In the 1880s, the government divided the Great Sioux Reservation into five smaller ones. Standing Rock reservation straddled the border of North and South Dakota. Directly to its south was Cheyenne River reservation, while to the southeast lay the Crow Creek reserve with the Missouri River flowing through its center. West of the Missouri, nestled along the southern border of South Dakota, sat the Rosebud and Pine Ridge reservations.

The Oglala Red Cloud offered his summation of the policy of Concentration and the efforts of the United States to solve the Indian question by that policy. Most other Indians probably would have shared his sentiment. Tinged with what for him must have been painful irony—for he was the only Plains Indian leader to defeat the United States in war, and his victory had forced the federal authority to offer generous terms in the Fort Laramie Treaty of 1868—Red Cloud concluded ruefully: "They made us many promises, more than I can remember, but they never kept but one. They promised to take our land, and they took it."

The struggle of arms between the United States and the Indians to realize, then enforce, the policy of Concentration effectively ended by 1877, leaving the government in complete control. The wars of Grant's "peace policy," wars conducted "to conquer a lasting peace," had destroyed the last vestige of self-determination of the once powerful tribes who had resisted the Concentration policy and who once dominated the middle of America. Now their lives would be devoted to adapting to a new and alien lifestyle: one of absolute confinement on a reservation. The army's job became easier following the Red River and the Great Sioux wars, with nearly all of its former adversaries restricted to reservations and relegated to the status of wards of the United States government. The primary responsibility of soldiers became rounding up those Indians who refused to report to, or remain on, their reservations. Occasional clashes still broke out, but they arose generally between individuals and usually ended quickly. The army clearly had the upper hand.

The final actions concluded in 1886 when Geronimo, the last to resist the policy of Concentration, surrendered to General Nelson A. Miles following brilliant campaigning by General George Crook. Geronimo, with a small following of Chiricahua Apaches, had hidden in the mountains of Arizona and New Mexico. For a while he effectively fought off a much larger federal force. Like a few other Indian groups, the Apaches briefly captured the imagination of the nation, and their leader Geronimo is probably one of a half dozen Indians recognized by name by the American public. As increasing attrition, weariness, and military pressure overcame them, these Apaches could not continue the fight. Following his surrender at Skeleton Canyon, Arizona, on September 4, 1886, federal officials sent Geronimo and nearly 500 Apache followers to a military prison at Fort Pickens in Pensacola, Florida.

The end of the Indian wars in 1877 concluded one long chapter of United States–Indian relations and began another. Spanning almost three decades, the United States first had fashioned, then implemented and enforced the policy of Concentration to solve the Indian question. The responsibility for inaugurating the new era fell to President Rutherford B. Hayes, who took office in March

1877. Even though the government had realized the Concentration policy, it proved to be neither the panacea nor the permanent solution Americans expected and predicted it to be. The end of the Indian wars raised an issue of great magnitude, too. The president was acutely aware of this: "How best can we aid them [the Indians]?" Hayes pondered in his diary. "How to deal with them is a problem which for nearly three centuries has remained almost unsolved." The answer to his introspective query proved elusive, as his eighteen predecessors had discovered before him. The United States government's search for the solution to the Indian question still had not ended.

The Wise Ones said we might have their religion, but when we tried to understand it we found that there were too many kinds of religion among white men for us to understand, and that scarcely any two white men agreed which was the right one to learn. This bothered us a good deal until we saw that the white man did not take his religion any more seriously than he did his laws, and that he kept both of them just behind him, like Helpers, to use when they might do him good in his dealings with strangers. These were not our ways. We kept the laws we made and lived our religion. We have never been able to understand the white man, who fools nobody but himself.

PLENTY-COUPS, CROW

The Search for a New Order

The year 1877 marked an important juncture in the history of United States–Indian relations. Centuries of struggle and armed conflict between the two races, culminating in the Plains Wars of the 1860s and 1870s, ended shortly after Rutherford B. Hayes's inauguration. The Great Sioux War, the last major conflict to enforce the policy of Concentration, and the mauling of George Armstrong Custer at the Little Bighorn, lay less than a year in the past. The crushing defeat sustained by the Sioux and their allies marked the end of Indian military power. Destroyed was the Indians' ability to defend and sustain their accustomed way of life and resist the Concentration policy through force of arms. By the spring of 1877, as Hayes commenced his duties as the nation's chief executive, the Indians had been humbled. Their military power was broken, never to revive; their lands were drastically reduced; many Indian leaders were confined in federal prison; the remnants of a fiercely independent people were reduced to emotional, cultural, and material bankruptcy on reservations. Although minor conflicts would continue into the early twentieth century, President Hayes correctly notified Congress in his first annual message that "after a series of most deplorable conflicts . . . we are now at peace with all Indian tribes within our borders."

The issue of how to govern the Indians in the aftermath of the Indian wars and to provide for their well-being demanded the immediate attention of the government. The challenge was clear: what policy should guide relations between the United States and the Indians in the transition between war and peace? The question excited much interest, both in government and among the general public. In response, Thorndyke Rice, editor of the *North American Review,* requested that General Nelson A. Miles write an article giving his views on the subject. Miles suggested that "the real issue [is to] devise some ways of still improving the practical and judicious system by which we can govern a quarter of a million of our population, secure and maintain their loyalty, raise them from the darkness of barbarism to the light of civilization, and put an end forever to these interminable and expensive Indian wars." Although the challenge was clear, the solution proved elusive and difficult.

The necessity of developing an effective and positive Indian policy in the aftermath of the Indian wars was underscored by a feeling of urgency. Those who were aware of the state of Indian life—the terrible conditions on western reservations, the distressing sense of dislocation among tribes, the near nonexistent means for them to provide for their needs by accustomed methods—feared for their survival. "The civilization or the utter destruction of the Indians is inevitable," surmised John Q. Smith in 1876, President Grant's fourth and last Indian commissioner. "If they cannot be taught, and taught very soon to accept the necessities of their situation and begin in earnest to provide for their own wants by labor in civilized pursuits," he predicted, "they are destined to speedy extinction."

The Hayes administration was the first to grapple with the Indian question following the era of warfare. The president himself characterized the transition period as an era "when old questions are settled, and the new are not yet brought forward." Although the agenda his administration advanced was not translated into an effective, a well-defined program until after Hayes's term of office, it followed a direction that evolved into the Indian policy of the United States for the next half century: the policy of Americanization.

Reforms and Jurisdictional Disputes

President Hayes realized that crucial to the success or failure of his administration's handling of Indian affairs was the individual appointed secretary of the Interior, for that official's jurisdiction included supervisory responsibility over the Indian commissioner and the Indian Bureau. Hayes selected Carl Schurz of Missouri to fill the post. Liberal Republican, outspoken critic of the rampant corruption in Grant's administration, and long-time champion of civil service reform, Schurz served with distinction in his cabinet post. With the support of the president, he introduced entrance examinations for civil servants (a constructive measure to dispense with the long tradition of patronage) and initiated conservation of the nation's forest resources. Of all the responsibilities under Schurz's jurisdiction, Indian affairs proved the most frustrating and involved him in the most controversy. The secretary knew almost nothing of the Indians and their problems upon assuming his post, but to his credit he labored diligently to educate himself on these matters. Journalist and historian Henry Adams, writing to Henry Cabot Lodge in December 1877, remarked of Schurz's singleminded determination, that "lumber and Indians are his sole mental food just at the present." Schurz's policies were instrumental in reforming the Indian Bureau, ridding the Indian service of incompetent and corrupt officials, maintaining civilian control of the service, and attending to the substantive problems of the Indian question in the aftermath of the era of warfare.

For years Carl Schurz had preached reform, and now as Interior secretary he had a chance to practice it. Rampant political graft and corruption, combined with the executive irresponsibility of Ulysses S. Grant, had driven the prestige of the presidency to one of its lowest levels in history. President Hayes's insistence upon efficient management and clean government quickly brought the Bureau of Indian Affairs under close scrutiny. Perhaps of all federal departments and bureaus, Indian Affairs was in greatest need of housecleaning. Almost from its inception in 1824 it was notorious for fraud, corruption, and inefficiency. Over the years, as the Bureau fell increasingly under the domain of political patronage, these problems were exacerbated. Agents were partisan appointees, often of unscrupulous character. They, in turn, distributed the spoils associated with their posts, often appointing subordinates who were minimally qualified at best. Patronage seekers clamored for Indian service positions, hoping to satiate their rapacity and lust for "honest graft" through readily available opportunities. General Henry Heth, who served as an inspector in the Indian service, commented about agents: "The Indian Bureau has been made the dumping ground for the sweepings of the political party that is in power." Episcopal Bishop Henry B. Whipple agreed. "They [Indian agents] are often men without any fitness, sometimes a disgrace to a Christian nation; whiskey sellers, barroom loungers, debauchees, selected to guide heathen people," charged this Indian rights advocate whom the Indians called "Straight Tongue." A job in the Indian service, as everyone realized, provided a cornucopia of opportunity for graft. Too many agents, earning an annual salary of a couple thousand dollars, banked outrageous sums of money during their service. One Indian recalled: "When he [the agent] come he bring everything in a little bag, when he leaves it take two steamboats to carry away his things." So riddled with corruption was the Indian service that Secretary Schurz lamented that "a thoroughly competent, honest, and devoted Indian agent is . . . so rare a jewel that . . . nothing could induce me to part with him."

President Hayes clearly recognized the pressing need to reform the Indian Bureau and to employ trained, honest, and efficient personnel. In his first annual address he affirmed the need for immediate reform and strongly supported Schurz's efforts. The secretary had acted with dispatch after assuming his cabinet post. To study the Indian Bureau in action, he made a six-week tour of the Indian Territory. The trip convinced him that the situation was even worse than he had feared. Schurz immediately ordered a full investigation of the Bureau, Indian agencies, and the agents' business methods. He appointed a board of three individuals—one each from the Justice, Interior, and War departments—to investigate. He also ordered Indian Commissioner Smith to assess the Bureau. Smith, in his report to Schurz, assured him that "I know of no custom in the Bureau which can properly be termed an abuse." The Inquiry Board came to a different conclusion. It discovered evidence of widespread inefficiency, manipulation, fraud, and other irregularities, including unethical activities by Commissioner Smith and the chief clerk, S. A. Galpin. The board's report, submitted in January 1878, accused the Indian Bureau of "cupidity, inefficiency, and most barefaced dishonesty," and it concluded that the Bureau was "simply a license to cheat and swindle the Indians in the name of the United States." It confirmed the worst suspicions of Hayes and Schurz. Schurz obtained Smith's resignation and dismissed Galpin, as well as the worst of his subordinates. The former commissioner appealed first to Secretary Schurz, who responded: "The fact is, you never knew what was going on in the office under your charge, and your clerks were well aware that you did not know it." A month later, in February 1878, Smith wrote a long letter to Hayes protesting the criticism of his management of the Indian Bureau, but his arguments failed to move the president to reverse the firings.

Next, Secretary Schurz promptly reorganized the Bureau. He ordered the end of nepotism, long a common Indian service hiring practice. All agents who continued to hire relatives were removed. A stricter system of keeping accounts and greater insistence that agents promptly submit their accounts for review was introduced, reducing fraud during the Hayes presidency. And finally, the Bureau for the first time issued a code of regulations outlining appropriate conduct for agents. As part of his housecleaning, Schurz sought a person of high integrity as the new commissioner. He wanted him to be "a man of thorough business training and habits, indefatigable industry, quick judgment and great power of resistance." When the reformer William Welsh declined the post,

Schurz turned to Ezra A. Hayt, a wealthy New York businessman, former chairman of the finance committee of the Board of Foreign Missions of the Reformed Church, and former member of the Board of Indian Commissioners. Although Hayt worked well with Schurz on Indian matters, scandal drove him from office in early 1880.

The reforms implemented by the Hayes administration improved the Indian service and its methods, thus decreasing possible agitation, or even open hostility, by the Indians. The changes so impressed General Philip Sheridan, long experienced with western Indians and corrupt Indian agents, that he fairly crowed, "The service of Indian affairs was finally lifted out of the mire of corruption that had long made it a discredit to our civilization." Schurz likewise was pleased: "I do not pretend that the Indian service, as at present organized, is all that it ought to be. But it has been and is my earnest endeavor to make and keep it as honest and efficient as any other branch of the public service, and I have reason to believe that considerable progress has been made in that direction."

Efforts to reform the Indian service soon brought Carl Schurz into bitter conflict with religious reformers, a conflict that undermined the reforms he had realized. From the earliest white settlement of North America onward, various Christian denominations had labored among the Indians. While the Spanish and the French enjoyed moderate success in the vineyard of saving souls, their British, and later American, counterparts lagged considerably behind in the progress of their own missionary efforts among native groups. The establishment of a network of western reservations in the 1850s and 1860s by the United States under the Concentration policy heartened missionaries, for access to Indians en masse would now be possible. Working together with sympathetic officials in Washington and various secular reform groups dedicated to the destruction of tribal ways and beliefs, missionaries could work industriously on reservations, toiling to transform the Indians into self-supporting, productive Christian Americans.

The fortunes of the missionaries received a bigger boost in 1866. In that year the government granted religious bodies permission to work on federal reserves, not only in the capacity of missionaries of their particular denomination, but as civilian agents of the Indian Bureau. At the same time, concern over rampant corruption within the Indian Bureau and the abuses of political patronage in selecting Indian service agents and administrators spurred religious and secular reformers to seek control over the Indian service and Indian policy. Their efforts were realized, and their influence dramatically increased when, in 1869, Congress authorized the ten-member Board of Indian Commissioners, whose members epitomized the evangelical religious attitudes of the nineteenth century.

The Board of Indian Commissioners, in theory, represented all Christian denominations, but trouble quickly arose when no Roman Catholics were appointed to the Board, although that church had been more active in the Indian mission field than any other denomination. The Roman Catholic Church also had contributed more than half of the funds for missions on reservations. The intense anti-Catholic sentiment of the nation also affected the low number of agencies assigned to the Roman Catholic Church, relative to those awarded to Protestant denominations, even though Grant's guidelines recommended that an agency should be assigned to the missionary sect that already worked there among the Indians. The Church pointed out, to little avail, that of the ninety-four initial agency appointments, Catholic missionaries were awarded only 7, or less than 8 percent of those available. Consequently, in 1874 a central Catholic agency was established in Washington, D.C., and five years later the Bureau of Catholic Indian Missions emerged in answer to the Protestant-controlled Board of Indian Commissioners. The Bureau of Catholic Indian Missions monitored Catholic missions and acted as agent to the federal government. The best account of Catholic activities and the problems encountered by that church is Peter J. Rahill, *Catholic Indian Missions and Grant's Peace Policy, 1870–1884*. Once Carl Schurz became secretary of the Interior, the Catholic Church pressed its demands with him for religious freedom on the reservations.

Religious reformers expected the Hayes administration to be as supportive of their efforts as had Grant's. They had badly misjudged Interior Secretary Schurz. "The present system which permits religious societies to nominate candidates for Indian agencies is, in some respects, undoubtedly an improvement upon the former practice of making appointments . . . on political grounds," he declared. Yet, Schurz vigorously disapproved of the heavy denominational influence on the Indian service and on the shaping of Indian policy for three principal reasons. First, the rancorous competition among sects for Indians' souls and the missionaries' lack of success in their work among the tribes colored his assessment. And Schurz was not the only one unsettled by religious reformers. Indians were too. They observed the ferocious discord among sects and the striking contradictions manifested by the sectarians and their work on reservations. The conflicting dogmas advanced by competing Christian denominations confused Indians, who scorned the obvious disparity between sermons advocating brotherly love and the absence of Christ-like deportment among the battling missionaries. The assessment of Chief Joseph of the Nez Percé provides a good example of the reasoning of many tribal leaders who refused to permit missionaries to work among their people. "They will teach us to quarrel about God as the Catholics and Protestants do," warned Joseph. "We may quarrel with men . . . but we never quarrel about God. We do not want to learn that." Indians scorned equally the hypocrisy of the society that had crushed them and now sent religious representatives to offer instruction in "proper" conduct and lifestyle. "It is your people, who you say have the Great Spirit's book, who bring us the firewater," a Sioux elder retorted acerbically when missionaries sought his permission to toil among the tribe. "It is your white men who corrupt our daughters. Go teach them to do right, and then come to us and I will believe you."

Schurz based the second criticism on his assessment that religious appointees lacked the appropriate business expertise to manage Indian agencies efficiently. The Inquiry Board that Schurz convened in June 1877 to assess the Indian Bureau and its agents reinforced this evaluation. In addition to detailing evidence of widespread abuses, as indicated earlier, the Board also criticized the appointment of agents "because of a sentiment," rather than because of business knowledge and administrative qualifications. The Board offered Schurz a harsh and sarcastic appraisal of religious reformers: "Pigmies [who undertake] the solution of a problem that has engaged the best efforts of statesmen and philanthropists ever since the days of the republic."

Finally, Schurz considered denominational influence and appointments as an unacceptable impingement upon his jurisdiction. Soon after taking the reins of the Interior Department, he moved purposefully to undercut the influence of Christian denominations in the Indian Bureau, the principal feature of Grant's "peace policy." Although accepted practice by 1877, the nomination of agents by religious groups lacked the force of statutory law, providing Schurz the necessary latitude to challenge the practice. The secretary moved quickly to undercut the religious reformers. He ordered the Indian office to assume responsibility for appointing agency clerks and physicians. Before the end of Hayes's first year in office, thirty-five of the seventy-four Indian agents had been replaced. The new policy of widespread replacements and central control under the Interior Department struck a blow to the churches from which they never recovered. When the controversy between Protestants and Catholics over exclusive religious jurisdiction on reservations did not subside, Schurz, in February 1881, ruled that all reservations would be open equally to missionaries of all denominations.

Late in the Hayes presidency churches increased their efforts to regain control of agent appointments, but it was too late. Christian missionaries steadily abandoned work among Indians in favor of a more "challenging" and, so they judged, equally deserving population: Asians, especially the Chinese. The shift in appointments from religious to government nominees ironically played into the hands of politicians and spoilsmen, who desperately hoped to regain their lost influence in the lucrative Indian service. By passing over religious sects to fill Indian Bureau and agent vacancies, the administration was forced to rely instead on political nominees—the "venerable pool of the spoils system." By 1883 and the passage of the Civil Service, or Pendleton, Act, the spoilsmen had nearly regained complete control of appointments to the Indian service. The conflict between Protestants and Catholics did not end here, and, in fact, the period of severest tension peaked between 1888 and 1912 as the two sides battled over control and apportionment of Indian mission schools, as Francis Paul Prucha details in *The Churches and the Indian School, 1888–1912.*

Reappraising the Concentration Policy

The Hayes administration's conduct toward Indians passed through two stages, paralleling a changing of United States Indian policy and its program for solving the Indian question. The first stage, characterized by further implementation of the Concentration policy, gradually shifted to the policy of Americanization, which emphasized "civilizing," then assimilating the Indians into the dominant society, while providing them the means for economic security. Hayes suggested that three principal results would accrue eventually from the Americanization policy. First, the federal government would no longer need to maintain land reserves for Indians or to defend Indians and reservation land from the constant threat of white encroachment. Second, Indians would be made productive, self-sufficient members of American society. And third, the nation's Indian question would, at long last, be solved. At first, however, the Hayes administration followed a well-worn road. The Concentration policy had served as the bedrock of federal Indian management since the early 1850s. The government's insistence on total compliance by western tribes precipitated a series of conflicts known as the Plains Wars. During the Grant presidency, the consensus of opinion was that it would now be in the best interests of both whites and Indians if Indians were consolidated further on smaller land reserves: zones of protection in Indian Territory and in an area on the northern plains for tribes newly displaced by white expansion. Consequently, the government modified the policy of Concentration to reflect a "small reservation approach." By 1877, as Hayes took office, over sixty tribes had been resettled in the Indian Territory, while many more were shifted from their homeland to new locales. Reflecting the frustration caused to tribes by frequent relocation, the Sioux chief Spotted Tail suggested with mock sincerity: "Why does not the Great Father put his red children on wheels, so he can move them as he will?" Yet the small reservation system seemed the best means of minimizing the hostility between Indians and whites, and it was certainly a better alternative to the wars that had reduced the Indians' land and their population. Because of his inexperience in dealing with Indians or in considering the Indian question carefully, Secretary Schurz supported this assumption and built his policy upon it.

Shurz's decision to sustain and further enforce the small reservation approach of the Concentration policy fell hard on Indians, eventually producing yet another round of armed conflict. "The period of tranquillity was not long to continue," lamented General Nelson Miles. "Over the Western Mountains came the rumbling of a coming storm. Another Indian war, or, more strictly speaking, another cruel unjustice, was to be enacted." Resentment by some tribes upon being relocated to smaller and less desirable reserves led to military conflicts with Chief Joseph and his band of Nez Percé in 1877, then against the Utes and the Apaches in 1879. Of the three conflicts, perhaps the most tragic and certainly the one that stirred the greatest public interest and indignation was that with Chief Joseph. More significantly, it became the first of three events that made the United States government begin to move away from the old answer for solving the Indian question.

The traditional domain of the Chopunnish, or Nez Percé, was the valley of the Clearwater River, which flows through the three northwestern states of Oregon, Washington, and Idaho. Their lands, like those of other western tribes, were reduced and defined in the 1850s when the federal government implemented the policy of Concentration (see Chapter Two). By means of a treaty signed at Camp Stevens, Washington Territory, on June 11, 1855, the Nez Percé surrendered one-half of their lands to the United States. The government organized the remaining half into the Lapwai reservation, where it expected the tribe to live and where, by the terms of the treaty, whites were forbidden to enter.

The treaty's provisions were clearly stated; indeed they were much like most other Concentration treaties. Also typical was its violation by whites almost immediately after its implementation. First to arrive were prospectors, after rich gold deposits were discovered on the Lapwai reservation, followed soon by white settlers who erected farms and towns. The Nez Percé, a warm and harmonious people who had always been friendly and helpful to whites, remained peaceful toward the Americans residing on their reservation land. *The Oregon Statesman,* on April 28, 1862, remarked about their commitment to peace. "If open hostilities have not commenced with the Nez Percés, it is not because they have not been outraged to that degree when 'forbearance ceases to be a virtue,'" William Purvine noted in the paper. "In return for the continued friendship in time of want, and generous acts of hospitality, always so readily extended towards the whites by these Indians, they now reap an abundant harvest of every species of villainy and insult." In time, the Nez Percé requested that the federal government enforce its own treaty, even as the Americans who had moved onto the reservation illegally and audaciously demanded that Washington remove the Nez Percé from the reservation's best lands. Per the usual pattern, a subsequent treaty in 1863 opened nearly three-quarters of the reservation to white homesteaders. This new accord shattered the unity of the Nez Percé. Many of the chiefs, led by Old Joseph (father of Chief Joseph), refused to sign the document, seeing in it nothing but futility; the federal government would no more honor these terms than those of the earlier treaty. As a result, some 600 Nez Percé, no longer in possession of any treaty at all, remained on the land of their former reservation.

By the 1870s, pressure from whites was building to force those Nez Percé not bound by a treaty onto the sharply constricted Lapwai reservation. In 1873 President Grant tried to forestall trouble by issuing an executive order setting aside for these Nez Percé a part of their old land in the Wallowa Valley, where no whites could settle. But the protest from Oregonians about Indians still residing on former lands swelled to such intensity that he rescinded the order two years later. A federal peace commission came west in November 1876 to convince these Nez Percé to move onto the Lapwai reservation. The chief with whom they negotiated was Hinmatonyalatkit, or Joseph. Born in 1840, Joseph succeeded his father, Old Joseph, as the leader of those Nez Percé who refused to participate in the renegotiation of the 1855 land cession treaty. Old Joseph died in 1871, but he left his son with a stern admonition: "Always remember that your father never sold his country. You must stop your ears whenever you are asked to sign a treaty selling your home. A few years more, and white men will be all around you. They have their eyes on this land. My son, never forget my dying words. This country holds your father's body. Never sell the bones of your father and your mother." The new Chief Joseph was calm, intelligent, self-assured, and commanding. Although his gentle but egalitarian behavior toward the Americans angered several of the commissioners, they returned to Washington agreeing that his claims were indeed right. Even so, these men were influenced by the ideas of their time, and they accepted Concentration as the best solution to the Indian question. Thus, their report recommended that unless Joseph moved his people to the Lapwai reservation "within a reasonable time," force should be used to relocate them.

Carl Schurz inherited the problem. He realized clearly its source: it springs "from the greedy encroachments of white men upon Indian lands, and that, hostilities being brought about in this manner, in which the Indians uniformly succumbed, old treaties and arrangements were overthrown to be supplanted by new ones of a similar character, which eventually led to the same results." Still, the secretary, secure in his decision to sustain and enforce the small reservation approach, decided to settle the issue without further negotiations. All of the Nez Percé were to be forced onto the reservation. General Oliver Otis Howard, the former head of the Freedmen's Bureau who was known as the "Christian General," now commanded the Department of the Columbia and was given the responsibility of enforcing the government's orders. Howard gave Chief Joseph one month to bring his people into the reservation and warned him that if they were late in arriving there, he would dispatch troops to bring them in forcibly. Joseph tried to reason with Howard. He explained that the deadline would be difficult to meet because of the many newborn animals in his cattle and horse herds. Even nature failed to move Howard to extend his deadline. Some of the cattle and horses had to be left behind, while the rest were rounded up for the journey to the Lapwai reservation.

Along the way trouble ensued when a few young men sought a final measure of revenge on local whites before accepting confinement on the reservation. General Howard immediately sent troops after the Nez Percé, attacking them twice—once in June 1877 at the Clearwater River and again in July in the Big Hole Valley. Even though the Indians repulsed both assaults, Howard's actions convinced the Nez Percé they faced one of two alternatives: war or flight. Following a council, they decided to avoid further conflict, quit the area, and seek haven east of the Rocky Mountains. "I would give up everything," Chief Joseph concluded, "rather than have the blood of my people on my hands." Thus, in late July 1877, 650 Nez Percé embarked on an arduous and dangerous journey over the Rockies.

Joseph expected that once they were outside of Howard's jurisdiction, the general would find no further reason to give chase. The error of this assumption quickly became clear as troopers relentlessly pursued Joseph's band. Throughout the summer of 1877 the Nez Percé traveled over the northern Rockies in an incredible effort to escape the soldiers; under the skilled direction of Looking Glass they eluded and, when necessary, defeated a much larger foe. By mid-September Chief Joseph and his people had swung far enough east to pass through the newly opened Yellowstone National Park. (They almost bumped into General William T. Sherman, who was in the park on a sightseeing tour.) Now more troops joined in the hunt, and for all the adroitness of the Indians, the murderous pace of their pursuers wore down the Nez Percé. Still, they stumbled on to Montana, where they would turn northward toward the Canadian border. In late September they made camp just above Bear Paw Mountain. These men, women, and children had traveled 1,700 miles since June over mountainous terrain, and now they were only thirty miles from Canada—a long day's ride. Had they stopped briefly and then pushed on, they might have made it. Instead, yielding to exhaustion, they rested. The decision proved fatal. Forces under General Nelson A. Miles caught up with them on September 30, blocking the way to Canada. Even though greatly outnumbered, the Nez Percé for the moment held the soldiers at bay.

A heavy snowfall on the first of October lasted for three days. Though the Federals could not fight under the conditions, the Nez Percé could not hope to slip through the cordon of troops to reach Canada. In the interim, the Nez Percé debated their next course of action. Joseph, unwilling to sacrifice the lives of his surviving people, counseled negotiation with the Americans. Looking Glass, who had directed the armed defense of the Nez Percé during their flight, urged a "do-or-die" dash for Canada. The matter was settled shortly after the meeting concluded, when a sniper's bullet struck Looking Glass in the forehead, killing him instantly. On October 4, 1877, Joseph surrendered conditionally to Generals Miles and Howard, who promised him that the Nez Percé would be treated with honor and returned to their homeland. Lieutenant Charles Erskine Scott Wood recorded Chief Joseph's words of capitulation, capturing the mood of tracked desperation felt by the Nez Percé, in their English translation. It became one of the most famous speeches in American history:

I am tired of fighting. Our chiefs are killed. . . . The old men are dead. . . . It is cold and we have no blankets. The little children are freezing to death. My people, some of them, have run away to the hills, and have no blankets, no food. No one knows where they are—perhaps freezing to death. I want to have time to look for my children and see how many I can find. Maybe I shall find them among the dead. Hear me, my chiefs, I am tired; my heart is sick and sad. From where the sun now stands, I will fight no more forever!

Six hundred and fifty Nez Percé had set out in June. Four hundred were taken prisoner and about fifty were able to escape to Canada where Sitting Bull took them in. The remainder had died on the long trek. Howard characterized their flight as "remarkable for the brilliant leadership of an Indian; . . . a feat that is perhaps without parallel in Indian warfare," while Miles stated in his report to Secretary of War George W. McCrary that "the Nez Percé are the boldest and best marksmen of any Indians I have ever encountered, and Chief Joseph is a man of more sagacity and intelligence than any Indian I have ever met." Regardless of the laudatory comments, General Sherman, fully aware of the administration's decision to sustain and further implement Concentration, overrode Miles's and Howard's pledges to return the Nez Percé to the Lapwai reservation in Idaho. Instead, he ordered them transported to the Indian Territory, where over a quarter of them quickly succumbed to malaria and other deleterious effects of the lowland climate. Commissioner Hayt noted matter-of-factly in his 1878 annual report that "the extinction of Joseph's title to the lands he held in Idaho will be a matter of great gain to the white settlers in that vicinity." An embittered Chief Joseph declared: "General Miles promised that we might return to our own country. I believed General Miles, or *I never would have surrendered.*"

In those same years two other tribes, the Bannocks and the Northern Cheyennes, took desperate action because of reservation conditions. Their discontent, Hayes accurately assessed, "appears to have been caused by an insufficiency of food on the reservation, and this insufficiency to have been owing to the inadequacy of the appropriations made by Congress to the want of the Indians at a time when the Indians were prevented from supplying the deficiency by hunting." In the case of the Northern Cheyennes, their exodus in 1878 from the Southern Cheyennes' reserve in the Indian Territory to return to their homeland on the northern plains had the additional impetus of intense homesickness, coupled with wretched conditions.

Following the Great Sioux War of 1876–1877, Washington relocated the Northern Cheyennes, allies of the Sioux in that conflict, in the Indian Territory at the Southern Cheyenne and Arapahoe agency. Here the government intended to force a consolidation of the two branches of the Cheyenne people, melding the northern wing with the southern. The Northern Cheyennes arrived among their kinfolk in the terrible heat of August 1877. Sickness and death, caused by the hot, damp, malarial climate, ravaged these displaced people during the winter of 1877–1878. Little Chief described his people as "homesick and heartsick in every way." The gall of their wretched existence in Indian Territory was made even more bitter by the contempt of the Southern Cheyennes, who scorned the Northern Cheyennes as "fools" and "Sioux." Desperately homesick and increasingly harried and distraught by conditions in their exile, many were driven to escape, to venture across the prairies in an all-or-nothing gamble to reach their homeland along the Rosebud, Bighorn, Powder, and Tongue rivers on the northern plains. On September 9, 1878, 273 Northern Cheyennes fled the reservation, led by Morning Star (also called Dull Knife) and Little Wolf.

The fugitives crossed the plains with caution, trying to elude both the army patrols searching for them and settlers who were always ready to turn them in. Reaching central Nebraska, they disagreed over their eventual destination and so separated. Morning Star and his group placed their hopes on reaching their old hunting grounds near the Sioux's Pine Ridge reservation. Little Wolf's band was set on reaching the Yellowstone Valley. After wintering in northern Nebraska, Little Wolf's group resumed its journey homeward. Little Wolf led his people across the Sioux reservation in South Dakota, around the Black Hills, and as far as the southeastern corner of Montana Territory before soldiers captured them. The group was confined at Fort Keough. Its fate would be shaped by the government's response to Morning Star's band, who were already in federal custody. After the bands split, Morning Star's had traveled as far as northwestern Nebraska before running into an army patrol during a heavy snowstorm. They were taken captive on October 23, 1878, and imprisoned at Fort Robinson.

The Northern Cheyennes' flight from the Indian Territory and Chief Joseph's attempt to reach Canada threatened the Concentration policy and shocked the War and Interior departments. General Sheridan acknowledged sympathetically that a common condition on reservations was "insufficient food and irregularity in its supply," and that this was a principal source of great Indian discontent. He and Secretary Shurz nevertheless agreed that "unless [the Indians] are sent back to where they came from, the whole reservation system will receive a shock which will endanger its stability."

On January 3, 1879, the Northern Cheyennes' fate was decided when Shurz ordered them returned to the Indian Territory. Morning Star and his people were anguished by the verdict, bluntly telling Captain Henry W. Wessells, Jr., Fort Robinson's commander, that they would never go back to a slow and agoniz-

ing death in the South. "Great Grandfather sends death in that letter [the removal order]. . . . You will have to kill us and take our
bodies back down that trail!" they warned. "We will not go!" Their
refusal to be relocated again prompted Wessells to break their will.
He cut off rations of food and water first. A few days later he deprived the Northern Cheyennes of fuel. The freezing cold of the
plains added to the torture of their hunger, but the prospect of returning to Indian Territory was unbearable. Morning Star and his
people resolved it would be better to die fighting on the open prairies than to perish on a reservation in Indian Territory. On January
9, 1879, they shot their way out of Fort Robinson, sustaining
heavy casualties in the process. Those who survived the breakout
did not get far. Soldiers tracked them down and, on January 21,
captured them after a bloody fight. Their unsuccessful escape had
cost them dearly; only seventy-eight of Morning Star's people,
half their number, were returned to Fort Robinson.

Widespread condemnation followed the government's handling of this affair. Compounded by strong criticism of the recent
episode with Chief Joseph, both incidents jolted the Hayes administration and forced it to reassess the government's Indian policy.
Commissioner Hayt wrote Secretary Shurz noting the "impolicy
of sending northern Indians to Indian Territory." Shurz did not
"hold the Government entirely guiltless of the wrongs inflicted
upon the Indians," reflecting on his decision to sustain and enforce
the small reservation approach of the policy of Concentration.
"Still less would I justify some high-handed proceedings on the
part of the Government in moving peaceable Indian tribes from
place to place without their consent, trying to rectify old blunders
by new acts of injustice." General Nelson A. Miles, who continued
to press for the return of Joseph and his Nez Percé to their homeland, published a stinging indictment of the government's Indian
policy in the *North American Review* in 1879. "The forcing of
strong, hardy mountain Indians from the extreme North to the
warmer malarial districts of the South was cruel, and the experiment should never be repeated." Criticism came from Congress,
too. "Mr. Shurz made one very unfortunate mistake quite early in
the course of his administration of the Interior Department," con-

cluded Senator George F. Hoar of Massachusetts. "He formed the opinion, I suppose without much practical experience in such matters, that it would be a good plan to get the civilized Indians of the country into the Indian Territory." Secretary Shurz, in his annual report for 1880, conceded that he had supported that policy in the belief "that [it] would be apt to keep the Indians out of hostile collision with their [white] neighbors, and in exclusive and congenial contact with their own." He conceded that it was "a mistaken policy."

One additional event bolstered the government's resolve that the Concentration policy must be eliminated. The event centered on a plan by whites to encroach on the lands of the Indian Territory. The reservation system annoyed westerners. Many refused to acknowledge the validity of federal pledges providing tribes with inalienable areas in which to live, the integrity of which Washington solemnly vowed to preserve and defend. Westerners preferred to view reservations as valuable public land that they as American citizens had an indisputable right to settle, but which for the moment Indian residents inconveniently encumbered. For the government, maintaining the integrity of reservations, the bedrock of the Concentration policy, became a problem of increasing difficulty after the army broke the Indians' military power, which deprived them of the ability to defend even their narrowly defined lands. "The settler and miner are beginning, or at least threatening, to invade every Indian reservation that offers any attraction, and it is a well-known fact that the frontiersman almost always looks upon Indian lands as the most valuable in the neighborhood," Carl Schurz observed. "From the articles in the newspapers of those remote Territories, it would sometimes appear as if, in the midst of millions of untouched acres, the white people were deprived of the necessary elbow-room as long as there is an Indian in the country." He concluded: "It is needless to say that the rights of the Indians are a matter of very small consideration in the eyes of those who covet their possessions."

The Indian Territory was critical to the government's plan to concentrate tribes. Established in the 1830s under the policy of Separation for the exclusive use of the removed members of the

Five Civilized Tribes, the United States reorganized it in the aftermath of the Civil War to facilitate the Concentration policy. The Reconstruction Treaties of 1866, imposed by the victorious Union government as penalty for the five tribes' involvement in the Civil War, stripped them of substantial territories (virtually the entire western half of the present state of Oklahoma). This area was then divided into reservations for the southern plains Indians, whom the government concentrated there after the Plains Wars of the 1860s and 1870s. It was then partitioned further to provide new homelands for dozens of relocated tribes under the small reservation approach.

Nonetheless, even what remained of Indian Territory was a powerful magnet for avaricious whites. Over the winter of 1878–1879, westerners organized an extensive scheme to take forcible possession of lands in Indian Territory. Parties interested in the project published letters and circulated them in the states surrounding the territory. The letters declared that these were public lands, not federal land that the government could reserve for Indian use, and as such were open to settlement by American citizens. A large number of persons from Missouri, Kansas, and Texas entered the Indian Territory in the spring of 1879, carrying their household goods and farming implements with the purpose of settling permanently. "The success of this invasion," declared Carl Schurz, "introducing into the heart of the Indian Territory a reckless, lawless, grasping element of adventurers, sure to grow and spread rapidly after once having gained a foothold, would bring upon the Indian population of that Territory in its present condition the most serious dangers."

President Hayes acted quickly and decisively. Issuing an executive proclamation on April 26, 1879, he forcefully enjoined "certain evil-disposed persons" to leave the Indian Territory immediately and abandon any further attempts to occupy land there. Hayes also warned that "any and all such persons who may so offend . . . will be speedily and immediately removed therefrom" by the military of the United States. Detachments of the U.S. Army promptly evicted the trespassers, and troops were posted at points along the lines between the Indian Territory and Texas, Missouri, and Kansas to prevent the entry of unauthorized parties. The president, in his third annual message to Congress, explained why he had taken these steps. "It is my purpose to protect the rights of the Indian inhabitants of that Territory to the full extent of the executive power." Hayes also expressed concern that attempts by whites to squat on Indian land and threaten the Concentration policy would continue. "It would be unwise to ignore the fact that a territory so large and so fertile, with a population so sparse and with so great a wealth of unused resources, will be found more exposed to the repetition of such attempts," he explained. "Under such circumstances, the difficulty of maintaining the Indian Territory in its present state will greatly increase, and the Indian tribes inhabiting it would do well to prepare for such a contingency." This realization, coupled with the tragic effects of sustaining the small reservation approach demonstrated by the Nez Percé and Northern Cheyenne cases, convinced the president that another direction in the federal management of Indians affairs was needed. Hayes's conclusion was reinforced in 1880, when westerners, casting their president's wishes and order aside, again attempted to occupy lands in the Indian Territory. Hayes issued a second presidential proclamation ordering them to desist and remove at once.

Americanization: Something Old and New

After 1879, emphasis on the relocation of tribes, especially to the Indian Territory, gradually decreased as the government slowly began to modify the long-standing Concentration policy. Instead, it sought the means to bring Indians into the American family, eventually eliminating the necessity for the government to maintain land reserves for Indians and to ceaselessly defend Indians and reservation land from the constant threat of white encroachment. Officials believed that only when Indians were freed of reservations and fully integrated into the American mainstream would their physical safety, material well-being, and legal and property rights be protected. By transforming Indians into productive and self-sufficient members of American society, the greatest benefit would accrue: the nation's Indian question would be solved. Government's active participation in the process was essential. "We can not expect them to improve . . . unless we keep faith with them in respecting the rights they possess," Rutherford Hayes stressed, "and unless, instead of depriving them of their opportunities, we lend them a helping hand."

The policy of Americanization drew upon recommendations proposed over the previous two decades by various reformers, Indian Bureau personnel, and chief executives. It was not so much an iron-clad, unchanging program as an ever-increasing commitment by Washington to seek the acculturation of the Indians and their assimilation into the dominant society. It provided the basis, and became the rationale, of federal Indian management for the next half century; although, as historian Frederick E. Hoxie pointed out in *A Final Promise*, the government's commitment to full acculturation and assimilation waned in the early twentieth century to the point where the goal became providing Indians only the minimal skills necessary to survive in the white man's world.

The policy of Americanization initially rested on two fundamental tenets: one, land reform centering on allotment in severalty; and two, a comprehensive government educational program for Indian children. The goals of the first measure were to teach Indians self-reliance and induce the habit of industry by the holding and working of private property, to direct them toward economic self-sufficiency, and to provide for the ultimate elimination of the reservation system. The purpose of the second was to foster the Americanization of Indians by destroying their "Indianness," thus giving them the capability of "self-protection in a civilized community." As Hayes stressed in a letter to both houses of Congress in 1881, "the time has come when the policy should be to place the Indians as rapidly as practicable on the same footing with the other permanent inhabitants of our country."

The program received the near universal approval of Indian reform and political action organizations, collectively calling themselves "Friends of Indians," that, with one exception, emerged in the late 1870s and early 1880s. The most important of these organizations included the Boston Indian Citizenship Committee; the

Women's National Indian Association, organized by Philadelphia churchwomen; the Indian Rights Association, founded by Herbert Welsh and Henry B. Pancoast; and the Board of Indian Commissioners, the only one directly affiliated with the federal government, established in 1869 by executive order of President Grant. The Friends of Indians gathered twice yearly to discuss and evaluate initiatives for solving the Indian question under the policy of Americanization. Each year they met in January in Washington for the annual meeting of the Board of Indian Commissioners, and in early fall they came together at the Lake Mohonk Conference in the Catskill Mountains of New York State. The National Indian Defense Association, headed by Dr. Thomas A. Bland, disagreed with the Friends of the Indians. Defending the Indians' right to self-determination, Bland stressed in the reformer Alfred B. Meacham's monthly publication, the *Council Fire,* that he "opposed rather than encouraged governmental action on the theory that Indians should be left alone." His stand drew frequent censure from the Friends of Indians. "Dr. Bland's efforts have been directed toward keeping the Indian as he is, his tribal relations untouched, his reservations intact; and in opposing the sale of his unused lands, upon no matter how equitable conditions, for white settlement," declared Herbert Welsh, leader of the Indian Rights Association.

Private or individual ownership of land was a concept foreign to most tribes, and, until the mid-1870s, except where laws had made special exceptions, Indians held their lands in common. Reformers during the late 1870s, led by individuals such as Senator Henry L. Dawes of Massachusetts who chaired the Senate Indian Affairs Committee, hoped to move Indians in the direction of embracing the concept of personal, private property. They promoted this partly as a pragmatic response to the rapid settlement of the trans-Mississippi West and to the incessant calls from westerners to open the remaining Indian landholdings to white settlement and exploitation. Commissioner Hayt expressed the feeling in January 1879 that "the experience of the Indian Department for the past fifty years goes to show that the government is impotent to protect the Indians . . . from the encroachment of its people." Proponents proclaimed that allotment would also serve as "the most effective civilizing agencies, . . . secure the Indians in their possessions [and] prevent them from becoming forever a race of homeless paupers and vagabonds." Carl Schurz concluded, "I am profoundly convinced that a stubborn maintenance of the system of large Indian reservations must eventually result in the destruction of the red man, however faithfully the Government may endeavor to protect their rights."

To encourage Indians to end tribal associations and take up agriculture, herding, or ranching as a private enterprise, Congress in 1875 passed general legislation that extended the land benefits of the 1862 Homestead Act to Indians willing to surrender tribal status. Few Indians availed themselves, however. Each succeeding year advocates of Indian welfare argued that Indians would be Americanized more quickly were the concept of private property successfully introduced among them. They stressed that this would elevate Indians from wretched living conditions on reservations, from the "contaminating" influence of tribal affiliation and activities, and from near absolute dependence on the national government for subsistence. Increasingly, they called for legislation permitting allotment in severalty of Indian land. As one agent commented: "As long as Indians lived in [communal] villages they will retain many of their old and injurious habits. . . . I trust that before another year is ended they will generally be located upon individual land or farms. From that date will begin their real and permanent progress." Other Americans, equally supportive of allotment legislation, were little more than potential land-grabbers. They exerted enormous and steady pressure on the government to liquidate most, if not all, of some 155 million acres of reservation land.

Allotment legislation was introduced in the closing session of the Forty-fifth Congress (1879) and at the beginning of the Forty-sixth Congress (1880). Those legislators in support of the proposed law agreed with the evaluation of Senator George H. Pendleton of Ohio, that "it must be our part to seek to foster and encourage within [the Indians] this trinity upon which all civilization depends—family, home, and [private ownership of] property." Yet the proposed legislation encountered unexpectedly heavy opposition. Both times it was defeated, in part out of fear that Indians were ill-prepared to hold and maintain private property, and because allotment seemed to stand little chance at the moment of achieving its intended results to advance the Indians' welfare. The minority report issued by the House Committee on Indian Affairs, typifying the opposition, stated, "However much we may differ from the humanitarians who are riding this hobby, we are certain that they will agree with us . . . that it does not make a farmer out of an Indian to give him a quarter section of land." Henry M. Teller of Colorado, the staunchest opponent of allotment in the Senate, characterized it as "a bill to despoil the Indians of their land and to make them vagabonds on the face of the earth." Teller predicted, with accuracy, that forty years after the passage of allotment legislation, when the Indians had been alienated by whites from their private allotments, they would "curse the hand that was raised professedly in their defense."

While allotment legislation failed during the Hayes presidency, the movement for it continued during the early 1880s. Hiram Pierce, both James A. Garfield's and Chester A. Arthur's Indian commissioner, pressed for congressional approval of allotment; although Henry Teller, now serving as Arthur's Secretary of Interior, strongly opposed it. Likewise, Grover Cleveland's Indian commissioner, John D. C. Atkins, firmly supported allotment proposals. Success finally came on February 8, 1887, when President Cleveland signed the Dawes General Allotment Act into law, legislation that President Theodore Roosevelt in a later message to Congress characterized correctly as "a mighty pulverizing engine to break up the tribal mass." The Dawes Act authorized the president to subdivide the Indians' land into private plots without the consent of the tribes affected. A quarter section, or a 160-acre lot (the traditional plot of a white homestead), was awarded to the head of a family and smaller plots to individual family members. The communal lands that the government designated as surplus (that is, unallocated) were offered for sale to whites. The allottees' lands were held in trust by the federal government for twenty-five years, while Indians mastered their new economic lifestyle and to protect them against loss of land to unscrupulous whites.

The allotment system proved an unqualified failure. Senator Henry Dawes's warning was correct: "Severalty must follow, not precede the transition from a wild blanket Indian to one having some aspirations for a better life." Accurate too was the cautious appraisal of Indian Commissioner John Atkins. Eight months after passage of the Dawes Act he suggested in his annual report: "There is danger that the advocates of land in severalty will expect from the measure too immediate and pronounced success. Character, habits, and antecedents can not be changed by an enactment." Not only did allotment in severalty threaten the cohesiveness of community and challenge gender-based tribal mores about the appropriateness of males being farmers, it violated the Indians' deepest feelings about the place of human beings in nature. Ultimately the legislation also took away from tribes nearly 108 million acres of unallocated land, or 70 percent of the total that was left them at the conclusion of the Indian wars. For the most part, the allotment system failed to transform Indians into self-supporting independent farmers, herders, or ranchers; and it did not eliminate the necessity for federal reservations. The avowed purpose of allotment in severalty was to teach reservation-bound Indians self-reliance and induce in them the habits of industry by the holding and working of private property. Once transformed, the Indians could proudly wear a badge of civilization. Instead, allotment hung like a millstone from the necks of most Indians, entrenching even more deeply Indian dependence on the government for subsistence, survival, and protection from land-hungry whites.

Americans widely viewed education, like allotment in severalty, as the panacea for solving the Indian question. It was not a new idea. As early as 1780, the Continental Congress appropriated $5,000, a large sum for that era, for the education of Indian students at Dartmouth College. For decades the national government relied on religious denominations to educate Indians at their missions. From 1819 onward, Congress authorized an annual appropriation for Indian education by missionary groups. By the end of the Indian wars in the 1870s, most Americans believed that the Indian could not continue to exist as an Indian and survive. The Board of Indian Commissioners surmised in 1875, "*education* must be regarded as a fundamental and indispensable factor," while one Indian commissioner remarked, "To educate the Indian in the ways of civilized . . . life is to preserve him from extinction." Survival for the Indians, however, would come at the steep price of their Indian identity.

Reformers and the Indian Bureau were in general agreement on a new course in educating Indian youths in "civilized" ways and skills. They argued that the best hope of educating Indian children lay in physically removing them from the influence of their elders and their cultural heritage—effectively breaking the bonds of family, neighborhood, and ethnic identity that white Americans valued so highly in their own cases. Supporters of this brand of education for Indian youths also hoped that adults on the reservations would be more inclined to remain peaceful and give up their traditional ways once their children were confined in government schools many miles away. Although this was tantamount to the taking of hostages, few Americans at the time would have seen it that way.

Although Indian day schools had functioned for decades throughout the United States, beginning in 1879 off-reservation vocational boarding schools became an important dimension in federal Indian education. The impetus for this type of school came from the success in educating Indian youths at the Hampton Normal and Agricultural Institute at Hampton, Virginia. President Hayes, in his second annual message of December 1878, called Congress's attention to "the experiment recently inaugurated, in taking fifty Indian children, boys and girls, from different tribes, to [Hampton] . . . where they are to receive an elementary English education and training in agriculture and other useful works, to be returned to their tribes, after the completed course, as interpreters, instructors, and examples." Subsequently, Army Lieutenant Richard H. Pratt (later Captain and finally Brigadier General) established the first off-reservation boarding school for Indians, Carlisle Indian Industrial School.

Situated in old military barracks at Carlisle, Pennsylvania, Carlisle opened in the fall of 1879 and soon boasted a student body of 158 pupils of both sexes, three-fourths of whom were males. The institution's motto, "Kill the Indian and save the man," succinctly summed up its mission. Pratt's two principal goals were to Americanize Indians through the classroom and to demonstrate to the American public that Indians were educable. Pratt elaborated on his educational theories in his volume, *How to Deal with the Indians: The Potency of Environment.* The key to Indian advancement lay in educating the children. "There is little hope of the civilization of the older wild Indians," concluded Commissioner Ezra Hayt, "and the only practical question is how to control and govern him, so that his savage instincts shall be kept from violent outbreak." Commissioner Hiram Price concurred fully: "Educational . . . activities among Indian youth would reclaim the Indian population from barbarism, idolatry and savage life."

Pratt patterned Carlisle, which became the model for subsequent government off-reservation boarding schools, after manual labor institutions. The curriculum included reading, writing, arithmetic, and spelling, but the greatest emphasis was placed on pragmatic training in domestic skills for females and on agricultural and manual arts for males. The Indian pupils also were instructed continually in the precepts of Christianity, American culture, and patriotic citizenship. Such instruction, neither wrong nor harmful in itself, took place at a time when the children's traditional culture was being systematically destroyed and when their relatives residing on the reservation were subjected to scorn and ridicule because they had not mastered the new learning. The subjects of history and geography proved the most useful tools in demonstrating to the children their rank on the scale of civilization. Educators hoped that pupils would accept the degradation of their own culture and history as an objective fact, and in turn would be spurred to seek improvement. An examination marked "excellent" was published by one school to demonstrate the institution's pedagogical triumph:

Question: To what race do we all belong?
Answer: The Human race.

Question: How many classes belong to this race?
Answer: There are five large classes belonging to the Human race.

Question: Which are the first?
Answer: The white people are the strongest.

Question: Which are the next?
Answer: The Mongolians or yellows.

Question: The next?
Answer: The Ethiopeans or blacks.

Question: Next?
Answer: The Americans or reds.

Question: Tell me something of the white people.
Answer: The Caucasian is away ahead of all of the other races—he thought more than any other race, he thought that somebody must made the earth, and if the white people did not find that out, nobody would never know it—it is God who made the world.

On another examination one Indian pupil surmised: "The red people they big savages; they don't know anything." Examination questions also stressed the white historical experience to the exclusion of that of the Indian youths. A third grade history test asked students to "tell about the voyage of Columbus and why he wanted to go," as well as "Who were the Pilgrims and where did they land?"In like manner, a fifth grade exam questioned, "Why did England tax the colonies? Tell about the 'Stamp Act'."

The schools the children were required to attend were strict and authoritarian. They were also, although perhaps not intentionally, cruel. Rarely allowed to go home to visit their families, the children were forbidden to speak their native language upon arrival at the boarding schools and were required to remain silent until they could speak English. "This language, which is good enough for a white man and black man, ought to be good enough for a red man," asserted Indian Commissioner Atkins. "It is also believed that teaching an Indian youth in his own barbarous dialect is a positive detriment to him. The first step to be taken to civilization, to teaching the Indian the mischief . . . of continuing in their barbarous practices, is to teach the English language." Matriculation typically resulted in rechristening, as youths forfeited their actual names in favor of "American" ones. The regimen at Carlisle, and other boarding schools, was steeped in military discipline. Students dressed in cadet uniforms, marched to the classroom and dormitory, and drilled daily in military formations.

Youths failing to follow rules were punished with denial of food, or even whippings.

The experiment at Carlisle, little less its putative success, so impressed the national government that the executive branch opened more off-reservation schools and Congress annually increased its appropriation for Indian education. In 1877 the general appropriation by Congress for the education of Indians was $30,000. In 1880 it jumped to $75,000; in 1885 to $992,800; and by 1890 appropriations reached $1,364,368. Eventually the government erected an elaborate three-tiered system of Indian education in the Far West, comprising reservation day schools, reservation boarding schools, and off-reservation boarding schools like Carlisle. As the number of institutions multiplied, school attendance increased from 3,598 Indian pupils in 1877 to 12,232 in 1890.

The system of Indian education was successful in accomplishing half of its intended aim: it destroyed much of the social cohesiveness and the tribal identification of the Indians. However it did not produce many "White Indians." On the contrary, it bred deeper resentment toward the dominant white society and its culture among students and the schools' graduates. It also produced in its wards a keener awareness of the plight of their people and, at least in some, a determination to resist. Some observers pointed out that Indians who attended government schools like Carlisle forgot their training and lessons in "civilization" upon their return to the reservation. Others charged that those who returned were a divisive, rather than enlightening, influence within their tribes and were often shunned by their own people. Historian Francis Paul Prucha has observed that Americanization measures, such as schooling, "did not quickly transform the Indians. Rather, it broke down their heritage and cultural pride without substituting anything in its place, until the Indians became a demoralized people, lost between their historic identity and the white culture they could not accept." Educator David Wallace Adams concludes that in the aftermath of the era of war "the next campaign was . . . waged in the classroom. The issue at hand was no longer the dispossession of the Indian's land, but rather the possession of his mind, heart, and soul. It was to be a gentle war, but a war just the same." Polingaysi Qoyawayma, rechristened Elizabeth Q. White, attended Sherman Institute at Riverside, California, for four years. Of her experience in the classroom she recalled in her autobiography *No Turning Back:* "As a Hopi, I was misunderstood by the white man; as a convert of the missionaries, I was looked upon with suspicion by the Hopi people. . . . The white man killed the buffalo because the buffalo presented a problem. Indian children are a problem too, but can't be so preemtorily disposed of." Reflecting her own inner confusion and chaos, she concluded with the plaintive assertion, "Don't ask them to peel off their brown skin and become white men."

"To Make the World Wiser and Better"

Federal Indian policy from 1879 onward was modified to reflect the belief that government's foremost responsibility was to Americanize the Indians, providing them the wherewithal to assimilate into the mainstream of American life and culture. Only in this manner could the Indians' actual survival be assured. No longer was it sufficient that the Indians simply accept absolute confinement on reservations. They now must forfeit their culture and sacrifice the traditional customs and values that had restored some meaning to their existence. If the Americanization program failed to transform the Indians and solve the Indian question, the Indians would become, as Commissioner Francis A. Walker predicted, "vagabonds in the midst of civilization, which will be festering sores on the communities near which they are located."

Hand in hand with this supposition was the belief that successful acculturation would produce another group of "hyphenated" American citizens. As Polish immigrants in the later nineteenth century became "Polish-Americans," or Italian immigrants became "Italian-Americans," so too Indians would be submerged in the American melting pot and come up "Indian-Americans." Government and civilian planners agreed that sooner or later the unique Indian type would be extinguished. Most Americans were convinced that would not be a bad outcome. And even those sympathetic to the Indians believed that outcome inevitable. Everyone, however, concurred on Americanization's chief result: there would no longer be an Indian question if there were no longer people identifiable as Indians, or people who identified themselves as Indians.

Supporters of Americanization gave little consideration to the idea that the policy might not be the correct, or fair, or even workable, course. "Savage and civilized life cannot live and prosper on the same ground," Commissioner Hiram Price declared in 1881. "If the Indians are to be civilized and become a happy and prosperous people, which is certainly the object and intention of our Government . . . the few must yield to the many." Nor would such distinctions have occurred to the great majority of policymakers and humanitarian reformers, considering their belief system. The program they erected was rooted in a series of deeply held premises and propositions about the nature of the American experience, the lessons of history, and the dominant self-image of American society in the latter third of the nineteenth century.

One premise stressed the desirability of a homogeneous American citizenry. The multiple political, social, and demographic forces propelled by the massive economic expansion of the post–Civil War period severely undermined America's cultural "island communities." Late-nineteenth-century modernization also provoked efforts to impose a heretofore unrealized degree of cultural uniformity upon the republic's social fabric. Increasingly, spokespeople of the dominant culture urged that the United States be blanketed by culturally homogeneous communities, woven into uniformity by common social, educational, and economic institutions. Conformity would be demanded and, if need be, imposed. Successful integration of "cultural aliens" (be they Indians or European and Asian immigrants, for example) would confirm the post–Civil War definition, expectation, and self-image of the United States.

Social evolution, a theory gaining widespread ascendancy in Europe and the United States in the last half of the nineteenth century, was another belief buttressing the Americanization policy. Americans have always had a strong tendency to accept that science provides ultimate truth. Society in turn adjusts to these truths.

The attitude of reformers and Indian policymakers found common ground with, and was reinforced by, the research and writings of practitioners in the emerging fields of anthropology and ethnology. Foremost among them was Lewis Henry Morgan of the Smithsonian Institution's Bureau of American Ethnology. Morgan's *The League of the Ho-de-no-sau-nee or Iroquois* (1855) pioneered the use of field observations in the study of Indian tribes. His widely acclaimed *Ancient Society,* published in 1877, buttressed social evolutionary ideas. Henry Adams, the insightful albeit skeptical commentator of the American experience, proclaimed this book to be nothing less than "the foundation of all future works in American historical science." History, to social evolution proponents such as L. H. Morgan and John Wesley Powell, founding director of the Bureau of Ethnology, was not merely the accurate chronicling of people and events of the past. It was a story infused with symbolic meaning. History's foremost purpose was to explain the progress of humankind's ascent on a vertical ladder. According to proponents of social evolution, peoples must pass through three principal stages of cultural development: from savagism, to barbarism, to civilization. (They would have accepted "Americanization" as a synonym for the final developmental stage.) Morgan taught that the degree of civilization, or the extent of social development of all peoples, could be accurately plotted along this continuum.

The scale of civilization was invested with three immutable laws. First, the stage of civilization was superior to the two preceding stages. Second, civilization would always triumph over barbarism and savagism. And third, those people highest on the ladder had a special responsibility to assist the development of those beneath them. This burden, the "white man's burden," to borrow a phrase from Rudyard Kipling, stressed the obligation of the white race both to Westernize and Christianize the "darker races" throughout the world. The Lake Mohonk platform of 1895 declared: "Our American civilization is founded upon Christianity. A pagan people can not be fitted for citizenship without learning the principles and acquiring something of the spirit of a Christian people." The burden also was underpinned by paternalism: "We must in a great measure do the necessary thinking for them, and then in the most humane way possible induce them to accept our conclusions," Carl Schurz stated. "This is in most cases much more easily accomplished than might generally be supposed; for, especially in the transition from savage to civilized life, the Indian looks up with natural respect to the superior wisdom of the 'Great Father.'" Reformers acknowledged that the transition would be difficult and often traumatic, but the results would be worth the price paid. The Indians are "in the middle of that swift and treacherous stream which divides civilization from barbarism and which all Indians must cross," asserted Herbert Welsh. "Doubtless its current will carry some away and its quicksands will engulf others, while those who succeed in getting safely over into the promised land will be both stronger and cleaner than they would have been were they not forced to cross it."

Social evolution provided a powerful rationale for why Indians needed immediate assistance. It also provided strong stimulus for reformers to labor diligently to Americanize Indians, and for the government to support such efforts. Indians clearly were relics of an earlier, more primitive, cultural order: "barbarous men" who must be taught to live in a "civilized way," proclaimed reformers. Once they affirmed this premise, reformers shouldered the attendant obligation to provide Indians the means for ascent. Many reformers had decried the wars that the United States had recently fought to effect the policy of Concentration. Now they reluctantly acknowledged them as the harsh but necessary means to fulfill the noble obligation of raising the Indians to a higher level of cultural development. Reservations would be the social laboratories—the "cultural hot-houses"—in which Americanization programs could germinate, blossom, and bear fruit under controlled conditions. There, Indians would be provided with the tools for ascent up the scale of civilization. Yet, in the end it was the Indians' choice alone whether they would become an "American beauty rose," in John D. Rockefeller's parabolic expression, or remain a cultural dinosaur. Those who refused the opportunity provided by white society invited extinction. Reflecting the era's faith in another dominant credo, Social Darwinism, Hampton Institute's newspaper the *Southern Workman* explained, "Put [the Indian] under the usual and natural conditions of life; the necessity of labor, law and order, with a good practical education for his children, and we shall see the survival of the fittest."

The policy of Americanization posed a grave threat to the Indians, and they realized it. Once confined within federal reservations under rigid supervision and scrutiny, Indians wrestled mightily with their new situation. Some actively sought to cooperate with the Americans. They believed that their accustomed way of life was gone forever and that their future depended on adaptation to their new role. Others advocated resistance to white society and the government's newest solution to the Indian question, but how? There was little consensus, because there was little in their environment that offered choices. Armed resistance, used to resist earlier "solutions," was out of the question. Flight from the reservation seemed increasingly an unattractive alternative, as white settlers and entrepreneurs transformed their old habitats. Passive resistance, a strategy difficult to implement effectively, held little hope of success among a people who still revered the ethos of a warrior culture. Passivity, in fact, ultimately proved more debilitating than fortifying for those Indians who attempted it, serving only to increase their alienation, discouragement, and dejection.

While a large number of Indians floundered in bewildered uncertainty, perplexed about how to deal with the present or the future, many refused to submit passively to the changes that Americans now tried to impose upon them. Gradually, various responses emerged in an effort to forestall or resist the policy of Americanization. Some resisted the new government system of education, hiding their children from educators and Indian Bureau agents. Others turned to the heavy consumption of alcohol as a means both of tempering the unpleasantness of reservation life and spurning white society. Some, grasping for vestiges of their old lifestyle, readily joined Wild West exhibitions and itinerant Wild West shows that toured the eastern United States and Europe, demonstrating for excited white audiences their prowess at riding horses and shooting. Still others, in defiance of Indian Bureau regulations and federal statutes, practiced time-honored religious rites such as the Sun Dance, the Snake Dance, or the Katchina ceremony.

Many Indians, clinging to the hope of throwing off white domination and reasserting an identity, resisted by means of new spiritual directions that stressed redemption and regeneration. The Ghost Dance, for example, based on the visions of the Paiute Wovoka, promised that God in the fullness of time would expel the white people and return the earth to the Indians, the living as well as the dead. Frustrated by a century-long struggle with the United States, some Indians turned to this new and exhilarating religion. However, the battle at Wounded Knee in 1890 destroyed people's faith in Wovoka's message and the Ghost Dance. The Peyote cult, based on the sacramental use of peyote buttons, also emerged in the latter nineteenth century. At first stressing the hallucinogenic effects of the peyote buttons, the Peyote cult gradually grew to include an ethical code of temperate behavior, honesty and truthfulness, devotion to one's family, and the merit of traditional customs and mores. By the early twentieth century, the Peyote cult had become institutionalized as the Native American Church.

United States Indian policy from the 1870s had two predominant goals: first, detribalization and the destruction of "Indianism" with its accompanying dress, traditions, religions, philosophies, languages, and social, economic, and political systems; and second, continual instruction in American cultural and economic ways and beliefs with the objective of molding natives into "White Indians," that is, an ethnic group indistinguishable from any other in the dominant society. The ultimate ambition of the the Americanization policy was to legitimate the new cultural experience as a dignified and proper way of life, not merely to coerce the Indians into being practitioners of it. Although Washington modified the policy from time to time, the modification never departed in any significant way from the basic objective: to solve the Indian question; an objective pursued, but never realized, since the founding of the republic, forming an organic whole in the history of the United States–Indian relations.

As the nineteenth century drew to a close, tempered optimism prevailed among whites that the vexed question was closer than ever to being solved, even though many Indians consciously, and often successfully, resisted the policy of Americanization. As Indian Commisssioner Hiram Price noted confidently in 1891, two months after the battle of Wounded Knee:

Since the plow and the sickle have, to a great extent, driven the tomahawk and the scalping knife from the field, thousands of Indians have learned that labor is ennobling and not degrading, and are beginning to see the dawn of a brighter future, where they may stand side by side with those whose aim is to make the world wiser and better.

Indian perception was notably different. Chief Seattle's observation perhaps best portrays a sentiment dramatically different from that of Price:

My people are few. They resemble the scattering trees of a storm-swept plain. . . . There was a time when our people covered the land as the waves of a ruffled sea cover its shell-paved floor, but that time long since passed away with the greatness of tribes that are now but a mournful memory.

We, the native Americans, reclaim the land known as Alcatraz Island in the name of all American Indians by right of discovery. . . . It would be fitting and symbolic that ships from all over the world, entering the Golden Gate, would first see Indian land, and thus be reminded of the true history of this nation. This tiny island would be a symbol of the great lands once ruled by free and noble Indians.

PROCLAMATION: TO THE GREAT WHITE FATHER
AND ALL HIS PEOPLE
NOVEMBER 1969

A Brief Profile of the Twentieth Century

Although there is a common assumption today, at least in the eastern half of the United States, that the American Indians vanished after the wars of the nineteenth century, they are in fact very much alive today. That it is little known may attest the shame it occasions. Certainly the twentieth century with which Indians have had to contend has been shameful in the extreme. Recently, however, Indians have begun to assert themselves as a united and proud people—if not a nation as Americans commonly use the word, then as an ethnic group. The growth of the American Indians rights movement, with its accompanying demands for equitable treatment by the United States (and in some cases even independence from the United States) is a force that has united the Indians nations in collective action on a scale unseen since the great wars of resistance. Their unity may even be greater now than it was during the wars of conquest.

The trend of federal Indian policy following the defeat of the Plains Indians can be divided into four periods. The first, from the mid-1870s until roughly 1933, witnessed confinement within a reservation (detailed in Chapter Six) under careful scrutiny and rigid supervision. Indians were not actually imprisoned, but experienced conditions disturbingly similar to prison camps. The entrance of the United States into World War I in 1917 may be seen as an important turning point for American Indians. Eight thousand of them volunteered for and served in the armed forces. Seven years later, in 1924, the United States granted national citizenship to all Indians. During the 1920s the acculturation policies and programs came under close scrutiny and criticism from a number of agencies, most significant among them the Brookings Institution and the United States Senate. Both bodies recommended drastic changes in America's Indian agenda.

The inauguration of Franklin D. Roosevelt in 1933 brought a new outlook to Indian affairs. During the second period, which flowered briefly in the 1930s, the federal government initiated a reorganization and reconstruction of Indian policy. This was chiefly the result of the dedication and imagination of John Collier, Roosevelt's commissioner of Indian Affairs. Collier terminated the program of Americanization and implemented a policy of Self-determination. He not only defended the Indians' right to their own cultural practices, but he believed there was much of value in those ways, value which could add a new depth to American society. Collier's policy also envisaged the creation of new Indian governments free to forge their own societies within the United States. Roosevelt liked what his commissioner was trying to do. He wrote of the status of the Indians in 1934: "The continuance of the autocratic rule by a federal department over the lives of more than 200,000 citizens of this nation is incompatible with American ideals of liberty. It is also destructive of the character and self-respect of a great race." Congress in 1934 approved the Indian Reorganization Act, which recognized the Indians' rights to traditional religion and religious practices, as well as a lifestyle free from federal interference and federally mandated norms. The U.S. government also ended allotment in severalty and tried to compensate tribes for lost lands.

The promise of the 1930s faded with the outbreak of World War II in 1939, followed by the entry of the United States into it in

1941. Many Indian males welcomed military service as a traditional and honorable activity in which manhood could triumph over the degradation of reservation life. More than 24,000 native men and women entered military service. (The Indian population numbered slightly more than 345,000 in 1940.) Many served at the front and earned awards for distinguished service. In addition, some 50,000 left their homes to work in defense industries. While legislation for Indians came to a virtual standstill during the war years, the experiences of those who departed the reservation produced greater acculturation than all the legislation that had acculturation as its aim. The war provided the first opportunity for a large number of Indians to observe the non-Indian world closely and over a prolonged period of time. The war years benefited Indians in another way too: military service and war work provided leadership opportunities and the training needed for dealing with the white world. Following World War II, many Indians decided to remain living, working, and raising their families in the non-Indian world.

Furthermore, during the war years an important step was taken to organize for the defense of Indian rights when peace came again. In 1944, the National Congress of American Indians (NCAI) was formed in Denver. As the first national, all-American Indian activist group, it identified its function as that of explaining and defending the Indian point of view to Congress. To facilitate that end it registered as a lobby in Washington, D.C.

In the third period, from the late 1940s to the early 1960s, the federal government opted for a new implementation of an old policy: a sped-up assimilation to be brought about by the termination of the federal trust and the integration of Indians into the mainstream of American society. Under one phase of the new policy of Termination and Relocation, those Indians still residing on the reservation would be gradually placed in the non-Indian world. In typical fashion, federal agents transferred Indian families to large U.S. cities where they would receive housing and employment assistance and vocational training. But when these Indians found little work in the cities, they clustered in ghettos as blacks had done a generation earlier. Indians strenuously opposed the government's newest policy, charging that it caused tribes extreme hardship and social disorganization. In the end, the United States did not terminate the federal trust with tribes, and many Indians never relocated from the reservation.

These experiences gave rise to the real beginnings of the American Indian rights movement. Although activists modeled it on the National Congress of American Indians, their new agenda moved them beyond mere lobbying. In August of 1946 they won a battle for redress of grievances against past infringements and violations of treaties. In that year Congress moved to create the Indian Claims Commission. Its purpose was to settle the myriad land claims of the American Indians that had risen over almost two centuries, but the method of settlement took a unique turn. For the first time Indians would be legally entitled to sue the federal government. Perhaps skeptical at first, they soon understood their opportunity and seized it. The United States government was besieged by claims, many successful. In the quarter century following creation of the commission, Indians won over $400 million in claims (a very large sum of money, since inflation had not yet gutted the value of the dollar).

The 1950s also saw the questioning of educational standards for all Americans, in large part because of the Soviet triumph over the United States in putting *Sputnik,* the first artificial satellite, in orbit. The value of learning, which had seemingly slipped in priority in an affluent and self-confident postwar American society, became important again as the United States recalibrated its tactics in fighting the Cold War. American Indian young people joined the trend toward more serious study. Their college registration rose dramatically in the late 1950s. Many Indians went on to graduate or professional school.

This development carried with it two important consequences. It exposed these students to the rapidly growing civil rights movement, which was particularly active on the nation's campuses. They inevitably perceived the relation of civil-rights grievances to the plight of their own people, both on and off the reservation. Further, it meant that Indians, for the first time in the twentieth century, could look to their own community for trained and qualified professionals to provide leadership, rather than to whites.

The fourth period originated in the 1960s. Stimulated by the turbulent events of that decade, political activism accelerated among American Indians as it did among other disadvantaged groups in the United States. Indian activists bitterly pointed out that of all minority groups in the United States, American Indians were the poorest: three out of five lived below the federally established poverty line. They demanded that something be done, and quickly, to address the blighted existence of their people, which was attributable in large measure to federal Indian policy as it developed in the nineteenth and continued into the twentieth century. Indians pressed for their long-buried rights and demanded that white America fulfill its many unkept promises to them.

Several consequential instances of this trend appeared in the 1960s. One protest conducted against the United States developed over the Kinzua Dam project in northwestern Pennsylvania and southwestern New York. The construction of a dam on the Allegheny reservation by the U.S. Corps of Army Engineers meant the flooding of more than 90 percent of the rich farming land of the Senecas' reservation. The sanctity of the reservation land had been guaranteed by federal treaty since 1794, and yet the Senecas were unable to stop the dam's construction. Obliged to concede they could not retain their land, they demanded reimbursement for it. Their answer came in the form of a Senate bill calling for termination of the remaining 10 percent of the reservation. Combined protests from Indian and non-Indian groups got the bill tabled and the federal government was forced to mediate. Nonetheless, the Senecas lost their fertile lands and were forced to relocate in low-grade allotments. They received minimal cash reimbursement for the roads, houses, farms, schools, and buildings destroyed by flooding.

Following the Kinzua failure the Indian rights movement became more militant. The non-Indian world's consciousness was jolted into recognition of this by three protests. The nineteen-month occupation of Alcatraz Island in San Francisco Bay came first in 1969. Alcatraz Island has been utilized for several centuries and for numerous purposes. California Indian tribes inhabited it before the arrival of Spanish explorers. Whites used the island at different times as a haven for fishermen and their boats, for an important lighthouse, and, finally, after World War I for a detention center to house the most incorrigible criminals. The penal installation finally closed in the 1960s, and the facilities were abandoned. In the fall of 1969, Indian activists occupied the island and offered to buy it back for $24, the supposed price for which Manhattan Island was purchased from the Manhattoe Indians in 1626. The island's newest occupants intended to use it for ecological study and as an Indigenous Nations cultural and spiritual center. The federal government threatened force and invasion to remove the squatters, but backed down when it became apparent numerous casualties could result. After nineteen months, and the virtual disappearance of media coverage of the occupation, government agents came ashore and peacefully escorted the remaining occupants to the mainland.

The outcome at Alcatraz did not dampen the determination of the Indians. On the contrary, in the early 1970s agitation increased both in volume and aggressiveness. The American Indian Movement, founded in 1968 by urban Indians, typified the trend toward "Red Power," analogous to that era's Black Power movement. AIM organizers led nearly 1,000 demonstrators in a forcible takeover of the Bureau of Indian Affairs in Washington, D.C., in November 1972. The building was occupied for six days and, when vacated, was left in shambles. AIM members confiscated numerous documents, including federal Indian treaties.

Shortly thereafter, in February 1973, the most dramatic and certainly the most reported event in the history of American Indians in the twentieth century occurred on the Pine Ridge reservation of the Sioux in South Dakota. About 300 AIM members seized the small village of Wounded Knee, taking eleven hostages and barricading themselves in a hilltop church from which they issued demands. The location had been carefully selected to correspond with the scene of the massacre of Big Foot's Sioux in December 1890. The protestors held out for seventy-one days. Far from leaving in obscurity like the holdouts at Alcatraz, the Wounded Knee protestors had gained and held the attention of the entire nation. Not all Sioux favored defiance of this sort. Some feared the federal government would use violence in which the

Sioux would inevitably be the principal sufferers. There was nonetheless much support and sympathy for them both inside and outside of the village.

As the U.S. war in Vietnam steadily decreased in the early 1970s, so too did most manifestations of 1960s radicalism, including Indian activism and any white support for it. Still, one legacy of the American Indian rights movement is an increased pride among Indians in being Indians and in their people's traditional ways and beliefs. Another legacy is that today there is somewhat more attention paid at national parks and museums, as well as in textbooks and school curriculums, to the history of the First Nations of America and the American Indians' role in, and perspective on, the past.

The future promises hope as well as discouragement for American Indians. Surely the road can be no harder than that already traveled by them.

BIBLIOGRAPHICAL ESSAY

It is hoped that the reader, especially the initiate, will seek out other viewpoints and interpretations of Indian-white relations. The most comprehensive compilations of published titles are *A Bibliographical Guide to the History of Indian-White Relations in the United States* (Chicago, 1977) and *Indian-White Relations in the United States: A Bibliography of Works Published 1975–1980* (Lincoln, NE, 1982), both edited by Francis Paul Prucha. For those who wish to go a step further in their investigation, the National Archives and Records Service holds the essential primary documents pertinent to the history of United States Indian policy. Most are contained in Record Group 75, *Records of the Bureau of Indian Affairs,* and Record Group 48, *Records of the Secretary of the Interior.* Helpful directories to the collections in the custody of the National Archives and Records Service are Edward E. Hill's two volumes: *Guide to Records in the National Archives of the United States Relating to American Indians* (Washington, 1981) and *Guide to Records in the National Archives of the United States Relating to Records in the National Archives of the United States* (Washington, 1981).

Since the 1960s a large and expanding literature has emerged about the history of Indian-white relations and the American Indians that presents them as interesting and important people. This attitude, however, has not always prevailed, as two prominent scholars of the American Indians have pointed out. Arrell Morgan Gibson noted that most historians have largely overlooked or ignored evidence that the Indians were more than mere "bit players in the American historical drama." Francis Paul Prucha asserted that "until recent decades Indians did not occupy a very prominent place in writings about American history, and this disinterest and disdain were reflected in high school and college textbooks." David Muzzey, for example, whose textbooks influenced generations of American school children in the early twentieth century, conceded, in his own words, that although the Indians "had some noble qualities . . . at bottom they were a treacherous, cruel people." Too frequently writers, until recently, have portrayed the Indians simply as a savage barrier to American pioneer progress, characterizing them as cruel, barbarous, half-civilized, and childlike.

The radical activisim of the 1960s, and especially the Indian Rights Movement, stirred an increasing number of writers and scholars to reinvestigate Indian history and the history of Indian-white relations and offer a new understanding of them. The resultant literary output divides into at least a half dozen groups. The first two groups, judgmental and conspicuously pro-Indian in an effort to awaken the consciences of Americans and redress the past, are Indian activist writings, such as *Custer Died for Your Sins: An Indian Manifesto* (New York, 1969) and *Behind the Trail of Broken Treaties* (New York, 1974) by Vine Deloria, Jr.; and the writing of white critics of federal policy and white actions toward Indians, such as Dee Brown's *Bury My Heart at Wounded Knee: An Indian History of the American West* (New York, 1970) and Richard Drinnon's *Facing West: The Metaphysics of Indian-Hating and Empire-Building* (Minneapolis, 1980).

The other four groups sought a less polemical, more impartial treatment of the subject. General histories of Indian-white relations, the third group, typically concentrating on governmental Indian policy as the vehicle for exposition and interpretation, provide an introduction to, and overview of, the subject. Among the most useful are Angie Debo, *A History of the Indians in the United*

States (Norman, OK, 1970); Arrell Morgan Gibson, *The American Indians: Prehistory to the Present* (Lexington, MA, 1980); D'Arcy McNickle, *Native American Tribalism: Indian Survivals and Renewals* (New York, 1973); Francis Paul Prucha, *The Great Father* (2 volumes, Lincoln, NE, 1984); Wilcomb E. Washburn, The Indian in America (New York, 1975); Philip Weeks, ed., *The American Indian Experience: A Profile, 1524 to the Present* (Wheeling, IL, 1988), and James Wilson, *The Earth Shall Weep: A History of Native America* (Berkeley, 1999). Two briefer accounts are William T. Hagan, *American Indians* (Chicago, 1979) and Francis Paul Prucha, *The Indian in American Society* (Berkeley, 1985).

The fourth group is tribal histories. While offering detailed accounts of Indian societies and their histories, most concentrate on the postcontact period for tribes and on their relationship with white society. For this reason they are helpful in gaining a greater understanding of Indian-white relations as well as of specific tribes. For example, tribal histories shed great light on the details of removal under the policy of Separation and the resettlement of tribes in the southern portion of the Indian Territory. They include Arthur H. DeRosier, Jr., *The Removal of the Choctaw Nation* (Knoxville, TN, 1970); Arrell Morgan Gibson, *The Chickasaws* (Norman, OK, 1971); Grace S. Woodward, *The Cherokees* (Norman, OK, 1963); Edwin C. McReynolds, *The Seminoles* (Norman, OK, 1957); and Angie Debo, *The Rise and Fall of the Choctaw Republic* (Norman, OK, 1934) and *The Road to Disappearance* (Norman, OK, 1941), which is about the Creeks. Tribes from the Ohio Country and the Old Northwest, later colonized in the northern portion of the Indian Territory as a result of the Separation policy, are treated in other tribal histories: Bert Anson, *The Miami Indians* (Norman, OK, 1970); Randolph C. Downes, *Council Fires on the Upper Ohio* (Pittsburgh, 1940); William T. Hagan, *The Sac and Fox Indians* (Norman, OK, 1958); Arrell Morgan Gibson, *The Kickapoos: Lords of the Middle Border* (Norman, OK, 1963); C. A. Weslager, *The Delaware Indians* (New Bruns-wick, NJ, 1972) and *The Delaware Indian Westward Migration* (Wallingford, PA, 1978); and Erminie Wheeler-Voegelin and Helen Hornbeck Tanner, *Indians of Ohio and Indiana Prior to 1795,* 2 vols. (New York, 1974).

Several excellent tribal histories are invaluable in gaining a fuller understanding of the era of the Plains Wars, particularly Donald J. Berthrong, *The Southern Cheyennes* (Norman, OK, 1963); Peter J. Powell, *Sweet Medicine: The Continuing Role of the Sacred Arrows, the Sun Dance, and the Sacred Buffalo Hat in Northern Cheyenne History* (2 volumes, Norman, OK, 1969) and *People of the Sacred Mountain: A History of the Northern Cheyenne Chiefs and Warrior Societies, 1830–1879* (2 volumes, New York, 1981), the latter an especially enlightening study because it provides an Indian view of Indian-white relations and interracial conflict; Mildred Mayhall, *The Kiowas* (Norman, OK, 1962); Roy W. Meyer's *History of the Santee Sioux: United States Indian Policy on Trial* (Lincoln, NE, 1967); Robert M. Utley, *The Last Days of the Sioux Nation* (New Haven, CT, 1963); Ernest Wallace and E. Adamson Hoebel, *The Comanches: Lords of the South Plains* (Norman, OK, 1952); and Donald L. Worcester, *The Apaches: Eagles of the Southwest* (Norman, OK, 1979). Two other tribal studies, William T. Hagan's *United States–Comanche Relations: The Reservation Years* (New Haven, CT, 1976) and Donald J. Berthrong's *The Cheyenne and Arapahoe Ordeal: Reservation and Agency Life in the Indian Territory, 1875–1907* (Norman, OK, 1976), stress conditions for Indians during the reservation period and specific tribal responses to the policy of Americanization.

Biographies, both about Indians and those whites who exerted influence upon relations with Indians, constitute the fifth group. R. David Edmunds's revisionist accounts *Tecumseh and the Quest for Indian Leadership* (Boston, 1984) and *The Shawnee Prophet* (Lincoln, NE, 1983) are important in examining the fate suffered by the northern tribes as the press of white settlement penetrated the Old Northwest, as are John Sugden's *Tecumseh's Last Stand* (Norman, OK, 1985) and *Tecumseh: A Life* (New York, 1998). Kenny A. Franks, *Stand Watie and the Agony of the Cherokee Nation* (Memphis, TN, 1979) and Gary E. Moulton, *John Ross, Cherokee Chief* (Athens, GA, 1978) provide interpretations of the struggle within Cherokee society, both in Georgia and after removal to Oklahoma, to chart that tribe's national course.

Important aspects of the efforts of the Plains Indian tribes to resist the policy of Concentration are developed in other biographies like James C. Olson, *Red Cloud and the Sioux Problem* (Lincoln, NE, 1965) and Angie Debo, *Geronimo the Man, His Time, His Place* (Norman, OK, 1976). William H. Armstrong's *Warrior in Two Camps: Ely S. Parker, Union General and Seneca Chief* (Syracuse, 1978) assesses another side to the era of the Plains Wars by detailing the role played by Ulysses S. Grant's friend and first commissioner of Indian Affairs.

Informative biographical essays of the commissioners of Indian Affairs and their role in shaping and executing federal Indian policy appear in Robert M. Kvasnicka and Herman J. Viola, eds., *The Commissioners of Indian Affairs, 1824–1977* (Lincoln, NE, 1979). Biographies of principal American military personnel in the Plains Wars are plentiful. Offering a vantage point different from that of the Indian biographies for understanding the wars to implement and enforce the policy of Concentration, they also frequently serve as a defense of federal Indian policy. Robert G. Athearn's *William Tecumseh Sherman and the Settlement of the West* (Norman, OK, 1956) describes the role played by one of the dominant military figures in that era. Volumes about other important U.S. commanders include Virginia W. Johnson, *The Unregimented General: A Biography of Nelson A. Miles* (Boston, 1962); John W. Bailey, *Pacifying the Plains: General Alfred Terry and the Decline of the Sioux, 1866–1890* (Westport, CT, 1979); John A. Carpenter, *Sword and Olive Branch: Oliver Otis Howard* (Pittsburg, KS, 1964), David Dixon, *Hero Of Beecher Island: The Life and Military career of George A. Forsyth* (Lincoln, NE, 1994). Shirley A. Leckie's *Elizabeth Bacon Custer and the Making of a Myth* (Norman, OK, 1993) offers an interesting look at George Custer's life and the role of Libby Custer in establishing her husband's legend.

Period and episodic studies make up the sixth group. A solid overview of the efforts to drive westward the Ohio Country tribes is Wiley Sword, *President Washington's Indian War: The Struggle for the Old Northwest, 1790–1795* (Norman, OK, 1985). Indian policy in the Jeffersonian era, underpinned by its intellectual rationalizations, is treated in Bernard W. Sheehan, *Seeds of Extinction: Jeffersonian Philanthropy and the American Indians* (Chapel Hill, NC, 1973) and Reginald Horsman, *Expansion and American In-*

dian Policy, 1783–1812 (East Lansing, MI, 1967); while important studies about the origins and implementation of the policy of Separation include Reginald Horsman, *The Origins of Indian Removal, 1815–1824* (East Lansing, MI, 1970), Ronald M. Satz, *American Indian Policy in the Jacksonian Era* (Lincoln, NE, 1975), and Anthony F. C. Wallace, *The Long, Bitter Trail: Andrew Jackson and the Indians* (New York, 1993). Examinations of American expansion into the trans-Mississippi West during the 1840s and 1850s and changing federal Indian policy leading to the policy of Concentration are few. The best account is Robert A. Trennert, Jr., *Alternatives to Extinction: Federal Indian Policy and the Beginnings of the Reservation System, 1846–51* (Philadelphia, 1975). Robert M. Utley, *The Indian Frontier of the American West, 1846–1890* (Albuquerque, NM, 1984), Robert Wooster, *The Military and United States Indian Policy, 1865–1903* (New Haven, CT, 1988), and Janet A. McDonnell, *The Dispossession of the American Indian, 1887–1934* (Bloomington, IN, 1991) are excellent period pieces about United States–Indian relations during the second half of the nineteenth century and beyond.

Much recent scholarly attention has been directed toward the post–Civil War period, especially Indian reform efforts and the Americanization policy. Important works include Robert W. Mardock, *The Reformers and the Indian* (Columbia, MO, 1971); Henry E. Fritz, *The Movement for Indian Assimilation, 1860–1890* (Philadelphia, 1963); Loring B. Priest, *Uncle Sam's Stepchildren: The Reformation of United States Indian Policy, 1865–1887* (New York, 1969); Francis Paul Prucha, *American Indian Policy in Crisis: Christian Reformers and the Indian, 1865–1900* (Norman, OK, 1976); and Frederick E. Hoxie, *A Final Promise: The Campaign to Assimilate the Indians, 1880–1920* (Lincoln, NE, 1984). The Americanization policy through educational efforts is explored in David Wallace Adams, *Education for Extinction: American Indians and the Boarding School Experience, 1875–1928* (Lawrence, KS, 1995) and Donal F. Lindsey, *Indians at Hampton Institute, 1877–1923* (Urbana, IL, 1995).

Episodic studies are bountiful. Many focus on the more dramatic martial events in Indian-white relations of late, especially in the West during the nineteenth century. The Santee Sioux uprising and its aftermath has been most fully explored in Kenneth Carley, *The Sioux Uprising of 1862* (St. Paul, 1961); and C. M. Oehler, *The Great Sioux Uprising* (New York, 1959). Stan Hoig's *The Sand Creek Massacre* (Norman, OK, 1961) is a good survey of events in Colorado and the assault on the Southern Cheyennes at Sand Creek by John Chivington's militia, as is also David Svaldi's *Sand Creek and the Rhetoric of Extermination: A Case Study in Indian-White Relations* (Lanham, MD, 1989). Dorothy M. Johnson, *The Bloody Bozeman: The Perilous Trail to Montana's Gold* (New York, 1971), explores the American conflict with the Oglala Red Cloud over the issue of the Bozeman Trail.

Examinations of the Red River War, the last major conflict on the southern plains, are contained in James L. Haley, *The Buffalo War: The History of the Red River Indian Uprising of 1874* (New York, 1976), and Stan Hoig, *The Battle of the Washita: The Sheridan-Custer Indian Campaign of 1867–69* (Garden City, NY, 1976). The concluding conflict of the Plains Wars has drawn considerable literary attention. Events surrounding the Great Sioux War are treated in Donald Jackson, *Custer's Gold: The United States Cavalry Expedition of 1874* (New Haven, CT, 1966); J. W. Vaughn, *The Reynolds Campaign on the Powder River* (Norman, OK, 1961); and John S. Gray, *Centennial Campaign: The Sioux War of 1876* (Fort Collins, CO, 1976).

These six groups dominate the literature of Indian-white relations, but new approaches in methodology have appeared in recent years, too. They include institutional studies such as Paul Stuart, *The Indian Office: Growth and Development of an American Institution, 1865–1900* (Ann Arbor, MI, 1979); land policy studies such as Leonard A. Carlson's *Indians, Bureaucrats, and Land* (Westport, CT, 1981), which explores the Dawes Act and its effects on Indians; and ecological and environmental studies such as Gary C. Goodwin's *Cherokees in Transition: A Study of Changing Culture and Environment Prior to 1775* (Chicago, 1977), William Cronon's *Changes in the Land: Indians, Colonists, and the Ecology of New England* (New York, 1983), and Christopher Vecsey and Robert W. Venables, eds., *American Indian Environments: Ecological Issues in Native American History* (Syracuse, 1980).

INDEX

Farewell, My Nation: The American Indian and the United States in the Nineteenth Century, Second Edition
Developmental Editor: Andrew J. Davidson
Copy editor and production editor: Lucy Herz
Proofreader: Claudia Siler
Cartographer: James Bier
Printer: McNaughton & Gunn, Inc.